The Meaning of Your Dreams

Dream Interpretation – The Secret
David F. Melbourne and Dr Keith Hearne, Blandford 1997

Your Dreams and Your Stars
David F. Melbourne and Helen Adams, Blandford 1998

The Meaning of Your Dreams

An Interactive Guide

~~

**DAVID F. MELBOURNE
& DR KEITH HEARNE**

BLANDFORD

First published in the United Kingdom in 1999 by Blandford

Text copyright © David F. Melbourne & Keith Hearne, 1999
Design and layout copyright © Blandford, 1999

Distributed in the United States by Sterling Publishing Co., Inc,
387 Park Avenue South, New York, NY 10016-8810

A Cataloguing-in-Publication Data entry for this title is available and may be obtained from the British Library

ISBN 0-7137-2778-0

Designed and typeset by Ben Cracknell Studios

Printed in Great Britain by Creative Print and Design Wales, Ebbw Vale

Blandford
Illustrated Division
The Orion Publishing Group
Wellington House
125 Strand
London WC2R 0BB

Contents

Introduction

More and more people are dissatisfied with dream dictionaries, and with good reason. Nowadays, there are so many versions, nearly all of which disagree on the meaning of dream symbols. For example, one of them informs us that to dream of the moon could have many interpretations, from enjoyment of life to the death of a prominent person. Another states that the same symbol signifies that the dreamer will come into silver. These disparities render dream dictionaries useless unless dreamers adhere religiously to just one version – in other words, programme their unconscious to learn the given definitions in advance.

Many ancient cultures believed that certain dreams carried set meanings. If all the people within a culture learnt and believed in those meanings, their unconscious minds would furnish appropriate dreams to impart accurate, predetermined messages.

For example, even today, some West Indians maintain that, if a woman dreams of fish, a pregnancy is imminent. Amazingly, this seems to hold true. However, according to their beliefs, dreams that feature fish could have a different meaning for people from another culture – and that also would be likely to hold true. This suggests that messages from the unconscious will conform to our conscious beliefs.

Nowadays, with the increase of world travel, cultures have become mixed, each contributing its own language of dream symbols. Add to that the fact that many dream dictionaries are in circulation, and the result is chaos.

It is hardly surprising, then, that people are looking for alternative methods of understanding their dreams. It is ironical, however, that if there were just one 'universal' dream dictionary, which was studied before the onset of sleep, it would be likely to yield accurate meanings. Unless the day comes when such a dream dictionary is accepted as bona fide by the entire world population, there can never be universal symbols that will hold true for all humanity.

In the West, during the days of the witch-hunts, sadly, much dream knowledge was lost – people were too afraid to impart such wisdom. As a consequence, we have ended up with the current hotchpotch of dream meanings and symbols. However, through our awareness of ancient knowledge, and because of more recent findings, particularly the understanding of the way in which dreams are structured, we are able to decode the messages of dreams without relying on so-called 'universal' symbols.

It is through our insight into the structure of dreams and the brain's limitations in producing imagery that we can now access messages by using other methods. For instance, recognizing that dreams flow along by a 'law of least effort', while adhering to certain consistent rules, facilitates other approaches. To illustrate this point, it is crucial for analysts to comprehend that dreams also flow along visual- and verbal-associative pathways. In addition, they will often play on words by using anagrams, homophones, and other devices. Add to this the fact that, in the West, there are few accepted symbols with universal meanings, and we can begin to make sense of dreams by assuming that they are personal to each specific dreamer.

For instance, if Westerners were to dream of houses, what would it mean? Not having a universal dream language, the symbolic representation could have numerous implications. To one individual a house might signify just that – a house, while to another it could reflect financial stability. To somebody experiencing difficulty with mortgage arrears, though, the opposite might be applicable. However, for anyone familiar with the ancient teachings that a house represented the dreamer, this would also very likely hold true.

It was for these reasons that the cross-reference flowchart method of interpretation was devised. This system relies on a methodical, analytical approach to deciphering dreams, which is more scientifically based. In addition, because dreams are specific to the individual, it is crucial for the interpreter to know something about each dreamer – psychological profile, life circumstances, etc. Essentially, the flowchart method relies on identifying a consistent theme that permeates a message-bearing dream. Once a theme has been established, the dream is reconstructed, and an accurate analysis should emerge quite naturally.

Many individuals favour Jung's theory that the best people to interpret dreams are the dreamers themselves. However, after researching dreams for a quarter of a century, it is our belief that this is an incorrect assumption. Indeed, if dreamers are asked to give definite meanings to their own dreams, they rarely respond with clear-cut interpretations. Furthermore, both authors find that it takes considerably longer to work out their own dreams than it does to render accurate analyses of clients' dreams.

The reasons for encountering problems in self-analysis are understandable. First, it is always more difficult to become detached and view your own dream dispassionately, as an impersonal observer would do. In other words, you are too involved and can rarely see the wood for the trees. Secondly, to come up with accurate interpretations, we need to acknowledge and accept that we have less savoury sides to our characters than we are probably willing to admit.

This is particularly relevant if we accede to another of Jung's hypotheses – that each individual's unconscious mind acts as a guide and friend. If we then consider that dreams often try to impart messages intended to help us along life's path, by alluding to less desirable aspects of the psyche, unless we are prepared to acknowledge our faults and take them into account we are hardly likely to recognize the message behind the dream.

Over the past few years, we have written several books on the subject of dreams and dream interpretation, which are listed in the references. Our aim has been to make the general public aware of the substantial rewards of understanding dreams, and our first book, *Dream Interpretation – The Secret*, went a long way towards achieving that goal.

However, since then, we have learnt that people understand the subject of dream interpretation much better if they try analysing other people's dreams for themselves, as opposed to simply reading examples. Also, to become proficient in the science of analysis, it is necessary to learn as much as possible about sleep and dreams in the first place – specifically the way in which dreams are structured, and the limitations of the brain where producing dream images is concerned.

Therefore, this book is divided into three parts. Part I gives comprehensive background information about sleep, dreams, and various unusual phenomena that might be encountered, such as lucid dreams, sleep paralysis, and false awakenings. Cases from our files are used to illustrate these phenomena.

Also covered is the subject of dream incubation through ritual, to produce a mind-set of expectation. Self-suggestion scripts and exercises are provided to assist such anticipation. Creative incubation demonstrates how creative ideas, arising from dream incubation, can be put to use in the material world.

Some people experience difficulty in remembering their dreams. Dream recall is dealt with by encouraging readers to enhance their memory of dreams by keeping a dream diary. In addition, there is an explanation of visual imagery and how to concentrate on the use of guided visualization techniques. Finally, Part I reaches a conclusion with a detailed description of the Melbourne cross-reference flowchart method of dream interpretation.

Part II consists of dreams (numbered) for you to attempt to interpret. Each one is accompanied by clues taken from dreamers' original questionnaires, which will be of assistance in arriving at accurate analyses.

Part III contains correct interpretations of the dreams given in Part II (correspondingly numbered). Brief explanations of how the solutions have been worked out accompany each dream. This will enable you to compare analyses, so that you will be able to see where you have gone wrong – if you have gone wrong. Good luck!

The College of Dream Interpretation Studies can be located at
http://ourworld.compuserve.com/homepages/dreamthemes.

PART I

Sleep and Dreams

• • • •

The Nature of Sleep and Dreams

Before we run with dream interpretation, let us walk and gain an understanding of sleep and dreams generally. There are several features of sleep and dreaming that are highly relevant to a full comprehension of what might be happening in a dream, so we need to look at these first.

The Study of Sleep

Sleep became a topic for scientific study when technical developments made it possible to monitor the various bodily changes that accompany the state. In 1875, Richard Caton, at Liverpool University, England, discovered electrical activity on the exposed surface of the brains of animals, using a sensitive galvanometer. Then, in 1929, in Germany, Hans Berger reported that, by placing electrodes on the scalp of human subjects, various frequencies of electrical activity in the brain could be measured.

The breakthrough in sleep research happened when physiology student Eugene Aserinsky, in Chicago, USA, noticed that the eyes of babies moved rapidly quite often when they were asleep. He interested his professor, Nathaniel Kleitman, in undertaking some research, and they established a sleep laboratory to monitor adults by using attached electrodes linked to powerful amplifiers and a chart-recorder. They recorded eye movements and brain activity.

Their tracings showed that subjects had periods of *rapid eye movement* (REM), which alternated with periods when the eyes were still. By waking subjects in the different states, it became apparent that, in general, REM sleep was associated with dreaming. Aserinsky and Kleitman published their initial findings in 1953.

A few years later, Ralph Berger discovered the *atonia* (lack of muscle tone, or paralysis) of REM sleep. The appropriate electrophysiological measures were now available to study sleep and dreaming objectively.

Monitoring Sleep

The scientific study of sleep and dreaming involves the electrophysiological monitoring of subjects in the sleep laboratory so that the precise condition of wakefulness or sleep can be objectively ascertained. There is usually a bedroom, where the 'wired-up' subject sleeps, physically attached via an electrical plug-and-socket system to the recording apparatus. The experimenter observes and monitors the subject from a separate control room.

The recording machine, known as a *polygraph*, traces out the considerably amplified (perhaps several million times) signals from electrodes placed on the head of the subject. Several channels are used so that the simultaneous monitoring of different factors can be displayed.

The chart paper or computer representation travels at 10 or 15 mm per second. Each 'page', or 'epoch', of the recording is 'scored', i.e. the particular stage of sleep or wakefulness is determined and logged. The scoring criteria were internationally standardized by Rechtschaffen and Kales in 1958, so that results from different laboratories could be validly compared.

The intention may be to observe, say, the sleep patterns of different groups of people, or the results on sleep of manipulating some variable (e.g. the effects of a drug).

Three basic factors are continuously monitored in sleep:

~ Brain waves (electroencephalogram, or EEG)
~ Eye movements (electro-oculogram, or EOG)
~ Muscle activity (electromyogram, or EMG).

The EEG is usually picked up by two electrodes placed in certain measured positions on the top of the head. The electrical difference between the two electrodes is measured. Electrodes are placed according to an internationally recognized 'ten-twenty electrode placement system' described by Jasper in 1958. Scalp electrodes, in the hair, are usually attached using collodion glue. Those attached to bare skin are taped on, using micropore tape. A conductive gel is introduced under the dome-shaped electrodes (which are silver, coated with silver chloride) to facilitate electrical potentials.

The human brain produces different frequencies of brain waves (measured in Hz, or cycles per second), which are named as follows:

- *Alpha* waves (8–13 Hz)
- *Beta* waves (14–30 Hz)
- *Delta* waves (0.5–3 Hz)
- *Gamma* waves (30–50 Hz)
- *Theta* waves (4–7 Hz).

There are great individual differences between people. Some people, Dr Hearne included, produce continuous alpha waves in wakefulness, while some show none. Most people fall between those two extremes. It is not possible to say with any confidence that the presence of a particular brain wave is linked to specific characteristics in the person.

The EOG movements are detected in two recording channels by electrodes placed above and below the outer edge of the eye (the canthus), so that ocular activity in any direction is registered. The EOG electrodes actually pick up the movement of an electrical charge between the retina and cornea of the eyes, rather than the activity of muscles around the eyes. The cornea is electrically positive relative to the retina because of the higher metabolic rate of the latter.

The EMG muscle movements are detected by electrodes placed on the lower jaw, thus measuring the general tonus of the muscles as well as monitoring individual contractions.

Stages of Sleep

The work of Aserinsky and Kleitman showed that sleep is not, in fact, a uniform condition. It consists of two very different states: *slow-wave sleep* (SWS) and *rapid eye-movement* (REM) *sleep*. Over the years many different nomenclatures have come and gone for these two states, including (for REM sleep) 'paradoxical', 'desynchronized', 'light', 'deep', 'active', and 'restless', and (for SWS) 'orthodoxical', 'synchronized', 'quiet', 'high voltage', 'telencephalic', and 'ordinary'.

These two distinct states alternate in a roughly 90-minute *ultradian* (faster than a day) cycle, controlled at the base of the brain by the ebb and flow of two brain-transmitter chemical systems.

Sleep has also been arbitrarily subdivided into four stages of increasing 'depth':

- *Stage 1*. At the onset of sleep, SWS overtakes the body, and the eyes begin to roll slightly in many people. This is identified in the polygraphic record. At the same time, in those individuals who exhibit much alpha-wave activity, there is a sudden cutting-out of that frequency. The EMG level is usually lower than that of relaxed wakefulness.

~ *Stage 2.* In this stage of SWS *k-complexes* appear. These are sudden, sharp (negative-to-positive) brain waves which occur in response to a sudden external or internal stimulus. Rather like epileptic activity, they do not appear in normal people in wakefulness, but are universal in SWS.

~ *Stage 3.* The amount of defined slow waves steadily increase until they constitute between 20 per cent and 50 per cent of the recording, and this stage is attained. The k-complexes may still be present in this stage.

~ *Stage 4.* In this, the final stage of SWS, 50 per cent or more of the polygraphic record shows slow waves of 2 Hz or less, and these rhythmic slow waves are mirrored in the EOG channels. This is because the EEG is representing masses of brain cells acting in unison to produce slow waves. The activity is so large that the EOG electrodes also pick up the concentrated effect. Rousing from stage 4 sleep is difficult – people feel decidedly disoriented and reluctant to awaken. It results in a condition of *sleep drunkenness.*

After about $1^1/_2$ hours, the slow-frequency brain waves are replaced by a fast, mixed-frequency pattern which is indicative of REM sleep. This roughly 90-minute cycle repeats throughout sleep.

In REM sleep there is 'low-voltage', mixed-frequency brain activity. Saw-toothed waves appear. No k-complexes are present. The EMG polygraphic trace becomes thin, reflecting the muscular atonia, and a heart-rate trace (which would have been swamped in the record of wakefulness and SWS) may then become observable.

An amazing characteristic of REM sleep is that the body's musculature becomes paralysed, although breathing is automatically maintained. There is active inhibition, so that only slight twitches are occasionally observed. Reflexes, such as the tendon reflex, are suppressed. The purpose of this paralysis would seem to be a protective ploy so that we do not physically act out our dreams!

While some imagery may be reported by people woken from SWS, the active dreams with a story-line, which we recognize as proper dreams, are linked with REM sleep. The first REM period may only last 2 or 3 minutes, but each successive appearance is longer in duration, so that, after 7 hours of sleep, the dreaming time may be, say, 30–40 minutes or more. Correspondingly, the amount of SWS decreases throughout the night, so essentially the first half of the night's sleep is mainly SWS while the second half consists mostly of REM dreaming sleep.

Men have substantial erections in REM sleep, and there is clitoral engorgement in women. The erections, though, may have nothing to do with the dream content. It is simply an arousal cycle that can actually shift out of phase with REM sleep if the individual is repeatedly woken on entering REM sleep in the sleep laboratory. The erection cycle is not affected by sexual gratification, as Karacan and his colleagues reported in 1966.

Physiology of Sleep

In SWS, breathing is steady – perhaps about 10 breaths a minute – and deep. The musculature is still capable of operating, so there are occasional body movements. Oxygen consumption falls off gradually, reaching a low point after about 6 hours. The pulse rate and breathing rate decline.

People may make between 20 and 60 postural adjustments, but the total time taken for these is only a few minutes. One piece of research, reported by Lienert and Othmer in 1965, indicated that emotionally stable people make more bodily movements in sleep than unstable subjects.

The REM state also has distinct characteristics. Breathing is noticeably faster (perhaps 20 breaths a minute), more variable, and shallower in REM sleep. By definition there are flickering eye movements, which can be observed under the eyelids (*phasic* REM), although the eyes are often quite still in REM sleep (*tonic* REM).

Sleep Patterns in Babies and Children

At birth, REM sleep is present in abundance, constituting perhaps half of the 16 hours or so of daily sleep during the first few weeks. The REMs can often be seen under the eyelids of babies in REM sleep. The total amount of sleep, and REM sleep, then decreases steadily over about 4 years.

The pattern of sleep changes from birth. The newborn baby has a *polyphasic* distribution of perhaps five or six periods of sleep, which reduce as night feeding declines. At a year old, most infants sleep for 12–14 hours at night, with some extra during the day.

Purpose of Sleep – Changing Concepts

An early scientific idea about sleep was that it occurs passively in order to prevent fatigue, or as a result of lack of stimulation. An opposite superseding notion arose, though – that the brain actively inhibits consciousness. For instance, Pavlov thought that sleep was the result of cortical inhibition spreading from certain areas. In further support, Hess discovered that cats could actually be put to sleep by electrical stimulation of part of the brain called the diencephalon. Stimulation of a different area of the brain – the *reticular formation* – wakens sleeping animals, as Moruzzi and Magoun reported in 1949. It has generally become accepted that the reticular formation stimulates the brain to consciousness.

In emergency situations during sleep, where there is a lack of oxygen or an excess of carbon dioxide in the blood, midbrain stimulation automatically occurs to rouse the individual. Wakening will also be instigated if the body's detectors register that it is too cold or too hot. Another form of stimulation that can keep a person awake is the psychological effect of worries, which again, acts as excitation to the reticular formation.

Duration of Dreaming Sleep and Forgetting

The total amount of dreaming sleep for each night is about 2 hours – maybe 6 years in the course of a lifetime – but most of that dreaming is forgotten. Dreams are not erased, but actively suppressed – something the next day can suddenly cause you to remember a dream, so the material is still stored away somewhere. The forgetting occurs, perhaps, because we might otherwise confuse the dream with reality. It seems that we remember dreams – usually fragments – only because we sometimes awaken briefly after them. The average recall is just one fragment every other night, but there are vast individual differences. Some people say they never recall their dreams, while others can give vivid and lengthy descriptions.

Drugs and Sleep

Treatment of Insomnia

The problem of insomnia has been approached, medically, in several different ways. Hypnotics (sleep-inducing drugs) affect various areas of the brain and suppress activity. Anxiety, which may indirectly cause insomnia, can be treated by tranquillizers, and depression, which might cause early-morning awakening, can be treated by antidepressants. In some persons, severe pain – which could be interfering with sleep – may be alleviated by morphine.

At one time, barbiturates were widely used as a powerful and effective soporific, despite their addictive qualities. They were fatal in overdose, because the medulla of the brain, which controls breathing, was affected. Later drugs did not affect the medulla and were safer. However, it is generally agreed now that sleeping-tablets cause or worsen insomnia.

Effect on Rapid Eye-movement (REM) Sleep

It was known that many drugs initially suppress the amount of REM sleep – which then recovers to its normal level – and also that, if REM sleep is prevented, by physically waking the individual, then an excessive, or 'rebound', amount of REM occurs. With the *delirium tremens* (DTs) of alcohol withdrawal, REM imagery spills over into wakefulness.

A major question is whether dreams are the important aspect of REM sleep, or whether they are sidelines to other processes. It has been found, somewhat surprisingly, that REM sleep is not essential to adults, despite the assumption some three decades ago that if you did not dream you would go mad.

Significantly, it has been observed that certain antidepressants (monoamine-oxidase [MAO] inhibitors) totally abolished REM sleep in users, and yet no negative consequences were manifested. Remarkably, it therefore seems that REM sleep is not a necessity in adult humans! It is possible that REM sleep may be important to the developing fetus and infant, considering the great abundance of REM sleep in a newborn baby, but the question is still a mystery to science.

Nevertheless, although the state with which dreaming is largely associated is not essential to our well-being, dreams themselves can have enormous effects on us and can be used by us to gain much self-insight and as a source of immense creativity – as we shall see later in this book.

Sleep-Onset Phenomena

Hypnagogic Imagery

A number of strange phenomena occur to some people in the nodding-off (stage 1) condition of sleep. To some individuals, *hypnagogic* images appear – often in the form of very clear and detailed pictures. The term 'hypnagogic' comes from two Greek words, *hypnos* (sleep) and *agogeus* (leader). There has been discussion between the 'peripheralists', who think such images are caused by stimulation in the retina, and the 'centralists', who say the images are formed in the brain.

In 1959, Oswald pointed out that sense-organ stimulation is not necessary. For instance, it has been noted that patients with a completely severed spinal cord can still experience sexual orgasm, despite there being no nerve connections between the genital organs and the brain.

A sensation of falling when going to sleep is frequently reported. Oswald found that 144 out of 182 students stated that they experienced the feeling when drowsy. Often linked with such a sensation is the *myoclonic jerk* – a sudden exaggerated movement of the body.

The hypnagogic state has been neglected in the past. Sleep-researchers have understandably focused on REM sleep and SWS in their attempts to discover the secrets of sleep and dreaming, but this first stepping-stone into sleep is beginning to be recognized as having its own quite remarkable features.

While some hypnagogic imagery consists of still images, some people, who have woken just a few minutes into sleep, report that they were experiencing a normal dream and having a sense of continuity. Indeed, in a paper published in 1965, Foulkes and Vogel thought that these dreams were very similar to the REM-state variety. So, we can have dreams without the usual accompaniment of REMs.

It seems as if there is a progressing sequence of imagery in the hypnagogic state, starting perhaps with simple colours, shapes, or clouds, going on to clear, single pictures, and then to story-line dreams. But, as with all human phenomena, there are considerable individual differences. Some people have never experienced hypnagogic phenomena, as far as they can recall, while, for others, the nodding-off picture-show is a regular precursor to sleep. Studies have given varying incidences of hypnagogic imagery in the population, but it does seem to be quite high: around 75 per cent of adults.

Dr Hearne wired up three people who said they could 'astral travel' at will. They reclined on a bed for several minutes and were then questioned. All reported being out of their body and going far away. The polygraphic records showed that they had all been in stage 1 sleep, with slow, rolling eye movements, muscular relaxation, and loss of alpha frequency. The experience was a hypnagogic condition. Of course, the state may indeed be especially conducive to the reception of paranormal information.

In the hypnagogic condition, a whole range of sensory phenomena happens. Naturally, the visual displays are the most frequently reported. Usually the individual is a passive observer, i.e. the pictures have their own autonomy.

Seeing faces is a common occurrence and they often bear a specific expression.

As I am drifting into sleep I often start to see people's faces. They drift into sight and are very clear – the minutest details are visible – lasting brilliantly for a while and then disappearing, but another will then come in its place. All sorts of people come, showing all types of emotions. They may be ravishingly beautiful or dreadfully misshapen. If they are ugly, I am often intrigued by them anyway. The pictures are three-dimensional and as vivid as in reality – sometimes more so.

The face phenomenon is so common that it may relate to a special face-recognition ability in the brain. One of the first functions – across species – of a newborn is to recognize its parents. From an evolutionary perspective it is an identification that may be necessary for survival. At birth, babies will look at patterns showing eyes. It may be that the hypnagogic state is touching on extremely primitive perceptual processes.

Other frequently reported pictures are designs (e.g. geometrical patterns and spirals), scenes of nature (wonderfully beautiful landscapes and seascapes), and scenes of congregating people. A plot is not usually present; they are just shown in ordinary situations.

The scenes are usually silent, but sometimes a voice may be heard. It may be the illusion of someone calling your name, or the telephone or doorbell ringing. Amusing cases have been reported of nonsense words and sentences heard in the hypnagogic state. They may or may not link somehow with the visual material. Sometimes, something heard is then immediately seen, demonstrating the operation of Hearne's observation concerning dreams that what you think (or hear) you will then see.

Hearne's scene-shift effect (see p.34) is also a reported phenomenon of the hypnagogic state. A picture will change to another, with the minimum of visual effort, by reusing the pictorial elements of one scene to construct the new one.

The other sensory modalities also make their appearance in hynagogia. Sudden smells can materialize, varying from the exquisite scent of flowers to the pungent smell of decaying organic matter. The hypnagogic smell of acrid smoke woke one experiencer, who was impressed enough to check the property for a sign of fire – there was none.

The sense of being touched or some other bodily sensation may also be present. This may be, say, an erotic stroking, but it can also take the unpleasant form of a sudden great blow to the body, or some painful internal stimulus which strikes. 'Electric shocks' may be felt, or 'a bullet striking the body'. These may be associated with the myoclonic jerk.

In the 1950s, Silberer observed that thoughts just before sleep can be symbolically shown in hypnagogic images, a process which he termed the *auto-symbolic phenomenon*. He noted that, in the twin situation of drowsiness and attempting to think, these images manifest themselves. He categorizes three types:

~ *Material.* He was thinking of improving a part of an essay. He saw himself planing wood.
~ *Functional.* He was thinking of something, but was distracted to another thought. He was mountain-climbing and the close mountains hid the distant ones which he wanted to reach.
~ *Somatic.* He took a deep breath and his chest rose. Someone helped him as he lifted a table.

Powerful drugs can give rise to specific images in wakefulness, and their relatedness to spontaneous hypnagogic imagery has been noted. In 1928, Klüver coined the term *form constants* for these universal images. Examples include gratings, lattice, chessboards, cobwebs, tunnels, and spirals. He found that mescaline hallucinations in wakefulness were like hypnagogia in that they were bright, with many colours, microscopic detail, autonomy, and change. Objects might appear to be distorted (*dysmorphopsia*) and perhaps extra large (*macropsia*) or very small (*micropsia*). Klüver concluded that the same processes were involved.

Hypnopompic Imagery

The other type of imagery experienced on waking is described as *hypnopompic* (following sleep). Hypnopompic images are usually dream images which continue to be seen after waking. If the experiencer is in a state of paralysis, the REM regime is still in operation and there would be doubt about whether the person were really awake. However, if waking has definitely taken place and yet images are observed, this constitutes the hypnopompic condition.

Towards the end of the nineteenth century de Manacéine wrote:

> The appearance of the national flag in my house surprised me so much that I awoke, and on opening my eyes still saw it in front of me, with the three national colours, the eagle, and the two golden tassels, while the staff was slightly bent towards me. It was still night, and the bedroom was in absolute darkness.

Hypnopompic images can seem totally real and may be reacted to accordingly. People have been known to leap out of bed and attack imaginary 'burglars', or objects which have been totally misperceived as sinister. More reticent experiencers have pulled the bedsheets over them after seeing a 'ghost' (perhaps they did). Others have had to switch on the light in order to dispel the scene of hundreds of spiders running over the bed.

An interesting finding concerning hypnopompic imagery, which indicates possible cultural differences, was that by de Manacéine. She discovered that, out of 84 persons reporting this form of imagery, 27 were from Finland.

Sleep in Animals

Different animal species have their own distinctive characteristics of sleep. Some (e.g. rats) are polyphasic – having separate short durations of sleep – while others, like humans, sleep for single long periods. Most mammals exhibit the same cycle of SWS and REM sleep as humans, although the spiny ant-eater, an egg-laying monotreme found in Australia, is a curious exception and puzzle in that it seems to evince no *paradoxical sleep* (the term usually employed instead of REM sleep for animals).

Some of the differences are useful indicators in theorizing about the function of SWS and REM sleep. The rabbit, for instance, does not exhibit paralysis in sleep. From an adaptational view, it would not perhaps be so useful for that species – living in a burrow is not as hazardous as, for example, resting in trees.

Cats can sleep sitting or crouching, but in paradoxical sleep the atonia ensures that they lie flat so that the head is resting on a surface or a paw. In general, predators sleep long and languidly, while those preyed upon, such as grazing animals, sleep for short periods.

Interesting results have emerged in the study of porpoises and dolphins. It was found that, while being constantly awake and swimming, they can alternately close down one hemisphere of their brain, then the other, so that each goes through a process like sleep, with slow waves. They showed none of the features of REM sleep. Some birds, it seems, that 'sleep on the wing' also have this half-sleep ability, but in other birds the usual alternation of SWS and REM sleep occurs. In some, paralysis is absent.

Looking to the future, it is not beyond the bounds of possibility that something like this phenomenon of *hemispheric-alternation sleep* might be artificially applied to humans, so that continuous, healthy wakefulness would be possible. Remarkably, the effect would be to give us a third more available time in our lives.

Theories About Sleep

It has to be admitted that there is no universally accepted theory of why we dream, or even why we sleep. The plethora of suggestions that have come forward simply reinforces the fact that we do not know.

As with many features concerning humans, there are individual differences in the amount of sleep required. Some people can get by with, say, 5 hours sleep each night, but others might feel groggy if they do not have, say, a full 9 hours sleep.

Theories that try to take into account evolutionary factors have been proposed. Thus, Snyder (1966) thought that sleep exists to conserve energy and to keep the organism out of danger from predators, and Meddis (1975) also proposed that sleep serves to maintain immobility in animals as an aid to survival.

Ephron and Carrington (1966) suggested that SWS may be rather harmful to the brain and so 'reafferentation' is periodically introduced in the form of REM sleep. However, Hartmann (1973) believed that SWS is restorative.

It is tempting to think that some kind of renewal occurs in sleep. As mentioned before, creatures like dolphins, which keep swimming and appear never to sleep, shut down first one hemisphere of their brain for a time, then the other. This seems to indicate that some necessary process is going on – but what?

Dreams and Ancient Cultures

There is evidence that dreams were of great interest in ancient societies. Going back to the earliest writings on clay tablets from Assyria and Babylonia, dating from about 5000 BC, some of the cuneiform scripts state specific meanings for dream themes. The universal notion of *opposites* – that the dream could in fact represent the reverse of what it appeared to reveal – had already been noted. Thus, a happy event like a birth or a wedding might in fact portray the sadness of an impending death. There were even temples dedicated to the goddess of dreams, Mamu. It seems that magical ceremonies were held in those places in order to ward off spirits that could cause unpleasant dreams.

Early surviving papyri from Egypt, dating from about 1300 BC, have provided interesting insights into the knowledge of dreams of that society. The revered status of dreams (*omina*) is indicated by the fact that, here too, great temples were built – in particular at Thebes and Memphis – to their god of dreams, Serapis.

At that time, there existed a great tradition of *dream incubation*, whereby a person requiring an answer to an important topic would sleep at a Serapeum in order to receive an appropriate wise message from the gods. The procedure would be preceded by various cleansing rituals, prayers, and fasting. The resulting dreams, even if only because of the high psychological expectation, were probably vivid and indeed meaningful. They would be interpreted by the 'learned men of the magic library'. The system must have been successful in order to survive for such a long period. Again, there were agreed interpretations, often listed as simply good or bad. Thus, to see a snake was a good sign, but for a woman to dream of kissing her husband was a bad indicator (by the rule of opposites).

The ancient Chinese were profoundly philosophically engrossed in the paradox of dreams as a separate existence and pointed out that life itself could be a great dream. McKenzie, in *Dreams and Dreaming* (1965), quotes these words from the famous philosopher Chuang-Tzu (350 BC):

> While men are dreaming, they do not perceive that it is a dream. Some will even have a dream in a dream and only when they wake will they know it was a

dream. And so, when the Great Awakening comes upon us, shall we know this life to be a great dream. Fools believe themselves to be awake now.

The ancient Chinese had the idea that, in sleep, the soul, or *hun*, was free to wander about and could communicate with the souls of the dead. They recognized six types of dream: ordinary dreams, terror dreams, dreams based on the day's thoughts, dreams of waking, dreams of joy, and dreams of fear. Imbalance in the forces of yin and yang could affect dreams.

In the early Hindu texts, such as the *Atharva Veda* (1500 BC) dreams also had their respected place. Active dreams were considered to be favourable, whereas passivity on the part of the dreamer was not propitious.

The ancient Greeks also embraced dreams as a channel for privileged information from the gods. Here, too, dream incubation was also practised, in temples dedicated to Aesculapius. An interesting observation made by them was that the universe, or *macrocosm*, may represent the body, or *microcosm*. Bright stars might therefore be a visual statement meaning a healthy body.

Dreams which were considered to give early warning of illness were termed *prodromic* dreams. Thus, a lung problem might be presaged by dreams of fire before any symptoms appeared. In this culture, seeing a snake might represent approaching illness.

In the fourth century, Plato, contemplating the apparent absence of reasoning in dreams, commented in his *Republic* that 'In all of us, even in good men, there is a lawless wild beast nature which peers out in sleep' – diverging from the idea of a divine source of dreams.

The problem for the Greeks – and indeed for other cultures – was to distinguish between divine (true) and demoniacal (false) dreams. Homer stated, based on a Greek pun, that true dreams entered via the gate of horn whereas false ones came through the gate of ivory.

The Romans, like the Greeks, considered dreams to be special communicatory devices capable of providing both current and future information. One famous second-century Roman treatise on dream interpretation which has survived is *Oneirocritica* (The Interpretation of Dreams) by Artemidorus of Daldis, a Greek who moved to Rome. In this five-volume work, he recorded over 3,000 dreams. His approach was pragmatic, naturalistic, and probably highly efficient. He insisted that the dream related to the dreamer, and that the symbols had to be interpreted taking into account the dreamer's lifestyle. Symbols could mean opposite things to different people, and yet there were some universal representations, e.g. ploughing as a representation of sexual activity.

A long hiatus occurred in writings on dreams, during which the Church linked any such interest with 'sorcery'. Only a few Christian writers mentioned dreams. St Augustine (AD 354–430) thought that demons could influence dreams. Referring to unwelcome sexual dreams, in a prayer attributed to him, he asks God to keep him in 'chaste desire' and protect him from 'animal images' which would cause 'pollution'. St Thomas Aquinas, in *Summa Theologica*, accepted that dreams could foretell the future.

But, after this, for the science of understanding dreams, time stood still – for centuries.

~ ~ ~

David Melbourne and Dr Hearne have proposed that in early, homogeneous societies, where there was common agreement on the meaning of dream symbols (often based on verbal puns, as we shall see later), dreams could be interpreted with relative ease.

Inevitably though, over time, much cultural mixing occurred and, especially because of language interactions, great confusion has resulted. Modern 'dream dictionaries' reflect this mishmash of ideas – of meanings which were originally based on verbal links from another language but which have now become useless.

Theories About Dreams

Before Freud

When thinking and theorizing about dreams began to be acceptable again – in the nineteenth century, in the Age of Rationalism – several writers in France and Germany came up with cogent observations concerning the many phenomena of dreams, this time free of what they considered to be 'supernatural' assumptions. Often, though, they were rediscovering truths which had been known long ago by the ancients.

Delboeuf (1885) showed how *hypermnesia* (extreme retentiveness of memory) can occur in dreams. Thus the name of a plant that he saw in a dream could be traced back to his having written it 2 years previously. Maury (1878) saw in a dream a man who gave his name. He subsequently discovered that he knew him as a small child. Robert (1886) stated that dreams often include events in the previous day. 'Typical' dreams were thought to be caused by somatic stimulation in sleep. Thus, the dream of flying was due to the sensation of the lungs sinking when the thorax was insensitive.

The question of why dreams are forgotten so rapidly and completely on waking was considered. Strumpell (1877) gave a number of reasons, e.g. weak pictures are soon forgotten, dreams lack order, inrushing sensory input swamps memories.

Schleiermacher (1862) pointed out that, in wakefulness, we think in ideas, whereas in dreams we think in pictures. It is an automatic process. Spitta (1882) applied the term dramatization to this transformation of an idea into a hallucination. Once an image was presented, the clear flow of associations along phonetic pathways (puns, etc.) was appreciated.

The ethical nature of dreams was also inspected. Radestock (1879) thought the dream only reveals to us what we do not want to accept in ourselves. Hildebrandt (1875) said inhibition slackens on entering sleep, so the dream reveals our true self.

As to the amount of mind activity in dreams, writers held differing opinions. Delboeuf (1885) believed that the mind continued to operate in sleep in an undiminished way, but most thinkers considered that the dream was a phenomenon linked to a 'partial waking' state. Binz (1878) said that sleep was caused by 'fatigued albumen' in the brain. In the morning, parts of the brain were operating, but not others – this was the time of dreaming.

Most writers, including Maury and Binz, were dismissive of dreams, describing them as 'useless', although a small number of writers actually proposed that dreams have a function. Robert (1886) was of the opinion that they represented a physical process of elimination, or excretion, of nonimportant thoughts. Delage (1891) believed that strong impressions which had been accidentally repressed were the subject of dreams, whose purpose was to resolve psychological tensions. Burdach (1838) thought the dream had a refreshing, recreational function, allowing the dreamer to indulge in free play. A common public belief was that dreams represented wishes.

Scherner (1861) had some thoughts on how dreams arose, which were considered by Freud to be particularly perspicacious. Scherner stated that decentralization occurs in sleep, so that internal fantasy dominates. It uses waking memories and depicts thoughts as symbols. The dream material may be based on sensory stimuli, but the organic source is represented symbolically. Thus, the body may be represented by a house, the penis by a clarinet, pubic hair by fur, or the vagina by a slippery footpath. However, Schnerner could not ascribe a useful function to the dream.

Many ideas, such as symbolization, repression, hypermnesia, childhood memories, dramatization, associations, wish fulfilments, and day residues, already existed before Freud imposed his own speculations on the nature of dreams.

Work of Freud (1856–1939)

Sigmund Freud pioneered the investigation of the unconscious mind and postulated a function of dreaming based on existing ideas and on his own, three-component conceptualization of personality as consisting of:

~ The unconscious *id*, seeking gratification of basic (primary) instincts, especially sex and aggression.
~ The conscious *ego*, in contact with the real world and aware of its behavioural restraints.
~ The *superego*, which reminds the individual on what the behaviour ought to be in a particular situation – based largely on parental example.

The dream, he believed, was the way to understanding the unconscious mind.

He thought that dreams were significant and represented unconscious, repressed, and largely sexual wishes – often of an infantile nature. He was probably influenced by the strong association that all men recognize between penile erection and dreaming. Correlation, however, does not guarantee a cause-and-effect link. We now know that the erection cycle is independent of the REM dreaming cycle, but that they usually coincide.

The bizarre features of dreams were thought of as manifestations of some elaborate disguise mechanism. In sleep, the ego is absent, so the id (like Plato's 'wild beast') reigns. Freud thought that the organism essentially seeks inactivity, and that the function of dreams involves trying to give some kind of vicarious gratification to the wayward id's requirements without rousing the individual. Thus, the dream was the 'guardian' of sleep, i.e. it maintained the state of sleep.

But in order that the ego and superego should not be horrified by blatant gratification in the form of internally generated imagery, the dream material had to be converted into something that was symbolic and could thus fool a hypothetical *censor* mechanism. Thus, the original and lustful dream thoughts (the *latent* content) became transformed into a symbolic and stilted version (the *manifest* content) that was acceptable to the higher sensibilities. The psychoanalyst would trace back the various links by a process known as *free association* and so uncover the basic wishes – which arose either from unconscious id urges or were triggered by some conscious desire, often from the previous day.

Freud went to town on sexual imagery in dreams. The male organ might be shown, after the 'dreamwork' process, as the number 3, a serpent, a machine, or a stick, while the female genitalia could be referred to as a pit, cave, or landscape. Masturbation might be represented by sliding or gliding. In trying to make sense of the manifest content on recollection, distortions could appear in the waking account: a process of revision, or *secondary elaboration*.

Freud could not really adequately explain anxiety dreams as wish fulfilments so he tried to explain them as the result of incompetent dreamwork, the fulfilment of the wish itself causing anxiety, and over-powering by the censor. He maintained, as did the ancients, that the emotional aspect of the dream is a key interpretational signifier, remaining the same in both latent and manifest content – unless it represents the contrary (again an old wisdom concerning dreams which is now termed *reaction-formation*).

A process of condensation might combine different wishes into a composite. Thus, a repressed desire for two people to resemble each other could result in a dream image in which one is seen in the typical clothes of the other. By the device of displacement, significant elements of the dream thoughts might be transferred to a seemingly insignificant feature. Causal connections between items were indicated by scenes transforming into other ones. Reversals could greatly assist the disguise process, e.g. a wish for someone's death might be portrayed as a birth dream.

Not surprisingly, many criticisms have been aimed at Freud's ideas. At a profound philosophical level, Carl Popper (1959) considered psychoanalytical theory – including dream theory – to be a myth. It was all too easily verifiable but not falsifiable, i.e. cases could always be found to support it, but it was difficult to disprove anything.

Eysenck (1953) thought that Freudian ideas were unscientific. Certainly, by modern methodological procedures, his work was not rigorous or experimental enough. He used no control groups, did not quantify data, and relied much on his memory – and memory, of course, can be highly selective. On the other hand, Kline (1972) claimed that several empirical studies gave support for Freudian notions.

Fisher and Dement (1963) argued that, if the primary urges of the id were not gratified (as illusion) in the dream, psychotic behaviour would result. A need to dream was postulated by Dement (1960). However, Dement (1976) later acknowledged that animals low down in the evolutionary scale have REM sleep. The finding that some drugs abolish REM sleep in humans, yet with no apparent negative effects, has quashed the need-to-dream idea.

The objective linking of penile erections with REM sleep seemed at first to support the idea of the sexual nature of dreams, but the finding, by Karacal and his colleagues (1965), that repeatedly waking subjects in REM sleep led to the erection cycle occurring outside REM sleep demolished a key piece of physiological evidence in support of Freud.

Much of what Freud said was, as we have seen, already known. With the removal of his own major contribution concerning sexual wishes involved in dreams, we are very much back to where we started.

Work of Jung (1875–1961)

It was foreseeable that some followers of Freud would deviate from his uncompromising stance on dreams, and so it was that his student Carl Gustav Jung took exception to his theorizing.

Jung had a totally different concept of the unconscious, seeing it as our friend, guide, and advisor rather than a dark place full of repressed desires. It would try to communicate important information in dreams and visions. It had a compensatory function, so that any imbalance in our nature might be recognized and changed. In life, we undergo individuation, involving the reconciliation of opposing factors in our personality.

In Jungian dream analysis a series of dreams is often investigated. The analyst maintains the associations about the dreams rather than keeping a distance from them, and the therapist's associations are also included. A dream containing an important message may be repeated until it is recognized. We need to take heed of the wisdom of our caring unconscious.

Some dreams are prospective and look to future events for the dreamer. This is in contrast to Freud's beliefs, in which dreams are very much stuck with the primitive urges of the infant. To Jung, the censor did not exist.

Apart from our personal unconscious, Jung asserted that there exists a collective unconscious, shared by all humankind. Certain rare dreams contain *archetypes*, or motifs – also recognized by Freud – which are images that seem to be universal. Thus, for example, within us we have both a male and female part, which can be projected into our dreams respectively as the *animus*, or *anima*. We also have a shadow – a dark side to our nature – which may appear as a symbol or be represented as an unpleasant dream character.

After Jung

Since Jung, some other writers and practitioners have carried on the idea that dreams can be decoded and can help substantially with self-improvement and discovery. Frederick (Fritz) Perls, a South African psychotherapist, developed a *Gestalt* approach in his workshops in California in the 1960s. The past is not so important – what matters is the present.

In his sessions, Perls would get clients, using an 'empty-chair' technique, to play the role of other dream characters and objects – to give them voice so as to understand the full dynamics of the dream.

Recent ideas on dreams have tended to concentrate more on REM sleep – the matrix in which the dream appears. Evans and Newman (1964) saw the dream as a mere by-product of memory organizational processes going on in the brain. By analogy, they noted that the computers of that age needed to go off-line for updating programs. They stated that human memory traces are adaptive to new situations and need to be modified.

Short rerouting of several items would be reflected in 'non-sensical' dreams, whereas modification of lengthy programmes would result in long 'sensible' dreams. Repeated dreams would be caused by constant interruptions in the process.

Crick and Michison (1986) also saw the brain as coping with overload during REM sleep. These fashionable computer-similarity ideas may have had a niche when there seemed to be a need to dream, but they are now somewhat obsolete.

Melbourne and Hearne (1997) have stressed the wisdom of the simple approach, used by the ancients, of seeking the dreamer's own associations with dream items and looking for wordplays and metaphors in providing the real, unbiased, interpretation.

We find ourselves now in the situation where dreaming sleep as such does not appear to be a necessary part of human experience but, if correctly identified and interpreted, dreams can provide extremely valuable information that can warn, advise, and encourage the dreamer.

Dream Phenomena

Lucid Dreams

In ordinary dreams there is very little insightful comprehension of what is going on. You may, for instance, encounter an elephant in your kitchen, but the impossibility of that does not bother you too much. Although there may indeed be a vibrant, second-by-second awareness of events in ordinary dreams, the attention span is extremely limited and there is no background frame of reference – as if the memories of your identity and other relevant information are switched off.

However, there exists a particular type of dream – the *lucid dream* – in which you suddenly realize, incredibly, that you are dreaming. If you have not experienced a lucid dream, it is difficult to describe adequately, but most people have experienced at least a short moment of dream lucidity. In some people lucidity can last for many minutes.

What happens is absolutely remarkable. Paradoxically and incongruously, you actually become fully cognisant, with the sort of clarity of thought you have in wakefulness, that you are in fact in an ongoing dream. It is like being awake, in possession of all your critical faculties, but knowing that the whole realistic setting in which you find yourself is a complete fake. You can talk to people sensibly, and yet you are aware that it is all an ongoing construction of your mind.

The other main characteristic of lucid dreams, apart from the conscious comprehension of the state, is that the dream itself may be manipulated by mere thought. There are individual differences in the ability to control lucid dreams, but theoretically, any situation can be conjured up. A technique to bring up a new location is to 'cover' your (dream) eyes for a moment and think very clearly where you want to be.

You can call up a specific person by willing them to appear when you open a door. Thus, it is possible to experience anything at all in these dreams. Some people revel in simply observing the cleverly produced images, while others indulge in unbridled sexual passions with dream characters. These dreams, as can be appreciated, have a vast potential in unlocking secrets of dreaming and the unconscious mind, and as a field for recreation and therapy. Lucidity in dreams most frequently happens when some glaring inconsistency is noticed in the dream scenery, e.g. seeing someone who is known to be dead in reality, or finding yourself wearing something which you just know you would never wear.

Dr Hearne conducted the world's first sleep-laboratory research into lucid dreams for his PhD in the mid-1970s. Some 18 months after starting that work he had his first lucid dream:

> Firstly, it was a very vivid and detailed ordinary dream in which I was walking along a beach. I saw some coins in the sand. As I dug them out they were as big as plates. It suddenly dawned upon me that I was dreaming. I stood up in the dream with an incredible feeling of elation. My mind was perfectly clear and the scene was absolutely like reality.

Lucid dreams were hardly known in the 1970s, and there had only been a few written accounts. In the nineteenth century a French nobleman and oriental scholar, the Marquis Hervey de St-Denys, published a book in France about his own frequent experience of these dreams, in which he described himself as being 'conscious of my true situation', often every night.

Taking advantage of the unusual condition, St-Denys conducted many important and useful experiments, including some where his manservant would administer different stimuli, such as sounds and perfumes, while St-Denys was sleeping. St-Denys noted the flow of associations in dreams and the transformation of images, e.g. a spinning dancer into a bobbin (*similarity of form*).

He was sure of the important role of verbal links in dream images. In one dream he met a girl named Sylvia. Instantly he found himself in a thick forest (Latin *silva*, meaning wood, or forest) and the girl had an attractive bird perched on her shoulder.

In similar vein, Dr Hearne had a dream in which he was on a train which drew into a station called *Akpinar*. This in fact was the name of psychologist whose research papers he had been reading that day. Immediately there was a change of location and Hearne was *in a park* (an anagram of the name 'Akpinar'). The anagram had been worked out unconsciously, and the result had acted as an instruction for the next dream image.

St-Denys recognized that dreams represented underlying thoughts. If something was thought in the dream, it then appeared in the dream scenery. The imagery, he considered, came from previous actual perceptions of the individual.

One of his dreams provided a good example of hypermnesia (where something is produced that seems new but is really based on forgotten experiences). In the dream, he found himself in Brussels, a place he had never visited. He could see the well-known church of St Gedule in the background. St-Denys, fully lucid, inspected a particular store carefully. Months later, he went to Brussels and looked for the store without success. Years later, he was in Frankfurt and stumbled across the store. He realized that he had been there before when he was 17 years old.

Prior indications of illness came up in some of his dreams. Headaches followed dreams of climbing mountains easily. He also noted that certain drugs, such as morphine, resulted in specific images.

An interesting memory phenomenon he discovered was that previous dreams could be recalled in subsequent dreams better than in the intervening period of wakefulness. In the next century, in the area of learning theory, this type of memory effect would be described as *state-dependent*.

Another important observation was that, when an image is selected from memory for the purposes of the dream, the original feeling attached to the image is also introduced. Thus, when, in a dream, he and his family were having dinner with his host and family, the door opened and his former art-teacher appeared with a naked model, no-one was bothered by the sight. St-Denys had seen the model before, in the matter-of-fact atmosphere of the artist's studio.

In one of his external stimuli studies, St-Denys painted a canvas on the theme of Pygmalion, all the while keeping a piece of orris root in his mouth. At a later date, his servant placed the substance between his lips while he was sleeping. A dream occurred about the same story.

It was the Dutchman Dr Frederik van Eeden who came up with the convenient term 'lucid dream' at a meeting in London in 1913, when he presented a paper entitled 'A study in dreams' to the Society for Psychical Research. He reported on his findings after having personally experienced some 350 such dreams.

He, too, used the situation to observe and conduct experiments within the dream. He found that bodily sensations did not enter into dreams at the time:

In April 1906 I was suffering from violent toothache. I was in Italy . . . I had a perfect recollection of my waking life; I knew that I was sleeping and that my tooth was still aching. Yet I did not feel it . . . Next morning the pain was felt again and I had the tooth extracted.

Van Eeden was aware there was no muscular activity in dreams. As an experiment he would sometimes sing and shout, but his wife assured him that he was always quiet during these episodes. He was also certain that these were genuine dreams, associated with 'deep sleep' and not a product of the near-waking state. He stated that, without exception, his lucid dreams happened between 5 a.m. and 8 a.m.

Perhaps reflecting his moralistic nature, van Eeden never experienced anything sexual or erotic in his dreams. In fact, he sometimes observed 'demons', which would try to lure him into lascivious situations.

Celia Green (1968) collected the small number of published reports on lucid dreaming and collated the data. Green noted a transitional, *prelucid* state in the ordinary dream, when the dreamer is close to deciding whether or not the experience is a dream.

She observed that lucidity appeared to occur as a result of emotional stress within the dream, the recognition of some incongruity, the initiation of analytical thought, or the noticing of some dream-like quality of the experience. The great physical and psychological realism of these dreams was reported by Green.

On the topic of memory in lucid dreams, she was of the opinion that a sort of hierarchy of memory exists. General psychological reflections and intentions are most easily recalled, and information on the physical world. Less well recalled are specific intentions concerning the lucid dream and long-term memories. Recent memories of the dreamer's life may be subject to inaccuracies. If this last point is correct, it may indicate that in lucid dreams, and perhaps in ordinary dreams, those areas of the brain dealing with the consolidation and storage of short- and medium-term memories are somewhat divorced from the areas dealing with dream consciousness.

Rather than experimentation, the Frenchman Yves Delage (1919) took to enjoying lucid dreams in a daredevil way. In one reported dream, when he was standing on a precipice and became lucid, he suddenly knew that everything was illusory, and that he was in no real danger, so he hurled himself off the cliff. On these occasions, he would either arrive at the ground without a shock or enjoy 'a delightful flight'.

These were some of the early pioneers of lucid dreaming. Since then, of course, many others have learnt to experience them and have discovered for themselves the curious and yet consistent world of the lucid state.

Signals from the Dream World

The first sleep-laboratory research into lucid dreaming was conducted by Keith Hearne, for his PhD in England in the 1970s.

Hearne followed up the suggestion of Charles Tart (1965) that communication might be established between the lucid-dreamer and waking world. The practical problem, though, was the muscular paralysis of REM sleep. If lucid dreams were true dreams in REM sleep, atonia would be present. Van Eeden's reports indicated strongly that lucid dreams were indeed a REM-state phenomenon. Hearne had the idea that volitional ocular movements might be possible in REM sleep. In any case, by definition, spontaneous random movements occurred there.

At Hull University, Hearne instructed a subject who had fairly frequent lucid dreams to make a series of eight side-to-side eye movements on attaining lucidity. On the morning of 12 April 1975, the first-ever ocular signals from within a lucid dream were recorded. The signals could act as event-markers and, in addition, specific information could be conveyed from within the lucid dream.

Hearne moved to Liverpool University and conducted 3 years of research into the psychology and physiology of lucid dreams. Among many discoveries, he found that lucid dreams were indeed true REM dreams, and that lucidity was invariably preceded by a 'prelucid REM burst' (perhaps paralleling cortical stimulation to the point of lucidity).

It was confirmed that the waking report was an accurate statement of what was experienced, within the limits of short-term memory. The sequence of reported events on waking corresponded with the sequence of signals given at certain points. Thus, for the first time, it was shown that a dream was indeed a dream occurring in REM sleep (there had been no real evidence until then), and that such dreams operated in real time. There is still a widespread misconception that dreams are 'over in a flash', an idea propagated by Maury in the nineteenth century.

During the course of this research, Hearne also invented the world's first 'dream machine'.

Lucid-dream Induction

There are various ways to induce lucid dreams, or to increase their frequency. A general prerequisite is to read as much as possible about lucid dreaming so that the various phenomena which might be encountered are understood. Keeping a dream diary is also a very useful aid. It increases dream recall and focuses much personal attention on your dreams.

Since lucidity is usually caused by the recognition of some incongruity that is noticed in the dream, it is often a good idea to 'practise' by stopping at random times in wakefulness, asking yourself whether you are dreaming, and looking for any 'anomalies'. At the same time think to yourself 'Am I dreaming?' The same questioning will begin to appear in your dreams. Before sleep, tell yourself to look out for anything unusual in dreams so that you can become lucid.

You can also instruct your unconscious to assist matters by producing a particular sign in the dream, which you will immediately recognize as a 'cue'. This could be anything from a particular person, object, or even an emotion.

One method, devised by Dr Hearne, is known as the FAST technique (*false awakening with state testing*). You get someone to come into your bedroom every half hour or so after about 6 a.m. They simply say a few words and then go out again. You do not have to respond. Expectation has a strong psychological effect, and unconsciously you will be anticipating the interruptions, so there will almost certainly be occasions when you actually dream that the person has come into the room.

If you religiously go through a series of 'state tests' to determine whether you are dreaming (even if you are convinced that you are awake), a time may come when you discover that you are, in fact, dreaming.

The sort of tests to conduct are these:

~ Can you switch on a light? If the light fails to come on for any reason, this can indicate dreaming (see below).
~ Is the light level correct for the time?
~ Are the sounds (e.g. a ticking clock or noises outside) as they should be?
~ Try floating or pushing your hand through the bed or a wall (in a dream these are both possible).

Light-switch Effect

The world of dreams has its own seeming laws of physics and there are certain very interesting, consistent effects. It is, of course, essential to be aware of these because they can reveal to us useful information about the *dream-producing process* (DPP). Also, importantly from the point of view of dream interpretation, we need to recognize them so as not to ascribe erroneous 'meanings'.

The first reliably determined, consistent effect in dreams was identified by Dr Hearne in a paper published in 1981. Hearne had read and heard many dream reports. People often referred to not being able to switch on a light in a dream. This *light-switch effect* was not a phenomenon that could have been anticipated from any dream theory, and yet it appeared as a frequent problem for dreamers.

Hearne realized that lucid dreaming was an ideal way of conducting an experiment on the matter. The experiment was simple: eight habitual lucid-dreamers from all over England were selected to perform the task of switching on an electric light in the dream scenery and reporting back what happened. No indications were given of what might occur, and all the subjects responded in isolation. They did not know one another. None of the lucid-dreamers could switch a light on in the dream scenery. Various reasons emerged:

> I switched it on and off several times and looked up at the light, which was a naked bulb. It kept sparking and flickering. I could see the filament glow orangey-red. I thought 'Typical of this place, nothing works'.

> I know I'm dreaming when the bedside lamp will not switch on.

> I tried switching on the lights in the corridor, but nothing happened.

These were typical responses. One subject found that all the light switches had mysteriously disappeared, and another found that the lights came on dimly in another room. Another stated that he could switch a light off and then on again, but could not increase the original 'illumination' in the dream. The effect provides insight into dream construction. It is as if, although the overall subjective 'brightness' of dreams alters over time (some dreams are dark, some very bright, and others in between), it is not possible suddenly to increase the level by dream-control techniques. The current subjective brightness level of dreams is set at the maximum. When, during lucidity, the individual tries to increase the 'brightness', the DPP has to come up with some reason for its inability to change the level. The DPP, in effect, deceives the dreamer.

There are probably many such limitations in dream construction, and research is going on in this area. To attempt to interpret them is a useless exercise. A Freudian might possibly dwell on the inability representing impotence in a male. A Jungian might stress the metaphor of 'not seeing the light'. Both explanations might sound compelling, but the more straight-forward explanation – that it is a basic limitation in the DPP –would have been missed by both schools. Unfortunately, there are many 'dream interpreters' today who are still unaware of these basic limitations.

Scene-shift Effect

The phenomenon of one dream scene changing into another scene has attracted the attention of various introspectionists. The strong rule of associations operating in the succession of thoughts in the dream state has suggested that dreams flow along *verbal-associative pathways*. The link may be via similar-sounding words, anagrams, acronyms, etc.

However, some research conducted by Dr Hearne, using good visualizers in hypnotic dreams, has provided evidence of another kind of associative process in visual imagery. He discovered the *scene-shift effect*. Hearne was trying to find a way of externalizing the internal imagery of hypnotic dreams. He had devised a technique of getting subjects to hold a still image, with eyes open, in a dark room and to scan the image at a distance using a slowly moving point of light. The subject would call out when the light hit an outline in the scene. However, a quicker and better method was perfected. The hypnotic subject was seated in front of a drawing-board, on an easel, in a dimly lit room. Hearne would induce hypnosis, and a hypnotic dream theme would be suggested. At any point in the dream Hearne would tap a pencil on a desk, which was the signal for the subject to stop the dream imagery.

The subject was then instructed to 'freeze-frame' the image, convert it into a two-dimensional representation, open his/her eyes, and 'project' the picture onto the drawing-board. Then, the subject was handed a pen and told to *trace* the image. Colours were described by the subject, noted down by Hearne, and added later.

Using a stop-start method, and thus obtaining a whole sequence of such traced images, Hearne soon discovered a consistent scene-change effect between and within subjects. These are two reported examples:

A scene shows the thick reddish-brown trunk of a tree, with a green snake around it in one coil. The next scene shows a cellar, with a brick-red wall. A green pipe, like a single coil, comes out of the wall and curves round to end at a background grey.

A schoolteacher stands behind a large desk, and two children sit at their small desks facing here. The carpet is blue, the wood is brown, and a blackboard is seen. The very next scene is an overhead view of a room. Three people can be seen, and there are three items of furniture: a large sofa and two smaller chairs. The carpet is blue and brown, and black items are present.

It is very likely that these *visual-associative pathways* in hypnotic imagery apply in all imaging situations, including dreams, daydreams, and hallucinations. In which case, it becomes evident that dreams progress by a 'law of least effort'. It is an efficient process to use all the pictorial elements and concepts of one scene and shift them around to make a new scene. It is indeed a change of picture, but it is a recycled version of the previous one. Once again, the dream – in a sense – fools the dreamer. Hearne has termed his technique *hypno-oneirography* (the tracing of dream images under hypnosis). It illustrates perhaps another limitation in dream construction. The dream may not be free to produce anything instantly; it looks very much as if the dream can only move on from one picture to another by association, while constantly coming back to the basic underlying thoughts or metaphor.

Trigger Effect

David Melbourne has discovered that the phenomenon of waking directly from an ongoing dream is often a determined effort by the unconscious to point out an important message. He has named this the *trigger effect*. Such stopped-dreams take on a special significance in dream interpretation.

Sleep Paralysis

Some people experience a sleep condition in which they feel that they have woken and yet are absolutely unable to move. The slightest twitch of a muscle is impossible, and any attempt to speak or attract attention is futile. This sensation of being 'trapped in sleep' can be extremely frightening, and when wakening does occur, perhaps some minutes later, the sufferer usually has a racing heartbeat and fast breathing rate. Some sufferers think they have died, or that it is a sign of some impending physical or mental illness. Equally though, some individuals are not bothered by it and may be interested in its very unusualness.

The condition is also known as 'night-nurse's paralysis'. Characteristically the night nurse would perhaps be asleep at a desk when the matron's approaching footsteps were heard. Unfortunately, at that point, the nurse would be quite unable to move. Dismissal was at hand! In fact, the footsteps were nearly always dreamt – the fear of being found asleep actually acted as an instruction to the DPP. The condition has been reported particularly by persons who are supposed to be vigilant but have fallen asleep.

The cause of the condition centres around the natural bodily paralysis, or atonia, of REM sleep. It seems that there may be a temporary out-of-synchronization situation between the mind-alerting brain system and the body-paralysis system. In effect, the brain is awake yet the body is still in REM sleep. The sensory information seemingly received in the state, though, is hallucinatory. These are two typical reports:

> I am aware that I am in bed and aware of everything around me. The room is exactly the same as normal. I have a terrible feeling of being frightened because I can't move a muscle. I become very desperate.

> I am aware that my husband is lying beside me so I shout to him at the top of my voice to help. He always insists that I made no sound.

Often, 'intruders' with some evil intent are hallucinated. One woman described to Dr Hearne how, a few years previously, in her late 20s, she experienced sleep paralysis for the first time and had no idea what it was. Worse was to come: the devil appeared and started licking her neck. The woman's hair actually went white overnight through the massive shock.

Another woman reported:

> I heard footsteps on the stairs. The bedroom door started opening and creaking. I was laid with my eyes open and I could see the door open but could not move because I was totally paralysed. When I woke up, the door was tightly shut.

In REM sleep only the eyes are mobile, but Dr Hearne discovered, during the course of his PhD researches into lucid dreams, that the breathing rate may be volitionally altered. One woman noticed that her mother was making peculiar breathing noises and called a physician. The mother had been suffering a period of sleep paralysis. Alarmingly, the doctor had no idea what it was.

Some ghost stories seem to originate from this strange condition, e.g. where an apparition is seen at the foot of the bed, and the observing individual finds that they cannot move. The latest version of this is the alien being which appears and produces a ray gun that paralyses the individual in bed.

A related condition to sleep paralysis is termed *narcolepsy*. Instead of going first into SWS and then into REM sleep, narcoleptics immediately enter REM sleep. These people tend to collapse easily when tired, and may even do so if they laugh, cry, or have an orgasm. Many are wrongly diagnosed as being schizophrenic. As soon as they fall asleep, they start to dream.

There is a simple way to deal with sleep paralysis. First the sufferer should recognize the condition and label it: 'It's sleep paralysis – I read about it.' Such labelling takes away the unknown element and is reassuring. Then, instead of trying desperately to move – which is an almost universal response – the sufferer should do the opposite and simply relax. Any seemingly untoward events going on around can be ignored – they are often there when this phenomenon occurs. The experiencer will then automatically fall back into ordinary REM sleep, which will come to an end naturally a short time later.

False Awakenings

A *false awakening* is the convincing illusion of having woken, when in fact you are still asleep and dreaming. It is different from the sleep-paralysis effect because there is no experience of sleep atonia. Of course, the body is actually paralysed, but the individual is in a full REM state, and everything is dreamt.

The false awakening is a halfway house to dream lucidity. The mind can be very clear, but there is no insight that the extremely realistic setting is really being dreamt. Sometimes, however, anomalies are noticed which can cause lucidity:

I thought I'd woken. My bedroom was exactly as it is in reality. I tried to switch on the bedside lamp but it didn't come on. I tried to put the radio on, but that too did not work. Then I got up and looked out of the window, and the scene was totally different from how it is really. It then dawned on me that I was dreaming.

Quite often a false awakening comes after a lucid dream: you 'wake' into another dream. Sometimes people seem to wake from a lucid dream and perhaps tell someone, only to wake up properly shortly afterwards.

An amazing phenomenon is repeated false awakenings, where you seem to come out of a false awakening several times, serially.

Celia Green classified two types of false awakening:

~ *Type 1*. This is the usual situation. The following example was cited from van Eeden: I had a lucid dream in which I made the following experiment. I drew with my finger, moistened by saliva, a wet cross on the palm of my hand, with the intention of seeing whether it would still be there after waking up. Then I dreamt that I woke up and felt the wet cross on my left hand by applying the palm of my hand to my cheek. And then a long time afterwards I woke up really and knew at once that the hand of my physical body had been lying in a closed position undisturbed on my chest all the while.

~ *Type 2*. In this variety the dreamer wakens into an atmosphere of suspense or drama. A nurse reported: I dreamt I was sleeping and had wakened on hearing what I thought was one of the nursing officers. I dived across the room, knocking over tables and chairs. Then I heard voices at the door and the door being locked. I then realized I was dreaming and decided to wake up. What I did not realize was that I 'woke' into another dream, and when I stood up everything was lying on the floor as it was in my first dream. The door was locked, so I began banging on it and shouting to get out. My relief nurse unlocked the door. Shortly afterwards I really woke up.

Shared Dreams

There exists an extremely puzzling phenomenon whereby two or more people share the same dream, either at the same time or on different occasions. These dreams are fairly frequent and probably occur much more often than we think, because people do not often compare their dreams. The synchronicities usually become apparent accidentally.

Typical is the case of John Flynn, who lives in Ireland. He experienced a dream of being in a large mansion situated in extensive grounds, with a pink gatehouse. There was a party, and an incident where his grandfather had been given a golf cart but it had not been plugged-in to recharge.

A short while later he visited his mother in England and discovered that she was having the same dream, including the party, the golf cart, and the pink gatehouse. The mansion was one that neither John nor his mother had ever visited. The only possible causative link was that, very close to the dreams, was the anniversary of the death of John's grandmother.

David Melbourne also reports:

Being married to an enthusiastic dream researcher, my wife has got used to some of my strange behaviour, as I scent the bedroom with essential oils, breathe erratically during hypnagogic meditations, write down dream accounts in the middle of the night, switch on the bedside light to establish if I am experiencing a false awakening and so forth. However, her patience is most often tested if I awaken from a particularly interesting or fantastic dream and begin describing it.

During October 1987, I awoke from a dream in which I had been wandering around a large empty house that had some unique features, a dome in one of the rooms, for instance. During this dream, I was strangely aware that I knew this house and had dreamt of it several times before, although I was unable to recall details. The entire dream was accompanied by feelings of excitement and anticipation.

As I described this house to Chris (my wife), she suddenly became wide awake and looked aghast at me. 'That's impossible!' she exclaimed. 'I've just been having the same dream.'

She then began to continue the description of the house, which left no doubt that it was indeed the same. However, the story doesn't end there. Some years later, my Uncle Fred, who lives hundreds of miles away, wrote to me to ask if I could make sense out of one of his dreams. He went on to explain that, in his dream, he had found himself in a strange house. As I read on, his description of a dome in one of the rooms sent a shiver down my back. I was reading an account of the same dream!

These barely researched dreams are massively important because they challenge current science head-on. It is not a case of trying to ascertain how close a dream is to an event – as when we consider telepathic or precognitive dreams. The association is obvious. The main question centres on determining the common connecting features.

There are certain points on which we need to know more. For instance, how many people can share the same dream? Can the dreamers be complete strangers who have never met? A range of explanations suggest themselves:

~ Tapping into a collective unconscious.
~ A common, psychological, initiating element unconsciously or consciously experienced (e.g. the anniversary of a related event, or something said the previous day).
~ Telepathy or precognition.
~ The playing of common in-built dream sequences which can be triggered by a physical stimulus – perhaps even solar radiation (which should show a correlation with the solar cycle) or barometric pressure.
~ Our existence in some kind of illusory, nonphysical world.

Major science-shaking discoveries could be made in this little-known area where ordinary logical reasoning seems not to apply. Just as the physics of the ordinary world have been shown to be inappropriate to high-energy physics, so the psychological and philosophical aspects of ordinary wakefulness seem to require a whole new scheme of things when considering the dream world.

Dream and Sleep Disorders

Nightmare Dreams

Some 96 per cent of reported nightmares are frightening REM-sleep dreams which awaken the individual. The sufferer may awaken in a state of extreme exhaustion and anxiety, with racing heart, rapid breathing, and profuse sweating. There are clearly dangers to sufferers from cardiac or respiratory problems. Surveys suggest that perhaps a million people in the UK experience nightmares at a frequency of two or more per week.

In a sample of predominantly female nightmare-sufferers, Dr Hearne found that the themes of nightmares were, in descending order of frequency: witnessing horror and violence, experiencing attack or danger, flight from someone or something, a sinister presence, being late and frustrated in travel, suffocation, seeing nasty creatures, and being paralysed. In nearly 80 per cent of these frequent sufferers (minimum of one nightmare per month, maximum of several per night) the nightmares started before they were 20 years of age. Nine out ten said they experienced recurring nightmare themes.

In the same study, Hearne obtained personality-test measurements of the sufferers. It emerged that nightmare-sufferers have a particular type of personality which is characterized by the following factors: affected by feelings (emotionally less stable), apprehensive, tense, undisciplined (following own urges), and self-sufficient.

We are all different in how we react to situations. One person may go through a trauma and cope with it, whereas another may go through the same event and have constant nightmares about it subsequently.

Many millions of people who have lived through the horror of war still relive some traumatic episode, sometimes nightly, in their dreams. Part of them is stuck at that particular time. It is the same for, say, rape or bullying victims. Just over half the subjects in Hearne's study stated that their nightmares could readily be traced back to such specific incidents.

The repeating nature of many nightmares shows that there is 'unfinished business' going on – that there needs to be a sense of finality or completion about the original events. Hypnotherapy is a good method of revisiting the original scene, releasing the trapped emotion, and informing the unconscious mind that the event was in the past and no longer has any relevance.

Sleep is a welcome balm to most of us, but some people suffer nightmares so severely that they are absolutely phobic about going to sleep and may become suicidal. In Hearne's sample, 44 per cent of the sample really disliked going to sleep.

One surprising finding was that these nightmares happen not in the second half of night (when there is abundant REM sleep, in which most lucid dreams occur) but in the first half of the night. The significance of this fact is crucial in understanding nightmares. It indicates that they are caused not by encountering images in dreams that would – by association – set off the nightmare, but that they are physiologically engendered.

Nightmare-sufferers are 'jumpy' people anyway, and it seems that this sensitivity level continues for a while into sleep. Any kind of sudden stimulus – external or internal – could cause the preset nightmare scenario to roll. It is an established routine in many people.

The Freudian approach to nightmares puts it all down to sex. In 1949, Jones stated the official psychoanalytical position: 'The nightmare is an expression of intense mental conflict centring about some form of repressed sexual desire'. Today, most psychologists would view that attitude as ludicrous.

Some nightmares appear when you suddenly stop taking a powerful drug. What happens is that, when you start taking the drug, REM sleep is powerfully suppressed so that little or no dreaming is present. Over time the body develops 'tolerance', and the amount of REM sleep and associated dreaming gradually come back to the usual amount. However, a sudden discontinuation of the drug results in an immediate 'rebound' effect, with superabundance of REM sleep. Unfortunately, severe nightmares often accompany this rebound. For this reason, many people tend to stay on powerful medications. They need to reduce their dosage slowly over a period.

Dealing with Nightmares
The development of a very successful new therapeutic method for dealing with nightmares was reported by Dr Hearne in 1993. Based on his work on

lucid dreams and his research into nightmares, he devised a method for converting nightmares into controllable lucid dreams.

The technique takes advantage of the fact that frequent nightmare-sufferers nearly always have some kind of anticipatory negative thought in the dream just before the nightmare starts. The negative mind-set of the sufferer is changed from 'Oh my God, here's the nightmare' (typical) to 'Great, wonderful – here's the nightmare! That means I'm dreaming and I can control my dreams.' Sufferers are encouraged to practise the new dream thought daily. It is pointed out to sufferers that they have an advantage over most people because a consistent 'cue' (the nightmare-onset thought) enters their dreams fairly frequently.

Dream-control methods are explained. For instance, a way to deal with any chasing monster or mad axeman is to turn and face them, point your fingers directly at them, and visualize laser beams emanating from your fingers. The pursuer will be demolished and your fears dissolved. With a feeling of great mastery, you may then 'will' yourself to some exotic new location of your choice – perhaps by the eye-covering method already described (see Lucid Dreams, p.28). Nightmare sufferers can then actually hope that the introductory thoughts continue to crop up in dreams so that they can further explore the tremendous joys of lucid dreaming.

Dr Hearne also produced an electronic way of alleviating nightmares. One of the operations of his 'dream-machine' invention is to detect the increased breathing rate during nightmares. The device then initiates an incrementing audible alarm to awaken the user without shock. The effect is to interrupt the nightmare at an early stage before it becomes too severe. The reassurance to users that any nightmare will be nipped in the bud in this way is clearly beneficial.

Slow-wave Sleep (SWS) Nightmares

About 4 per cent of all nightmares are of this variety. Also known as *sleep terrors*, or *pavor nocturnus*, they happen in SWS – usually in the first half of the night's sleep and often within 90 minutes of sleep onset. They are interesting because they occur suddenly, with no prior warning – heart rate and breathing rate do not build up over a few minutes, as with REM nightmares. The sufferer often screams and perhaps jumps out of bed, in great agitation. There is much disorientation – the person may be incoherent and shaking. When questioned, there is usually only a mention of some fearful situation, not of a long preceding dream.

Surprisingly, for those others who were around and woken by the alarming event, sufferers usually have no recall of it in the morning, and they may be disbelieving or embarrassed on hearing about their nocturnal crisis. Like several SWS disorders, these nightmares are no problem to the sufferers, because they are not aware of the disturbance. It is the people who live with them who are concerned for the sufferer.

The abruptness of the initiation of these nightmares tends to indicate that they are precipitated by a sudden stimulus. They can be caused by sudden noises and probably the sort of internal stimuli that cause a jumpiness in some people, resulting in the myoclonic jerk. Dr Hearne has suggested that wearing earplugs can be a remedy for some people whose night terrors are triggered by external sounds, such as the switching on or off of electrical or heating systems.

Some night terrors are action replays of a trauma that the sufferer actually experienced at some time. A person who was once traumatized in a minefield may suddenly awaken terrified and, on all fours on the bed, shout 'Don't move! There are mines here!'

Dr Hearne treated one man who was regularly trying to strangle his wife in sleep. He thought he was being attacked and was retaliating. Hypnotherapy banished the problem in one session.

Relaxation tapes (using a player that will not click loudly at the end!) or self-hypnosis are ways of reducing presleep stress, which may help some sufferers of SWS nightmares. For those who are essentially nervous and may fear intrusion, the simple expedient of locking the bedroom door may provide an unconscious sense of protection that will allay anxiety.

Insomnia

The inability to sleep is a cause of great frustration and concern to some people. There are two types of insomnia:

~ *Initial insomnia*, in which the problem is going off to sleep. Such insomniacs count sheep, etc., but their mind is alert and the annoyance of not sleeping further adds to the general state of arousal.

~ *Sleep-maintenance insomnia*, in which going off to sleep occurs naturally, but the person wakes in the night and then finds it difficult to go back into sleep. Sufferers may have one or both of these varieties.

It is well known, though, that insomniacs often grossly overestimate the time that they are awake. Perhaps they go in and out of sleep without realizing it. The mind-set of an insomniac puts emphasis on the sleeplessness rather than on the amount of sleep. Therapists are aware that they often get starkly different reports about the patient's insomnia from the patient's sleeping partner. The condition of overestimated sleeplessness is termed *pseudo-insomnia*. It is possible, too, that some individuals dream that they are awake: the false-awakening phenomenon.

Some people have been taking powerful drugs for insomnia for many years. Such medications are discouraged now and these people now exhibit chronic insomnia. The way to treat insomnia is to deal with it practically. If the individual is a light sleeper, then a quiet bedroom is necessary. This must be achieved by soundproofing, using earplugs, or moving home.

It is generally recognized that insomniacs are either over- or under-stimulated. If your mind is buzzing when you go to bed, you need to relax. This may involve taking a warm bath, listening to peaceful music, relaxation tapes, or whatever you find removes stress. It could be sex – with a partner or alone. Self-hypnosis is a good technique for inducing a state of calmness. You can train yourself to re-enter a profound state of quietude.

If you are living a life of understimulation, then try jogging, crossword puzzles, or something to activate your brain. A nip of brandy may help you go to sleep. Alcohol is a cerebral stimulant in small doses, but becomes a depressant in large amounts.

One method (*associative imaging*) employed by Dr Hearne on people who are thinking too much about matters in their life when they go to bed – hence causing anxious or exciting thoughts – is slowly to recite a list of associated words. The insomniac visualizes (if they have good visual imagery) each scene. The idea is to distract the person's mind from daily concerns and also to encourage the sort of thinking that happens in sleep, where notions flow from one to another. It can lead the person into sleep by mimicking a characteristic of the sleeping mind.

Sleep-walking and Sleep-talking

These are both phenomena of SWS, in which the body's musculature is not inhibited. Since most SWS is associated with the first half of the sleep period, this is when these curiosities are witnessed. Again, as with other SWS conditions, the sleep-walker or sleep-talker is not aware of what is happening. Sleep-walkers have been known to get themselves into very hair-raising situations, e.g. walking on the parapets of high buildings – oblivious of any danger. Some, of course, have died from their unaware ambulations.

One woman whose boyfriend had a history of sleep-walking described how he would sometimes get up in the night, go downstairs, wash dishes, and generally clean up. The next morning he thought that she had been responsible for the work. She coyly omitted to inform him of his nocturnal unconscious industry.

For people who are likely to get into trouble through sleep-walking, it is advisable to have an alarm fitted to the door to awaken the sleeper – or someone else in the house.

There does seem to be a genetic element connected with the condition. Whole families have been reported to wander around while asleep.

Some individuals find that they sleep-walk when they are stressed. Methods of relaxation need to be employed in such cases. Hypnotherapy has a special way of treating the condition. The suggestion is given that, as soon as the unconscious mind finds that the person is about to start sleep-walking, a different form of behaviour will be substituted, e.g. to turn over in bed and relax into deep sleep.

Sleep-talking is not a life-threatening condition, but it can be a nuisance to a sleeping partner. A conversation can sometimes be held with a sleep-talker. One woman reported how she asked her husband about women he fancied when he was sleep-talking. Another woman told Dr Hearne that she once went to check on her two young daughters in bed and found they were talking to each other while asleep.

Snoring

This also constitutes a condition of SWS – especially in stage 4 – and also mostly affects the first few hours of sleep. The soft palate is so relaxed in SWS that a strong, sonorous vibration can be established as air is inhaled and exhaled. The noise can be relatively mild or, if the individual lies on his/her back, extremely loud. With some people it becomes so annoying and aversive to the partner that separate bedrooms – and even divorce – have resulted.

Here, too, hypnotherapy can be particularly effective for snorers. The 'as soon as – then – something else' procedure is invoked so that, when snoring is about to begin, the unconscious brings in a new action, which is to turn over in bed; this will lighten sleep and stop or reduce the snoring.

Teeth-grinding

The strange technical name for teeth-grinding in sleep is *bruxism*. The jaw muscles can exert tremendous power, and in some people this is a severe problem. They may have to wear a dental plate to prevent extensive damage to the teeth. The sound of bruxism is very eerie and often cannot even be reproduced by the individual in wakefulness. Psychodynamic psychologists say that the behaviour is an expression of frustrated anger. One therapy technique is to get the person to re-enact grinding their teeth (mildly) and to uncover any accompanying thoughts, emotions, or images. This can reveal the unexpressed aggression that might be responsible.

Bedwetting

Bedwetting, or *enuresis*, is usually thought of as being a problem of the very young or the very old, but it occurs in other age ranges, to the extent perhaps of about one or two per 100 people. Sometimes there is a physical cause, but various psychological reasons may also be responsible, including emotional upset and attention-seeking.

Electronic alarms have been used for several years. At the first sign of wetness, these rouse the person in order to go to the lavatory, but the alarm tends to wake others around.

Hypnotherapy can be utilized to explore any psychological basis, or simply to reprogramme the individual into a new behavioural sequence. There are also different methods of dealing with these and other sleep disorders, about which an analyst might be asked, so let us take a look at a few examples from our case files. Each of these people benefited from our suggestions – even if it only served to make them aware of their conditions.

Illustrative Case Histories

Case 1 Sleep Paralysis

Ruth wrote:

> A few weeks ago, I woke up in the morning with a strong sense of foreboding –
> I live on my own, yet could hear my bedroom door being opened. I was horrified
> to see large, gnarled fingers curl round the door.
>
> My first reaction was to scream, but no sound left my lips. Then I attempted
> to leap out of bed, but discovered that I couldn't move a muscle – I was
> paralysed with unimaginable fear!
>
> I struggled desperately to move, but the harder I tried the more exhausted I
> became. Then I was horrified to observe a sinister, dark silhouette enter the
> room. I think I must have passed out, because the next thing I remember was
> the sound of my alarm clock.
>
> When I finally plucked up the courage to get out of bed and inspect my flat,
> there were no signs of a disturbance. Now I am questioning my own sanity –
> did this really happen, or did I imagine it? Please help.

The reply:

This is a classic case of sleep paralysis, which is fairly common and occurs on the very edge of consciousness. To begin with, no matter how certain you were that you were awake, a polygraph would have proved that you were in unambiguous REM sleep. However, this in no way detracts from the apparent reality of your experience: sleep-paralysis sufferers are always convinced that they are wide awake.

What makes this strange condition even more disturbing is the fact that, because subjects are hovering on the edge of consciousness, they may indeed perceive the real world at the same time as dream images and be unable to distinguish between the two. In addition, in 70 per cent of cases, sleep-paralysis sufferers believe, like you, that a threatening, sinister presence is nearby.

In this respect, ghost sightings are common, but nowadays, reports of aliens are becoming popular. It seems likely, therefore, that many reported alien abductions might be the result of sleep paralysis.

However, apart from essential functions, REM dreaming sleep is always accompanied by bodily paralysis. Sleep-walking, sleep-talking, and teeth-grinding occur during SWS, which is not subject to lack of muscular activity.

Because sleep paralysis can be such a harrowing experience, readers will find it useful to learn how to deal with it. By following a few simple guidelines, it can be dealt with effectively. First, label it! If you believe you have woken up, but are unable to move, tell yourself 'I remember reading about this. This is sleep paralysis'. Next, ignore any imagery, smells, change in temperature, etc. You will exacerbate the condition if you fight against it, so relax. By following these three steps – labelling, ignoring, and relaxing – you will find that you slip back into a conventional dream or wake up naturally.

Case 2 Nightmares in Adults
Maureen, from Fort William, in Scotland, wrote:

> I have a recurring nightmare, sometimes two or three times a week. It always starts the same, with me walking along a path in a park. I come to a shady area near some trees, when a man appears in front of me. Somehow, I know instinctively that he wants to rape me. I have had this dream so many times that, at this point, I know that I am dreaming. I think to myself 'Oh no, here comes the nightmare, again!'
>
> I turn and begin running towards a group of women, who are playing hockey. However, they seem oblivious to my screams for help and ignore me. I run through a gate and onto a street. Now I can hear the man's running footsteps growing louder and louder. I can almost feel his breath on the back of my neck, and I know that my legs are turning to jelly.
>
> I am terrified as a hand clasps the back of my neck, at which point I always wake up, breathless, my heart pounding in my chest, and my pillow wet with sweat. Please can you help me? I don't know how much longer I can put up with this.

The reply:
Nightmares are usually powerful, message-bearing dreams demanding attention. Once a recurrent bad dream is interpreted accurately and explained to the subject, who then acknowledges and acts upon the dream's message, the nightmares invariably cease – the subconscious has done its

job and has no reason to persist. Nevertheless, it takes up to 4 hours to analyse a dream thoroughly, and competent dream interpreters are difficult to find.

However, in this instance, you have a golden opportunity to transform this nightmare into a pleasant lucid dream (where people become fully conscious within the dream and can control the ensuing events). In this respect, people who suffer recurring nightmares, as you do, can, for a brief moment at the onset of the dream, recognize that they are indeed dreaming.

Therefore, the next time the man appears in front of you, all you have to do is change your mind-set from 'Oh no, here comes the nightmare again' to 'Great, wonderful, here comes the nightmare, which means that I'm dreaming and can control my dreams!' Once you have done that, you will become lucid, or fully aware that you are dreaming.

This presents you with an opportunity to get your own back on the object of your fear. Many lucid-dreamers point their fingers at the thing, then fire imaginary laser beams from their fingertips which destroy or shrivel it.

There is an alternative, however, which is much more fun and which utilizes the golden rule of lucid dreaming: 'What you think, you will then dream'. That being the case, why not will the man to shrink to a height of only a few inches. Then think him into a pretty pink dress and high heels before introducing him to some sort of fate worse than death – ballet lessons, perhaps? Good luck!

Case 3 Nightmares in Babies
Christine wrote:

> Our 3-month-old daughter, Kirstie, suffers from the occasional nightmare. Usually, the first thing my husband and I are aware of is a blood-curdling scream coming from the nursery – it actually sounds quite alarming.
>
> I am well able to tell the difference between a cry of sudden pain and this cry of terror. We would like to know what causes these frightening dreams, and how, at such an early age, they are possible at all?

The reply:
Nightmares are extremely common in children from around the age of 5 years until the onset of puberty, but nobody knows why. In adults, bad dreams are usually trying to impart important messages, or forcing individuals to face their pain until an issue is resolved. This is common in cases of trauma, e.g. rape. In children, however, these criteria are less likely to apply.

There is plenty of evidence to show that babies also suffer from nightmares. Notwithstanding sudden attacks of pain, such as tummy gripes, babies sometimes waken with a start, then scream as if responding to a frightening experience.

In fact, even a foetus in the womb spends much of its time in REM dreaming sleep. It is during these periods that a mother will feel her unborn child kick – in response to dreaming sleep. This raises some interesting questions: what on earth could an unborn child be dreaming about, and are the sudden kicks a direct response to events in dreams? Unfortunately, until technology advances, we will never know the answers.

The fact that extremely young babies seem to endure nightmares also provokes the same questions, especially as they have not lived for long enough outside the protection of caring parents to experience things on which to base such dreams, or which would be likely to trigger off these frightening episodes.

There is another controversial theory, however, and one which perhaps deserves some serious consideration – reincarnation! It may come as a surprise to readers to learn that the early Christians accepted the premise of reincarnation in its entirety. More than 500 years after the death of Christ, that all changed.

In AD 553, at the Second Council of Constantinople, it was decided by just three political votes that we live only once. Apparently, it was decided that it would be easier to keep the masses in order if they believed hellfire and brimstone awaited them if they did not behave. However, if they had faith in the idea of several opportunities of reincarnation to get things right, what chance did the Church have of making them conform to its teachings?

It is not my intention to force any particular belief or doctrine upon you, but simply to present the facts. In this context, there is a growing mountain of evidence in favour of the notion of reincarnation. This is particularly noticeable when we examine reports from eminent heart specialists who, after reviving clinically dead people, are supporting the idea in increasing numbers. At first, these same physicians were putting their reputations on the line! Nowadays, however, they are met with almost no resistance from the establishment at all. Food for thought?

It seems incredible even to contemplate the scenario of dreams based on past life memories, but what are the alternatives?

Case 4 Insomnia
Mary wrote:

No matter how hard I try, I just can't seem to fall asleep very quickly. Each time I open my eyes to look at the bedside clock, another 20 minutes has gone by. By my reckoning, I must be losing about 1½ hours sleep a night. I've tried avoiding rich food, cheese, chocolate, and caffeine, and have developed a routine, but nothing seems to work.

To make matters worse, my husband just doesn't seem to understand how frustrating it can be. He makes light of it and even insists that I go straight to sleep, often kicking him just before I pass a comment concerning my insomnia. I am worried that, as the years pass, the time it takes me to get to sleep is going to increase until I stay awake most of the night.

The reply:

Nowadays, the biggest single cause of insomnia is stress, which manifests in two ways: initial insomnia and sleep-maintenance insomnia. Initial insomniacs find it difficult to 'shut down' their thought processes and continue mulling over problems, etc.

Sleep-maintenance insomniacs manage to fall asleep easily, but wake up in the middle of the night, then find that they cannot nod off again; they too, begin mentally going round in circles. Strangely, under certain circumstances, caffeine is thought to help this type of sleeplessness.

Stress-related insomnia is an extensive subject and can be fought on several fronts. However, it is important to establish that insomnia is the problem in the first place. From your account, Mary, it would seem that you might be blaming your husband's whimsical treatment of your claims inappropriately; he may actually be telling the truth!

As we have seen, sleep is divided arbitrarily into several levels: stage 1 (nodding-off sleep); stages 2, 3, and 4 (SWS, or nondreaming sleep); and REM sleep. Sleep-walking, sleep-talking, bedwetting, teeth-grinding, and restlessness can occur during SWS.

REM sleep is triggered throughout the night in 90-minute cycles, at the end of a SWS period. Apart from essential functions and eye movement, the body is subject to total paralysis during this stage. This is thought to be a safety mechanism inherited from our ancestors, designed to prevent us from acting out our dreams. The alternative is almost unthinkable: at night the streets would be alive with dreamers attempting to fly, enjoying romantic encounters, fleeing from monsters, etc.

However, the hypnagogic state (stage 1) is the transitional interval between consciousness and deeper sleep: the nodding-off period. This phase bears certain hallmarks which render it unmistakable: phantom-like imagery, hearing voices or one's name being called out, bright flashes of light and colour, a sense of being struck on the head, and, in Mary's case most important of all, myoclonic jerks.

Myoclonic jerks include imagining tripping over an object, a sensation of falling, etc. It is because stage 1 sleep is not subject to bodily paralysis that dreamers often attempt to save themselves during these experiences by punching or kicking out. In addition, individuals who wake up during this stage are likely to dispute, vehemently, the fact that they have been asleep.

Therefore, in this instance, it seems likely that your husband has indeed detected the telltale breathing which assures him correctly that you are asleep – poor man!

Case 5 Sleep-walking

Margaret wrote:

> Since having central heating installed, my 5-year-old son, Justin, has taken to sleep-walking. At first, my partner and I found this rather amusing. When we woke him, he was totally disoriented and didn't seem to recognize us, or know what was going on – he was so cute. When, the morning after, we mentioned it to him, he had no memory of it whatsoever and even denied it.
>
> Recently, however, we didn't discover that he was sleep-walking until neighbours phoned and told us that they had seen Justin walking past their house – it was the early hours of the morning, and he was heading towards a main road. We raced out of the house and caught up with him just before he reached it. I shudder to think what could have happened. Again, the following morning, he had no memory of it. Is there anything we can do to avoid this happening again?

The reply:

Unlike REM dreaming sleep, where people are paralysed, sleep-walking occurs during SWS, when muscle control is available. It is thought that the paralysis during REM sleep is a safety mechanism which prevents us from acting out our dreams (see Case 4 above).

Apart from physiological conditions, there is an interesting difference between the two distinctive sleep states. If you were to waken people who were experiencing REM sleep, they would be likely to recall a dream; this is not so with SWS. When subjects are wakened at these times, they rarely remember dreaming. Moreover, even an adult sleep-walker who has been awakened, then held a lengthy conversation, is likely to have little or no memory of the event in the morning. In addition they often display disorientation, or sleep drunkenness.

The lack of dreaming and memory during SWS makes it difficult to study, and less is known about it. However, in this particular instance, there is a clue as to what might be causing Justin's late-night excursions. His mother pointed out that these incidents first started after central heating was installed.

There is evidence that sudden noises can trigger certain SWS phenomena, and this includes sleep-walking. Therefore it seems likely that the electric pump on the new central-heating system could be clicking in and out throughout the night and might be responsible for Justin's problem. As he is too young to suffer the indignity of earplugs, I recommend that you introduce some 'white' noise into his bedroom. This could be in the form of a water fountain, an electric fan, or even a loudly ticking clock. Alternatively, you could organize background music.

Finally, remove any objects from Justin's room that could be a danger, put a lock on his door, and ensure that windows cannot open more than an inch or two.

Case 6 Bedwetting

Jenny wrote:

> My son, Robby, stopped wetting the bed when he was 2 years old, which is early for boys. Recently, however, now aged 6, he suffered a blow to the head from a cricket ball and has started wetting again. Could there be a connection, and is this likely to be a temporary problem? A neighbour told me that it would pass, but it has been 6 weeks without any promising signs. A doctor saw him at the time and found nothing wrong.

The reply:

Bedwetting is more common in boys, and they usually take considerably longer than girls to become dry. Once they do, it is unusual for them to start wetting again. However, even a seemingly small trauma can be responsible for accidents to begin happening again. The danger is that it can sometimes undermine a child's confidence and therefore become a self-perpetuating habit: the more they wet the bed, the lower their self-esteem becomes, and so on.

In this particular instance, though, Robby's tender years are an advantage: he will be more susceptible to the influence of positive suggestion than a much older child would be. In psychology, it is established that expectation can have a powerful effect. You have only to view a televized meeting of evangelical healers to see it in action. If, at the touch of a healer, people expect to collapse and writhe on the ground in a trance-like state, they are likely to do just that – expectation at work!

Therefore, a similar, less aggressive approach can be used here. Tell Robby, enthusiastically, that you have written to a North American Indian medicine man (or someone similar), who has sent a magic charm that will solve the problem. Be convincing. If he thinks that you believe in it, then he will. Next, get him an appropriate talisman or charm (an old piece of costume jewellery perhaps). Then write him a magic spell along the following lines:

This is a charm from Big Chief Ned,
To stop you, young Robby, from wetting the bed.
Place it under your pillow when you retire at night,
And think of these words as you turn out the light.
Try hard to remember them, really try,
And in the morning your bed will be dry!
[Great poetry it ain't, but it often works!]

If done convincingly, this can be an extremely effective method, but there are a few golden rules to observe. In the early days, Robby may have the odd accident. Remember: reward success but under no circumstances punish failure. Instead, sympathize and give positive encouragement. Tell him not to worry and explain that the magic will take a little time to build up to its full power. Good luck and please let us know how you get on.

Case 7 Sleep Apnea
Mrs B. wrote:

Since my husband Donald has put on weight, he seems to wake up in the morning with headaches, feeling tired and foggy, not ready to face the day. A colleague of his recently told me that, on occasions, Donald has fallen asleep at work.

More recently, he has become too sensitive to everyday issues in the home and often snaps at me. In addition, I have noticed that he is becoming forgetful and seems to be slipping into a depression. Are these symptoms of insomnia?

The reply:
Insomnia has many causes, none more likely than stress. However, in this instance, that does not seem probable. Your observation concerning his weight increase, taken together with the other symptoms you list, suggests that he is suffering from a sleep condition known as *sleep apnea*.

In Scotland alone, every night, sleep apnea steals sleep from thousands of unwitting victims. Apart from all the classic symptoms you have described, snoring, choking halts in breathing, and gasping attempts to breathe are telltale signs of this miserable and sometimes dangerous complaint, which affects people to varying degrees.

By definition, sleep apnea is the termination of breathing during sleep, and there are thought to be three types:

~ *Central apnea*, which is comparatively rare and neurological in origin, i.e. triggered in the brain.
~ *Obstructive apnea*, resulting from a blockage of the trachea, or airway, by the tongue or fatty tissue in the neck. This is the most widespread cause

and occurs in overweight people,

~ *Mixed apnea*, which is a combination of the other two.

Episodes when a sufferer stops breathing might last only a few seconds, but they can also last for about 2 minutes. Not only does this place tremendous strain on the heart but, over long periods, sufferers tend to display symptoms of high blood-pressure. These breathless attacks can occur many times throughout the night. On each occasion, sleepers usually waken (unwittingly) for a moment. It is hardly surprising that they wake up feeling groggy, with headaches and exhibiting symptoms of depression and insomnia.

Many cases of obstructive sleep apnea can be cured by nonaggressive methods: simply losing weight, which prevents the fatty tissue in the back of the throat from collapsing into the airway, cutting out alcohol, and refraining from smoking can be effective measures.

In severe cases there are surgical procedures that can be employed to defeat the effects of obstructive sleep apnea. This usually involves removing part of the soft palate that obstructs the back of the throat. If present, the tonsils and any other soft tissue that is deemed to be excessive are also taken out.

On occasion, a variety of oral splints can be used to prevent a large tongue from collapsing into the back of the throat. Techniques including surgery can be practised to hold the lower jaw in a forward position.

However, it is because this condition can lead to serious consequences – death, in extreme cases – that it is *always* advisable to seek medical help. Before resorting to surgery, doctors have at their disposal the resources to provide optional therapy, such as positive-pressure pumps, which are designed to keep the airway open by simply wearing a nasal mask.

More importantly, your doctor will be able to monitor and assess any risk to Donald, then administer the appropriate treatment.

Case 8 Delayed Sleep-phase Syndrome

Margaret wrote:

Lately, getting my 15-year-old son, Jason, out of bed in time for school is becoming almost impossible. I can hammer on his bedroom door for ages before I get a response, in the form of a grunt or groan. Then, every few minutes, I have to repeat what has now become a tiresome routine before he finally emerges looking washed-out.

His lateness and continual tiredness throughout the day have begun to affect his schoolwork. Perhaps I could understand it if he was a regular party-goer and kept unsociable hours. Instead, in an attempt to catch up, he stays home most nights studying. Yet when it comes to bedtime, he maintains that he cannot get to sleep and lies awake for hours. Is he developing some sort of insomnia?

The reply:

Jason's behaviour, as you describe it, is fairly common in teenagers. Often, they will lie awake until about 4 a.m. then, in their perception, what seems to be the next second, it is time to get up. These children are likely to feel pretty hungover for the rest of the day, their eyes can be sensitive to sunlight, and their minds are liable to wander. However, when the sun sets, their bodies tend to awaken. They still feel tired, but at the same time wide awake – something of an anomaly.

In addition to adolescent spots and budding sexuality, teenagers have to endure several chemical changes, some of which can lead to a state something like permanent jet-lag, and it sounds as if Jason falls into this category. In other words, it would seem that he might be afflicted by a little-known medical condition called *delayed sleep-phase syndrome* (DSPS).

Essentially, in response to different light levels, our brain controls our body clocks by sending signals from the pineal gland and the hypothalamus. When the level of daylight hitting the retina in the eye drops, a message is triggered by the hypothalamus, instructing the pineal gland to produce more of the hormone melatonin. This has the effect of making us feel sleepy.

Under normal circumstances our natural body-clocks are fairly adaptable and can reset themselves. However, in the case of DSPS sufferers, this self-adjusting mechanism appears to be lacking – and nobody knows why.

By the time many adolescents with DSPS reach the age of 20 years, they have tried every insomnia cure in the book, but without success. There is a certain amount of scanty evidence which supports treatment by the use of melatonin, but the results have generally been inconclusive. Similarly, findings of studies employing full-spectrum light used for *seasonal affective disorder* (SAD) syndrome are also somewhat hit-and-miss. In fact, the treatment – having to endure bright light being shone into the eyes for an hour or two during the early hours of the morning – might be worse than the disease.

However, there is light, in the form of good news, at the end of the tunnel. Once DSPS victims emerge from adolescence the symptoms usually decrease. By the time they are in their mid-20s, normal sleeping patterns usually return. Nevertheless, simply understanding the condition can alleviate stress in the sufferer and enables family members to offer comfort and support.

Dreaming the Future

How is science likely to advance in the area of sleep and dreams? It looks as if spectacular developments could happen in a matter of decades. As stated previously (see Sleep in Animals, p.19), it might be possible, using drugs, to mimic the behaviour of dolphins, porpoises, and some birds, which can selectively shut down one cerebral hemisphere at a time while maintaining awareness. Such a process could result in a third more time in our lives being available for other things – with no feelings of tiredness or fatigue.

In a sense, our evolutionarily established bodies are lagging behind our newly created environment, in which night is no longer a great inhibitory period of darkness and enforced inactivity. Research into other species which remain active at all times could show us how it is done, and we could emulate that trick. Such a discovery could change our species drastically. The notion may seem bizarre, but from the perspective of *ahypnos* (ever-wakeful) *humans*, the idea of wasting a third of one's life in unawareness would sound much more strange and unacceptable.

In the area of dreams, some really remarkable developments are likely too. Already the notion of establishing a universal dream code, based on letters of the alphabet and enabling messages to be obtained directly from the unconscious via dreams, has been devised by David Melbourne (see Melbourne and Hearne, *The Dream Oracle*, 1998). This is proving to be a powerful tool alongside conventional dream interpretation.

Lucid dreams are a major area of potential significance and are likely to be experienced by many more people. The unique situation of being able to control a dream while it is running should prove useful for creative people. The dream state has the facility to synthesize new concepts from elements not usually linked in our minds. It is that degree of novelty which can be exploited by e.g. composers, writers and architects.

There is evidence from the dream telepathy work of Ullman and Krippner that the dream state is conducive to the paranormal perception of distant material and thoughts. The lucid dream is an ideal research vehicle for such experimentation. Some lucid-dreamers may find they can devise techniques for acquiring useful information.

The induction of lucidity will no doubt be aided by various electronic devices. Dr Hearne invented the world's first dream machine during his PhD researches. The device detects dreaming sleep by monitoring respiration and then administers pulses to the dreamer. The stimuli become incorporated into the dream without causing waking. Developments of Hearne's invention have been taken up by people in the USA, and Dr Hearne is about to launch a new version of his dream machine.

The next major technical advance will be when we can actually see what people are dreaming. Appropriate monitoring of the brain will enable this to be achieved, reckons Dr Hearne, within 20 years. Dream pictures and sounds will be recorded for replay. At that time, the dream will be fully exposed to inspection, and we shall be able to say with certainty how dreams are constructed. The consequences will be considerable. We will no longer be able to withdraw to our own secret dream world.

Even thoughts will be monitored. How? Well, think the word 'No' strongly to yourself. Notice how, involuntarily, you make very small movements in your mouth. The vocal musculature, especially the tongue, cannot help but accompany the thought. Imagine a sophisticated future technology – not too far away actually – that could detect those minute movements, perhaps at a distance of a few yards.

Imagine too, a corresponding device which records or says aloud those thoughts. That will be the end of all privacy, and it may then be necessary to legislate against the use of such equipment in certain circumstances. But, thought-controlled devices – particularly in the field of virtual reality (VR) – will be commonplace.

An even stranger inevitability is that your dreams – converted into data by the dream recorder – will be capable of being fed into a VR system so that dream characters can take on a 'life of their own' during wakefulness. In VR, an apparatus is worn which provides computer-generated images, sounds, and even tactile sensations. The devices are very crude at this time, but pretty soon special micro-electronic contact lenses will be available, linked by radio to a small supercomputer in your pocket. The visual display of these units will be perfect and completely indistinguishable from actual vision.

This VR system will be able to produce any kind of images, sounds and sensations. It will be capable of:

~ Altering visual input (so that, for instance, the inside of a box-like concrete home will look like Buckingham Palace to every VR-ist entering, down to the most microscopic detail of a Rembrandt on the wall; and faces will be changed so that everyone looks incredibly beautiful).
~ Creating entirely novel scenarios and characters. The system will automatically link in to that of other people around. If you say (or think) 'Let's be on the surface of the moon', instantly you will all be there, seeing things from the correct relative position.

You could encounter a person in a dream who would become an ageless, lifelong companion – the personality and character crafted to your needs by the powerful VR computer.

The topic of VR should be the most important matter for discussion in the world. It will be the biggest revolution in the history of mankind, and it is only about 20 years away. People will not have to go anywhere; the whole universe will come to them. There is a real danger that actual interactions between human beings will cease to occur. Computer-made friends and lovers could be programmed to be always perfect and real people will not be able to match up to them.

It seems that we are the last experiencers of harsh reality. When VR takes over, our lives will be vastly enriched, but in a way we shall all be living in the ultimate material illusion – a permanent dream world.

2

Creativity in Sleep and Dream Incubation

The term 'dream incubation' is very appropriate. Just as a mother hen has the ability to incubate an egg, which grows and hatches into a chick, humans, too, are able to sow a seed – in the form of a question – and incubate a dream, which can then hatch an answer in the guise of a message which can be decoded.

Dreams, as we know, can be wonderfully entertaining and fascinating in their extremely unusual combinations of images and thoughts. Rather than passively experiencing the fountain of originality that presents itself in dreams, though, some people have actually brought to fruition something novel from a dream. In both the arts and sciences, many cases have been recorded of such creativity.

Dreams and Science

Many of us have dreamt of finding a valuable physical treasure, such as a jewel, which of course we cannot bring into wakefulness. But, as we shall see, some treasures – ideas – have been recovered from dreams, to the advantage of all of us. It is exciting to think that perhaps we could learn to exploit the great treasure-house of the dream world. The lucid dream would seem to be an ideal means for achieving that goal.

In fact some really significant scientific advances owe their existence to people's dreams. The first person to show the chemical conduction of nervous impulses at synapses (nerve junctions) was Otto Loewi – as the consequence of a dream – and the discovery earned him the 1936 Nobel Prize.

Loewi thought as early as 1906 that such a process operated but could not think how to demonstrate it experimentally. Loewi actually had the dream twice. The first time he scribbled some notes after he awoke but could not decipher them the next day. The dream presented itself the following night, however, and Loewi duly carried out the experiment.

What he did, just as he saw in the dream, was to use two frog's hearts, only one of which had the nerves intact. After stimulating the intact heart (increasing or decreasing the beating rate), he found that transferring a salt solution from the intact heart to the other heart caused a corresponding change in its beating rate. A chemical conduction was thus demonstrated.

There was also the discovery of the benzene ring by the chemist Friedrich August Kékulé von Stradonitz in a hypnagogic dream. He noted:

I turned my chair to the fire and dozed. Again the atoms were gambolling before my eyes. This time the smaller group kept modestly in the background. My mental eye, rendered more acute by visions of this kind, could now distinguish larger structures, of manifold conformations; long rows, sometimes more closely fitted together, all twining and twisting in snake-like motion. But look! What was that? One of the snakes had seized hold of its own tail, and the form whirled mockingly in front of my eyes. As if by a flash of lightning, I awoke.

Kékulé knew instantly that the carbon and hydrogen atoms constituted a hexagonal ring structure in various molecules. It was a major step forward in chemistry.

An archeologist, Herman Hilprecht, solved a particular problem in sleep. He was dealing with two fragments of agate which had cuneiform script on them. They looked to him as if they came from finger rings. A tall priest appeared to him in a dream (perhaps representing his knowledgeable and wise unconscious mind) and took him to the treasure-room at the site of a temple. The priest explained to him that the two pieces belonged together and came from earrings made from a cylinder of agate. The information was later confirmed.

As a direct result of a dream, David Melbourne came up with what Dr Hearne has described as 'the most significant development ever concerning dreams'. It consists of an alphabetical code that produces accurate dream interpretations without the user requiring any knowledge of the subject. You simply have to read the instructions, then start having message-bearing dreams to order, and know what they mean. It is as simple as that!

An amusing case of a dream influencing human inventiveness concerned the construction of the first lock-stitch sewing machine in 1844. Elias Howe, in the USA, had been toiling for some time on the prototype, but it was not successful. The needle had its hole in the middle. Then, in a dream, he was captured by a tribe whose king ordered him to complete the machine immediately, or he would be killed. He was having no success, and was about to be killed, when he noticed that the warriors' spears had an elongated hole at the pointed end. Howe woke and jumped out of bed to make a new needle of the same design as the spears. The design was perfectly successful!

There have probably been very many similar, but unreported, cases of dreams having boosted scientific progress.

Dreams and the Arts

The arts, too, have a large number of examples of dream creativity. Many of the great composers – Mozart, Schumann, and Saint-Saëns – obtained themes from their dreams. Some music came to Beethoven while he was asleep in a coach. The tune was to the words 'O Tobias, O Tobias, Dominus Haslinger O! O! O Tobias!' He could not quite recollect the music when he awoke, but the dream repeated itself the next day, and this time he remembered the music and wrote it down.

A main motif came to Wagner as he was dozing in a dream-like state. He refers to it in his autobiography *My Life*. Wagner felt he was immersed in fast-flowing water, and the experience suggested music centred on E flat major. Wagner used the wonderful sounds in his operatic cycle *The Ring of the Nibelung*.

The eighteenth-century Italian composer Giuseppe Tartini told the astronomer Joseph Lalande that he had experienced a dream in which the Devil had become Tartini's slave. He handed the Devil a violin, and he played a sonata 'of such exquisite beauty as surpassed the boldest flights of my imagination'. Unfortunately, on waking, Tartini could only recall the trill, which he included in his composition *The Devil's Sonata*.

Dr Hearne is also a composer and reports that several pieces of music have come to him either in dreams or on waking. He commented that, when you are immersed in writing music during the day, the activity seems to continue in dreams.

Literary writers, too, have gained rich material from mere dreams. Robert Louis Stevenson stated in an essay that he regularly used stories from his dreams. He would ask his 'Little People, or Brownies' – presumably aspects of his unconscious mind – for an interesting theatrical production. A story would be told, sometimes in serial dreams. Stevenson would then describe what he experienced. In this way he produced tales such as *Treasure Island* and *Kidnapped*.

The plot for his great classic *The Strange Case of Dr Jekyll and Mr Hyde* came in a dream, in which he saw Hyde being chased after committing a crime, taking a potion, and changing to the other character. From a few scenes, and the basic idea of a potion to alter a person's character and appearance, his book was formed.

There is also the case of Samuel Taylor Coleridge who, in 1798, while under the influence of opium (supposedly medicinal), had a vivid dream, or sequence of dozing imagery, in which he composed a long poem. Before sleep he had been reading from *Purchas from Pilgrimage*:

> In Xamdu did Cublai Can build a stately Palace, encompassing sixteene miles of plaine ground with a wall, wherein are fertile Meddowes, pleasant springs, delightful Streames, and all sorts of beasts of chase and game, and in the middest thereof, a sumptuous house of pleasure.

He awoke, ecstatic, to write down the long poem that was in his mind, but was interrupted by a visitor from Porlock. What he could recall constituted his masterpiece, *Kubla Khan*, which starts:

> In Xanadu did Kubla Khan
> A stately pleasure-dome decree:
> Where Alph, the sacred river, ran
> Through caverns measureless to man
> Down to a sunless sea.

The British poet John Masefield had a dream in which he saw a tall woman dressed in furs and a tall hat. He seemed to know instinctively about her background as she gazed toward Lincoln's Inn Fields. The dream was vivid and detailed: he noticed the sun shining, and pigeons pecking for food. The woman disappeared, and he clearly saw a poem engraved on an oblong metal plate, explaining the woman's life and feelings. Masefield wrote it down on waking, and it became the poem entitled *The Woman Speaks*.

The French philosopher Descartes had three dreams one night in 1619, which enabled him to establish his aims in philosophy. In the third, summarizing dream, he observed a poetry book and a dictionary on a table. One verse stated 'What way of life should I follow?' Someone came in and requested him to look up a poem called *Yes*. *No*, which he was unable to do. He then apparently became lucid and, while still in the dream, attempted to understand its meaning. He was sure it represented the fusion of philosophy and reason, and that poets could reveal more wisdom than philosophers. When he awoke he thought that the *Yes*. *No* referred to the Truth and Falsity in Pythagoras. He saw that the whole dream was 'the Spirit of Truth who had sought to open to him the treasures of all sciences by this dream'.

There is no doubt that, if creative people could learn to dream lucidly, they could visit a veritable El Dorado of originality in their unconscious. By volitionally controlling the locations in these dreams, they could set up scenes conducive to obtaining new ideas. Thus, composers might visit a concert hall and hear their own music, artists might enter a gallery of works designed by their own unconscious, and architects might visit a futuristic place in order to gain new concepts of style.

At a more ordinary level, we can enjoy dreams for their sheer recreational value. A good dream can make your day, and a few minutes of spectacular, exciting, or relaxing unusual experience can have a greatly beneficial effect.

Originality of Dreams

What is the source of originality in dreams? In the nineteenth century, Maury wrote:

> The eye, and the ear and the senses in general, have an ability to fuse and construct – relating to the creative power of the imagination. The components used are provided by past-perceived sensations, but their arrangement and method of assembly is original and results in visual images and sounds which are different from those perceived before.

St-Denys, who observed details carefully within his lucid dreams, found that the basis was often a waking source, but that the dream would then continue along a plausible associative pathway. The degree of recombination of perceptual components varies, so the amount of originality differs.

He sometimes described things that he would not have seen in wakefulness. For instance, in 1867, he wrote:

> I dreamed I saw a young woman dressed in an old-fashioned way, who was fooling with some pieces of red-hot metal, it seemed without harm. Whenever she touched them, long protuberances of flame stayed hanging from her fingers; and when she rubbed her hands there was a shower of sparks and a loud bang.

St-Denys also noted how his face changed when he looked in a mirror:

> I was looking at myself in a magic mirror, where I saw myself by sequence in a number of different guises: my hair and beard were in several different conditions – youthful and very flawless; then I was fat-faced, yellowing, ill-looking, toothless, several years older. My face passed through these successive alterations and eventually looked so frightening that I awoke with a jump.

St-Denys accepted that, in dreams, completely new perceptions could be constructed from existing memories.

It would be useful to be able to ascertain some index of originality in a dream, so that if, for example, a new composition presented itself, it could be determined to what extent it was based on something previously heard. The degree of bizarreness in the dream might reflect originality, so the more unusual the visual features the greater the likelihood of originality generally.

Dream Incubation

Perhaps more importantly, tremendous rewards can be forthcoming from learning to incubate message-bearing dreams which, when decoded, can reveal ways to improve our lives by enabling us to better understand what makes us tick as individuals. Therefore, people who are able to incubate and then comprehend their dreams are likely to have an advantage over the rest of the population.

In Chapter 1 we have already noted how ancient societies used to incubate dreams in special temples, but how does this process work? Essentially, there is a simple, one-word answer: expectation. In psychology it is widely known that expectation can produce potent effects. In this sense, the power of the human mind must not be underestimated. Without overstating the case, one day in the not-too-distant future, it might be realized that it is the most powerful force in the universe.

Apart from the very real evidence that exists confirming the placebo effect (the relief of medical conditions by administering inert substances which patients believe are beneficial drugs), there are many other examples of expectation at work. In one case, Alison, aged 32, was given an injection of distilled water and told that it would put her to sleep. Believing that the syringe contained a powerful anesthetic, she fell asleep almost the moment the needle penetrated her skin.

Perhaps a rather more disturbing effect of expectation can be observed at certain religious healing meetings. Some people have come to expect that the moment a healer lays hands on them they will succumb to a trance-like state and writhe around on the ground. Indeed, most of us will have witnessed this on television.

However, the power of the human mind, through the effect of expectation, can be seen at its most awesome when we consider that it has the ability to end human life. Death, seemingly of natural causes, sometimes occurs when a long-term loving relationship comes to its close through the demise of a partner. The bereaved husband or wife loses the will to live and passes away soon afterwards – a sort of death wish!

The most frightening illustration, however, can be found in different cultures all around the world. If a witch-doctor or medicine man, for instance, invokes a death curse on individuals, those same people, believing in the power of the curse, create a mind-set of expectation and are likely to just sit down and die. The Australian Aboriginal bone-pointing curse is a prime example.

If, therefore, expectation can be employed to bring about such incredibly potent effects, it is a relatively minor challenge to use it to incubate meaningful dreams. Nevertheless, to be successful in the first place, the matter has to be taken seriously. Remember, just like the bone-pointing curse, developing the degree of expectation necessary to produce results relies on the individual believing that it will work.

Some people fail to incubate dreams because the thought of following ritualistic behaviour and self-suggestion scripts makes them feel rather silly – especially if a third party is in a position to bear witness to these actions. It is particularly important to send a clear message to your unconscious mind that you mean business. If, for example, you live with a family member who tends to pour scorn on such activities, announce your intentions quite boldly. In doing this, you will declare your sincerity, and your subconscious will be likely to respond positively.

The process of dreaming is associated mainly with the right hemisphere of the brain. Therefore, it makes sense that, in order to incubate sufficient dreams, we learn how to stimulate and employ more right-brain thinking. Just like a muscle, the more you use the right side of your brain the more likely it will be to respond with right-hemisphere results, such as more vivid, meaningful dreams.

Dream incubation can be used for many purposes: to help resolve relationship problems, financial difficulties, stressful situations, etc. – even for financial gain. As pursuits of a creative nature – painting, poetry, writing fiction, etc. – tend to stimulate the right hemisphere of the brain, perhaps dream incubation to inspire, say, writing a short story for financial gain is a good place to start.

Building Expectation

First, set an entire day aside for the sole purpose of dream incubation. Make sure that you will not be disturbed. If appropriate, even unplug the phone. Make it a special day, by changing the appearance of your bedroom and the room in which you will spend most of the daylight hours. You could, for instance, drape some soft, pastel-coloured materials around the walls. Arrange some kind of special lighting and play music that is conducive to meditation. Fragrances, too, can have an influential role in generating a high degree of expectation; you could burn incense, perhaps. Indeed, do anything that you feel will help. In addition, before you retire for the night, change the position of your bed and fit clean, crisp sheets.

From the moment you arise on your special day, ensure that you break with all traditional routines. Everything you do should be different from the norm and suitable for the purpose of dream incubation. For example, first thing in the morning you might take an aromatherapy bath. Perhaps you are fortunate enough to be able to arrange a relaxing massage. Really pamper yourself!

If it is medically acceptable, forgo breakfast. Instead, drink only distilled water. When you do dine, make sure that the food is prepared in a way that is somehow special and eat it slowly by candlelight. Ponder over each morsel and give every mouthful a special thought related to the incubation.

Throughout the entire day concentrate on the issue you would like resolved: the inspiration for the short story, the answer to a relationship problem, a way out of financial difficulties, etc. Spend time engaging the right hemisphere of the brain. This can be achieved by attempting to create a fairly short chant, which should be repeated and developed as the day progresses. Initially, something along the following lines could be used:

> I ask my unconscious mind, that part of me which is ever vigilant and which has access to the limitless wisdom of the inner universe, to create a dream that will provide the inspiration for a short story [or provide an answer to a marital relationship problem, or guide me in matters of finance so that I can reduce my debts].

Once you have learnt the chant off by heart, expand upon it in a way that is directly relevant to your goal; each word must be pertinent and fight to earn its place. Throughout the day, keep learning and adding to it until you have about a hundred words that are directly related to the issue at hand. Another step that will help to galvanize a high level of expectation is to write about 500 words on how expectation can serve to incubate dreams successfully.

Before you retire for the night, take another relaxing, perfumed bath. From the moment you slide between the crisp sheets until you nod off to sleep, keep repeating the chant. Allow no thoughts other than the expectation of a suitable dream to enter your mind.

Paranormal Dream Messages

As we have seen, the unconscious is good at evaluating information which, for one reason or another, has eluded conscious examination, and then presenting that useful knowledge in the form of a message-bearing dream. But there is also evidence – in the form of accounts going back millennia, as well as modern scientific experiments – which indicates convincingly that some of the information presented in dreams could have a paranormal basis.

We should not, as reasonable people, be so foolish as to ignore such bodies of information because of any modern preconceptions that might have been imposed upon us. We are here in the areas of *telepathy* (mind-to-mind communication), *clairvoyance* (seeing at a distance, like remote-viewing), and *precognition* (premonitions, or seeing the future).

There is no shortage of cases where dreams have apparently described unanticipated events yet to happen at the time of the dream. Indeed, the earliest human records catalogue such phenomena. Clay tablets bearing engraved cuneiform scripts from ancient Assyria and Babylonia stated the clear acceptance that such knowledge – conceptualized as emanating from the gods – could be conveyed within the dream state.

A well-known precognitive dream from ancient Egypt is the one mentioned in the Bible: the Pharaoh's dream about the cattle, which was interpreted by Joseph (Genesis 41–43). A second dream on the same topic also occurred to the Pharaoh on the same night.

In the Biblical account, Joseph had previously interpreted dreams. He had been imprisoned, unjustly, because of the deceit of his master's wife. While he was there, two of the Pharaoh's servants (the chief butler and a baker) also became prisoners after having angered their master. On the same night, in jail, the servants each had a dream, which Joseph interpreted for them. It is enlightening to examine these two earlier interpretations by Joseph. First is the chief butler's dream:

> In my dream there was a vine before me and on the vine there were three branches; as soon as it budded, its blossoms shot forth, and the clusters ripened into grapes. Pharaoh's cup was in my hand; and I took the grapes and pressed them into Pharaoh's cup and placed the cup in Pharaoh's hand.

Joseph said that the three branches represented 3 days, and that the Pharaoh would restore the butler to his job so that he could once again place a cup in the Pharaoh's hand. The baker's dream also featured the number three:

> There were three cake baskets on my head, and in the uppermost basket there were all sorts of baked food for Pharaoh, but the birds were eating it out of the basket on my head.

In this case, Joseph responded here that, in 3 days, the Pharaoh would 'lift up the baker's head', hang him from a tree, and the birds would feed on him.

That is precisely what occurred 3 days later – on the Pharaoh's birthday. Both interpretations were correct. Unfortunately, Joseph continued to languish in prison for another 2 years until the Pharaoh had his famous precognitive dreams. The chief butler then, rather belatedly, remembered Joseph's ability to understand dreams and mentioned him to the Pharaoh.

A stark forewarning was provided in the Pharaoh's two highly symbolic dreams, which obviously agitated and puzzled him. In the first dream, Pharaoh was standing by the Nile and saw seven well-nourished cattle coming out of the water, followed by seven skeletal ones. The gaunt ones then proceeded to eat the fat ones. The dream's message was communicated again in the Pharaoh's next dream. This time, he observed seven ears of grain growing on one stalk, and then seven blighted ears of grain which swallowed up the healthy ones.

Joseph pointed out that the dreams encoded an identical prophetic message that required major action. In both of the servants' dreams, a reported number represented a time period, and so it was in the Pharaoh's dreams. Here, the seven cattle and seven ears of corn represented 7 years. There would be 7 years of bountiful harvest followed by 7 years of famine. The fact that the dream was 'doubled' gave it particular significance, added Joseph.

The Pharaoh, very wisely, accepted the interpretation and established a 7-year food-hoarding programme in order to cope with the anticipated hardships. Joseph, now 30 years old, was given a wife and placed second in command only to the Pharaoh, in order to supervise the reserving of foodstocks.

The massive famine came on time and lasted 7 years, as foreseen. Had the dreams not been interpreted, the historical consequences would have been profound, but, as it turned out, the kingdom survived the massive climatic disaster – 'severe all over the earth' – which culminated in a disastrous shortage of rain in the Nile region. The Biblical record clearly asserts that some dreams provide information which can avert impending catastrophes. Some 15 such dreams are reported in the Old Testament.

In India, long ago, dreams were also regarded as containing privileged information which could be uncovered by proper inspection. The Hindu book of wisdom, *Atharva Veda*, written in about 1500 BC, propounded the acquired knowledge about dreams of that culture. Aggressive dreams were considered to be generally favourable, whereas passivity in the dream, or some physical loss, e.g. of teeth or hair, was seen as a bad omen.

The treatise states an interesting negative correlation between the time of night at which the dream occurs and when the events actually happen. Thus, events foreseen in a dream at dawn would come to fruition sooner than those in a dream earlier in the night. Another view was that, if a series of dreams presented themselves, the final one contained the refined message and should be interpreted. Indeed, as we have seen with the Pharaoh's second dream, the ears of grain indicated very precisely the nature of the coming problem.

Many other significant dreams from history have been recorded. For instance, Julius Caesar decided to cross the Rubicon and attack Rome after experiencing a dream of incest with his mother. His oracles saw this as a symbol of territorial conquest. His wife Calpurnia is said to have dreamt of his assassination the night before it happened.

Edmund Halley was known for the comet which bears his name, but according to his friend Sir John Aubrey he also had a striking premonition. Writing in the seventeenth century, Aubrey states that Halley dreamt of the island of St Helena before he went there for astronomical observations. Halley was amazed to find the place exactly as he had seen it in his dream.

A notable premonitory dream of the early nineteenth century concerned the assassination of the then British Prime Minister, Mr Spencer Perceval. In a direct, nonsymbolic dream of the event, Cornishman John Williams saw a man dressed in a blue coat and white waistcoat shoot Mr Perceval. The dream then repeated itself twice more. Williams wanted to warn the Prime Minister, but was dissuaded by friends. Ten days later, Williams' son hurried home and informed his father that the dream had come true. John Bellingham, the assassin, was hanged.

At 3.30 a.m. on the morning of 28 June 1914, Bishop Joseph de Lanyi woke from a dream in which he received a letter with a black seal, bearing the motif of the Archduke Ferdinand. On the letterhead was a scene showing the Archduke's assassination in a motor vehicle. The letter stated that he and his wife Sophie would be killed the next day at Sarajevo. The Bishop held a special mass for the victims. Later that day the murders really happened. The Archduke was the heir to the Austro-Hungarian throne, and the killing was instrumental in starting World War I.

Science and Paranormal Dreams

While telepathic and precognitive dreams have been reported throughout history, little scientific work has been conducted on them, largely because of the strangely hostile attitude of conventional science. That frame of mind was probably a left-over from the massive repression by the Church of any perceived aspect of 'sorcery', including any interest in dreams, in the Middle Ages. Such edicts can influence many generations without people quite knowing why they think negatively about a topic.

It is rather like the ballot at the Second Council of Constantinople, concerning reincarnation (see p.49). The Emperor Justinian 'fixed' the proceedings. The Pope was not present and none of the Western bishops attended. It then became a punishable heresy to subscribe to the view of rebirth – an attitude that has prevailed right up to the end of the second millennium AD in the West.

Perhaps the most interesting scientific research into paranormal dreams was conducted at the Maimonides sleep laboratory in New York, USA, in the 1970s. The research team was headed by Drs Montague Ullman and Stanley Krippner. In a very well-thought-out and scientifically rigorous series of experiments, subjects were wired up in a sleep laboratory. When they started to dream, 'senders' tried to transmit randomly chosen images to them. Subjects were woken after dream periods and asked to report any dreams. Later, 'blind' judges rated how closely the subjects' dreams corresponded with the target material. Several of the dream-telepathy studies produced statistically significant results.

The team also investigated dream precognition using a British sensitive, Malcolm Bessent. In this study, dream reports were obtained from Malcolm over several nights. Each morning, a random experience was selected (after he had reported the night's dreams). For instance, in one trial, the word 'corridor' was selected, and an art print entitled Corridor of the St Paul Hospital was obtained. Malcolm had to play the role of a mental patient walking through a corridor in a mental asylum. Shortly before, he had dreamt of a large concrete building from which a patient had been trying to escape. Independent judges found very highly significant results in favour of the precognitive hypothesis.

Anecdotal cases absolutely abound. Simply asking one's friends and family about any dream of the future they might have had often produces a positive response. In a survey carried out in 1980 in the UK, 896 people were interviewed – all representative of the population. About two-thirds (63 per cent) believed that premonitions occurred, and 26 per cent – about a quarter of the sample (29 per cent females, 23 per cent males) – said they had actually experienced premonitions. The dream is the most frequent vehicle for precognition.

As a typical modern case, reported in Time-Life's *Dreams and Dreaming* (1990), aerospace chemist Edward Butler had a dream in 1959, when he was 25 years old. Edward was working on rocket fuels, and in his dream there was an explosion at work. He dashed out and saw that a nearby building was on fire. He ran in and found a colleague, Rita Dudak, on fire from head to foot. Grabbing her by the leg, he dragged her into his laboratory and doused her under a shower.

This disturbing dream recurred frequently over several months. Then, on 23 April 1959, it came true. Edward was working at a desk when an explosion happened next door. His colleague Rita Dudak was in flames. As if instructed by his recurring dream, Edward grabbed her leg and pulled her to the shower. Rita, badly burnt, spent 7 months in hospital. Edward admitted on a television programme in 1988 that he had not until then told anyone of his premonitory dream (except Rita) because it did not fit into his concept of science. 'I was almost ashamed that something mystical happened to me,' he said.

If a recurring premonitory dream is not enough to urge some kind of avoidance response, sometimes warnings also occur to others around. Thus, one woman informed Dr Hearne that she had a recurring dream each night for a week. In the dream, her deceased mother told her that she would not see her brother Doug and his wife, Joy, again. The informant wanted to alert the couple, but her husband told her 'Don't be daft'. Two days after she last had the dream, the woman bought a local paper and discovered to her horror that Doug and Joy had been killed in an air crash. The informant's other brother, Pete, also had a premonition and, while taking the couple to the airport, had asked them not to fly.

One of Dr Hearne's correspondents stated that a recurring premonitory dream saved his life, although it meant that someone else died in his place. After having completed his apprenticeship as an aircraft engineer, Philip Lammiman left London to work in the Midlands. One of his duties was to act as observer on test flights, with the managing director as pilot. At first he enjoyed the thrill of flying, but he soon became dogged by a repeating dream of sitting in the right-hand seat, attempting to pilot the plane, with his boss next to him, unconscious. One day, he reports, his nerve failed, and he refused to fly. The aircraft crashed, killing both the managing director and an apprentice.

One of Dr Hearne's case studies involved a man who knew what to do in a plane crash because he had experienced it already in vivid dream. Guy Stafford dreamt that he was in a plane which made a rough landing and burst into flames. People died.

A few days later Guy went on a business trip to China. By a seemingly random chain of events, he changed seats with his colleague Eric and found himself sitting in the same seat as in the dream. The plane reached Athens and started to land. The aircraft veered off the runway and went through the perimeter fence, as had happened in his dream. The plane then fell down a steep slope and started to burn. Although the nearest exit was towards the rear, Guy remembered that, in his dream, he went forwards – more than twice as far as the nearest exit. He did so and jumped 15 feet (5 metres) to the ground – slightly injuring himself. People at the back of the plane became trapped. Of the 142 passengers, 14 died, and of the six persons in row 25 (his original row), five died, including his colleague Eric.

Sometimes, the events are so specific and unlikely to have occurred by chance as to be amazing. Another of Dr Hearne's informants told how she went to stay with her niece and her husband, who lived in married quarters at a military camp. There was to be a party. The night before, the woman dreamt that the furniture had been piled against the wall. A couple came in and asked if she had heard of the accident at the camp in which three soldiers had been killed. The dream was so vivid that the woman asked if such an accident had occurred, but it had not. That night, the woman arrived at the party. The room was exactly as she had seen it. A couple came in and asked the same question as in her dream. There had been an accident during the day. The woman's niece and husband were incredulous. 'You mentioned that this morning,' they said.

The Percipients

Dr Hearne has studied premonitions for many years. In his book, *Visions of the Future*, he has collected cases of apparent foreknowledge and analysed the different types. Hearne noted that premonition dreams often contain symbols which the dreamer has learnt, by trial and error, to recognize. He studied some individual 'percipients' in depth. How do they decode their premonitions? We shall look at two people to see what they do.

Chris Robinson

Chris, in his 40s, is a lively-minded and colourful Londoner who has intelligently seen the link between certain of his dreams and future events, and learnt to decipher the dream material. He seems to have developed this to the point where he can actually request psychic information on specific topics.

He was particularly engaged in detecting Irish Republican Army (IRA) bombings in England when Dr Hearne studied him. The whole exercise was engrossing to Chris, who worked hard at understanding his dreams and communicating his predictions to the security services. He saw it as a worthwhile cause that could help to save lives.

Typically, before sleep, Chris would ask his 'spirit guides' for a dream that would provide useful information about the next attack. While in a somnambulistic state in the night, he would occasionally write things on a notepad, and, on waking, he was often surprised by what he had written. In the morning Chris would recall his dreams and see how they linked to the almost automatically written material. The feeling he had on waking was important too: a panicky feeling would mean that a bomb would soon go off.

His automatic writing was cryptic, linked to things that he had just dreamt and having associations relevant only to Chris. A number of consistent items could readily be decoded in the writing:

dogs, gits   = IRA terrorists

cups   = victims

cakes   = VIPs

TV chassis   = a bomb

fish   = a terrorist who would be caught.

Chris first realized that there were coded messages in his dreams when a postcode appeared. On 17 February 1990, 'LE1' was present in his dream notes. A few days later a bomb exploded in the centre of Leicester. 'BT', the Belfast postcode, would appear before a bomb exploded in that city. It might be shown in the dream and the dream notes as e.g. 'blood test' or 'Betamax tape', or, conversely, 'Thames Barrier' or 'The Bank'. The postcode identifier was a major discovery for Chris.

Anagrams and acronyms were also noticeable in his dream data. Thus 'A Boat On The River' became *abort* – in reference to an aborted IRA attack, or 'Better Make Our Breakfast' meant a *bomb*. The concept of opposites often applied in his dreams, so that words placed in a box were reversed, e.g. woman meant man, etc.

Chris has provided numerous cases of foretelling IRA attacks, and an early one concerned the IRA attack at the railway station in Lichfield, UK. At 5.52 p.m. on Friday 1 June 1991, two IRA gunmen in balaclavas picked out a group of three young soldiers in civilian clothes at Lichfield City station in Staffordshire and shot them at point-blank range. One was killed and the others badly injured. The gunmen escaped along the railway track.

The psychic indications started to appear in Chris's dreams a month before the incident. Lichfield station has a Walsall postcode (WS) and is adjacent to Stafford (postcode ST). From 4 May, various allusions to both postcodes were present: 'water stays', 'white stone', 'stop train', 'single track' – and opposites – 'swimming water', 'The Saint'. There were also references to trains, railway tracks, and escape. In a vivid dream on the night of 31 May (the day before the attack), Chris saw three soldiers in civilian uniform being shot by an IRA gunman on a station platform. The gunman then ran along the railway track to meet another man in a car.

From his dream-book information, Chris deduced that the station was to be Lichfield and felt that the attack was imminent. Chris had told his brother Keith and ex-wife Lorraine of his prediction concerning the attack at Lichfield station, and as they all watched the early evening news-broadcast on 1 June the news came in: three soldiers had been shot by IRA gunmen on Lichfield station, and the two gunmen had run along the track to escape. Keith and Lorraine confirmed all this in writing to Dr Hearne.

Chris has really become attuned to his dream language. He seems to have developed the skill of using his unconscious mind to communicate paranormally acquired information to conscious awareness. It is a great achievement and yet, as he asserts in his book, *Dream Detective*, it is an ability that is within everyone if we care to search for it.

Barbara Garwell

Barbara, who lives in Hull, UK, is in her 60s and is the seventh child of a seventh child – reputedly a psychic combination. She has had psychic experiences since childhood. Some of her precognitive dreams are direct representations of events that will occur, and some are cryptic, requiring decoding. A remarkable feature of her major premonitions is the often-consistent 21-day latency period between the premonition and the foreseen event.

One fairly accurate direct premonition was of the unexpected assassination of President Sadat of Egypt. In September 1981, Barbara dreamt of a stadium in which she saw a row of seated men, all wearing pin-striped suits. The men had 'coffee-coloured' skin. Barbara 'knew' that sand was nearby, and that the setting was somewhere in the Middle East. Two soldiers, also 'coffee-coloured', were seen to go up to the row of dignitaries and spray them with automatic fire. Barbara woke suddenly from the violent and vivid dream convinced, from previous experience, that the events would come to pass. She told the dream to witnesses.

Precisely 21 days later, on 6 October 1981, President Sadat was assassinated, and several others were killed and wounded, at the annual parade commemorating the Yom Kippur War with Israel. Some soldiers ran from a vehicle in the parade to the saluting base, where the guests were seated in rows. The attackers threw grenades and used automatic guns to fire at the President and dignitaries.

People who have precognitive dreams often tend to have them on the same general topic. Assassination was again the theme when Barbara had a cryptic dream 21 days before the assassination attempt on President Reagan in 1981. In early March, Barbara dreamt of being in a large, squarish, old car. In the car were two German soldiers in SS uniform. A limousine was approaching. It stopped and a man got out. He had a 'pock-marked' face, and she 'knew' he was an ex-actor. The two SS men got out of their car, and one of them drew a pistol from his leather holster and fired several shots at the actor, who fell. The victim in the dream appeared to be Trevor Howard, and yet she knew this was not the case.

On Monday 30 March 1981, an attempt was made on the life of President Reagan, well-known as a former actor. He was getting into a car near the Hilton Hotel in Washington DC. Several shots were fired from a pistol by John Hinckley, the 25-year-old son of a Denver oil tycoon. Reagan was shot in the chest and injured, as were his press secretary, a secret-service agent, and a police officer. Hinckley had joined the National Socialist Party (a neo-Nazi group) in 1978, but was expelled in 1979 because his views were too extreme and violent.

Although the victim in the dream was wrongly identified, the links with the Reagan incident are certainly close. It springs to mind at once that the 'Nazi' attacker could have been representative of Hinckley's political persuasion.

The way in which Barbara receives feedback about the foreseen event is often reflected in the original premonition. Thus, when Barbara has a premonition of a disaster, she often hears the voice of a television commentator using words similar to those actually broadcast. When the unexpected invasion of the Malvinas/Falkland Islands occurred on 2 April 1982, Barbara had already experienced a precognitive dream in which she saw the invasion as if on a television screen – with 'foreign words across the front of the screen'. British viewers saw much footage from Argentinian sources in subsequent news broadcasts, often with Spanish text across the screen.

Other Examples of Precognitive Dreams

There is some evidence that tragic situations can be avoided by acting on premonitions. Therefore, the more people find out about their psychic abilities, the greater the personal advantage. For instance, Louisa Rhine, in her 1954 study of such intervention, reported a case where, in 1942, a couple stopped for the night at a small hotel in Selma, North Carolina, USA. Early the next morning the wife dreamt that the hotel was reduced to burning ruins by an explosion. The dream woke her, and she was unable to go back to sleep. She became so agitated that she insisted that they leave at once, which they did.

A day later they saw, in a morning paper, that a truck loaded with dynamite had crashed into a small hotel and destroyed the building. The hotel was the one in which the pair had stayed the night before. If they had kept to their original schedule they would have been killed.

Sometimes the message of disaster is received, but no avoiding action is taken. There was the sad case of Aberfan, in Wales, on 21 October 1966. A huge coal-tip shifted and engulfed a school, killing 144 people, including 128 children. On the same morning, one little girl, 10-year-old Eryl Jones, told her mother that she had just dreamt that 'something black had come down over the school'. Eryl was killed in the catastrophe.

Although the majority of reported premonitions are about unpleasant events – indeed, the word 'premonition' comes from the Latin *praemonere*, meaning 'to warn in advance' – some cases are about trivial things, and a minority (9 per cent) actually foretell positive events.

There are other dreams that, it could be argued, are not precognitive, because the places witnessed in these dreams are so realistic that dreamers are prompted to search them out in real life, thus fulfilling the premonition. One such psychic dream, from Norman Brown, was sent to David Melbourne, who researched and validated it. Norman can be described as an easy-going, sincere person, and this strange dream still leaves many unanswered questions.

At the time of the dream, Norman (born in 1933), a retired computer-installation technician, lived with his wife, Camille, in the small French village of St André d'Apchon, not far from Lyon.

On the night of 26 May 1994, Norman had an unusually vivid dream in which he found himself in England, walking along a narrow path, with hedgerows on his right and a mist-laden lake on his left. The path meandered its way to well-kept lawns, which opened out in front of him. Standing on a gravel driveway, in front of a large red-brick mansion, was a group of people dressed in period costume. Norman recalled that he felt a great sense of relief at their appearance. As he approached them, he noticed that their thin faces were indistinguishable. Then, they all announced, 'Come and stay with us at South Walsham, we have never been so happy since we came to South Walsham.'

This statement jarred Norman awake (the trigger effect). He felt puzzled. Did such a place as South Walsham exist? When he got up, Norman studied several maps of the UK before he found what he was looking for: a small village in the county of Norfolk, east of Norwich.

On his next visit to England, Norman described his dream to his son, Jean' Pierre, who lives in the vicinity of Luton. Without further ado, Jean' Pierre, his wife Bella, and their 8-year-old daughter, Danielle, set out with Norman on a family outing in search of South Walsham. When they found it, Norman was amazed to find the path, the hedgerows, the lake, the lawns, the gravel driveway, and the mansion were just as they had appeared to him in his dream.

It transpired that the red-brick mansion, as Norman described it, was in fact South Walsham Hall, an historic English country-house, dating back to the *Domesday Book* in the eleventh century but now a plush hotel. Everything fitted Norman's dream – but why?

Perhaps the answer can be found in the next incredible sequence to Norman's visit to this country estate. As the family explored the grounds and South Walsham Hall, Norman felt a compulsion to visit the church, which is situated near the country-house. They looked around the grounds and then entered the church.

There, inside the church, Jean' Pierre and Danielle were astonished to discover a plaque on the wall which bore the name 'Norman Brown', who, it was discovered, met his end during World War 2. Upon contacting the family of the deceased Norman Brown, Norman discovered that his namesake had been an 18-year-old who had met his end during the first landing of the invasion of Normandy.

In summary, it appears that some people experience direct simultaneous and precognitive dreams which can be linked easily to events elsewhere, but that some material is consistently represented in ways that need to be decoded.

Searching for Paranormal Information in Dreams

If you sometimes have dreams that seem to correspond to later events, although not directly, you may find that you can develop a decoding system if you start to collect enough data. Obtain a notebook and, immediately on waking from vivid dreams, write down the key points: details of the characters involved, the setting (which country, indoors, outdoors, etc.), the activities observed. There may be a particular 'feeling' or vividness associated with precognitive dreams.

Observe, by daily reference to news items, whether any links with your dreams seem to exist. Then list any differences and see if such possible representations come up on other occasions. In this way, you may be able gradually to work out an accurate deciphering procedure.

Be aware that premonitions often seem to be based on experiences in your own life. Thus, for instance, you may dream of a situation from childhood which is, nevertheless, linked to a car crash with modern cars. It may be that you had a particular friend in childhood with the same name as a person about to have an accident now. That is how the unconscious seems to construct premonitions – even in the short term.

As an example, one Friday, years ago, Dr Hearne was studying zoology at university. A dogfish was being dissected, the concentration being on the branchial basket – the cartilages of the gill region. Of the seven cartilages, numbers four and five are fused. The next night he dreamt that he opened the Sunday paper and saw the football results listed. The first seven games were draws, except games four and five. It was clear to him that there was a compelling association between the pattern of scores and the cartilage arrangement that he had been studying. Technically, the experience was not precognition, because the games had already been played, but he certainly did not know the results on Saturday night.

Also, look for opposites occurring in dreams. Sometimes the unconscious seems to identify something by portraying its opposite, which happens to be more convenient to produce as an image. In particular, note things heard in dreams. They are often significant. Analyse the words as a metaphor, anagram, or acronym.

You could even establish a code of your own to identify a precognitive dream, by telling yourself before sleep that a dream in which a certain colour predominates will contain precognitive material, and that you will awake immediately from such a dream. That will limit your search area considerably so that you can analyse the material.

This whole area of coded paranormal information in dreams is open to investigation, and major discoveries may be waiting to be made.

New Science

Of course, if precognition exists, then the whole of science is fundamentally wrong. Premonitions cannot fit into a physical universe – where an effect cannot precede a cause – and yet, paradoxically, the evidence for precognition is overwhelming. However, there is an alternative philosophy – that we exist in a shared-mind world. This is an enticing vista for postulating and theorizing in the new millennium.

And now that we are almost in the new millennium, the sense of advance will hopefully put behind us the physicalist straitjacket of the last century which, on principle, refused permission for anomalous human experiences, such as telepathy and premonitions, to exist.

That extreme negativity, as bad as old-fashioned racism and sexism, became in itself a belief system, which was rigorously adhered to by some people who were out to forbid 'wrong' thoughts. They wanted to impose their cosy and conventional views on everyone, wilfully stunting and warping the progress of science. They were authoritarian and censorious scientific ostriches, hindering mankind's advance towards truth.

Official science was unscientific and fraudulent in its selectivity of data, and the refusal of so-called 'scientific' journals even to consider for publication serious research by parapsychologists was a scandal and crime against human development. However, the technological revolution has changed and freed the communication of ideas, so the era of strict control of published research is over.

Science progresses – as Jacob Bronowski observed – when awkward people ask impertinent questions. Now is the age for the rejection of orthodox science and the establishment of a New Science which will look, reasonably, and for the first time, at all viewpoints without bias.

Dream Recall

Assuming that you are now able to incubate meaningful dreams, the next step is to develop the capacity to remember them. There are several ways in which to achieve this end, and understanding how dreams are structured will make the task much easier.

As a general rule, in order to recall a dream, you must either wake up, become momentarily lucid (so that conscious awareness is attained), or have the memory triggered by a word, sound, smell, event, etc. For example, you might waken with no recollections of having experienced a dream, yet, on the following day, someone might say something that will trigger remembrance of a dream in its entirety.

All too often, in a state of frustration, people try hard to recollect dreams, but discover that they remain tantalizingly out of reach, or evaporate the moment the eyes are opened. It seems reasonable to assume that this is a safety mechanism to prevent us from getting the two states of consciousness mixed up. Otherwise dream events could be believed to have taken place in waking reality.

However, there are secret (until now) clues that we can follow which will assist greatly in dream recall. It depends on comprehending the brain's limitations in producing dream images and verbal utterances, as well as the way in which the brain puts dreams together.

Dream Structure

As we have already seen, Dr Hearne devised a way to externalize (make sketches of) hypnotic dreams, for which he coined the term *hypno-oneirography* (dream tracing), which meant that they could actually be seen and studied.

Remember, Dr Hearne noticed some striking consistencies – consistencies that were to revolutionize dream-interpretation techniques and open up new dimensions to our understanding of dreams. Incredibly, it was apparent that the brain was using trickery in the way dreams progressed from one scene to the next. This led Dr Hearne to conclude that the brain has limitations in the way it structures dream content, which is by a sort of 'law of least effort'!

It is worth restating that these experiments also revealed other consistencies that have long been suspected: dreams follow visual- and verbal-associative pathways. In other words, a banana could become a sausage in the next scene. The appearance of a flower could be followed by hearing the word 'follower' (flower).

Dr Hearne noticed that elements from one dream scene were being cleverly incorporated into the next, albeit in disguised form. For instance, a girl might dream of a black and white bullock grazing in a green field. The next scene might show a black and white dog, cat, snake, or bird, or even a black and white overcoat on a green carpet. Clearly, this has major ramifications in our understanding of dreams and their interpretation.

To illustrate this, let us imagine that a dream to be interpreted contained the black and white bullock grazing in a green field, then in the next scene a black and white cat curled up on a green mat. Which symbol should the analyst interpret: the bullock or the cat, the green field or the green mat? Perhaps the brain wanted to feature the cat as the principal element of the dream, but was only able to present it after transforming the bullock, i.e. dream construction by the law of least effort.

Furthermore, one aspect of importance in the dream could have been a black and white truck, which the brain might have clearly represented. However, to feature the next relevant element – the cat – it might have been forced to change the truck into an intermediate-sized object (the bullock) before it moved on to the image of a cat. Under these circumstances then, other than serving to assist the brain, it is possible that the bullock had no significance to the meaning behind the dream. It seems that dream scenes might have to travel around the houses before they are able to get to the point. Unless prospective dream analysts understand the scene-shift effect, there are clearly going to be many inaccurate interpretations.

Understanding these limitations of the brain in constructing dreams illustrates the reason why, if the unconscious mind wants to give us messages, it cannot succeed in straightforward terms. In other words, because it has to follow certain rules (perhaps many of which are still waiting to be discovered), the brain appears to lack the capacity to present a clear-cut, unambiguous message. This theory is supported by the fact that dreams are mainly the product of the right hemisphere of the brain which, among other things, is allied to creativity and imagery. The left hemisphere, on the other hand, lends itself to logic, language, and speech. It seems likely, therefore, that, in dream construction, the brain might be unable to make an unambiguous link between the two. Thus, our black and white cat could represent a play on words and really be symbolizing the mat (cat = mat).

It was for precisely this reason that David Melbourne devised the cross-reference flowchart method of dream interpretation. This system identifies a single theme that permeates the entire dream. Then, using that theme, it becomes fairly obvious which symbols the unconscious mind is trying to communicate as the central focus of the message. Symbols that crop up in scene changes but appear to bear no relationship to the theme of the dream can, with reasonable confidence, be discarded. Thus, the dream becomes much easier to decode and the process takes far less time.

The Written or Spoken Word

Although dreams are more of a right-brain activity, the left brain also has its part to play. Therefore words also come into the equation, but not necessarily as we would expect.

One dream from our files featured three women sitting in glass-fronted premises overlooking the sea. The woman in the middle was the dreamer herself, flanked on either side by an aunt and her mother. Suddenly, out of a blue sky, a meteorite plummeted into the sea, leaving an enormous hole. In this instance, by making the meteorite serve two distinct purposes, the unconscious mind proved how brilliant it can be at utilizing the resources available to overcome its own limitations.

First, it transpired that the meteorite symbolized an emotional catastrophe – which came like a bolt from the blue – in the dreamer's life and then left a big hole. Amazingly though, the meteorite even revealed on whom this emotional upheaval was focused. The dreamer's aunt was sitting to her left and so could be excluded as the main character. However, the person on the right of the dreamer (her mother) was clearly the dream's focal point. In fact, the dream was almost screaming it out, 'Me to your right!' (meteorite).

We have discovered that people who enjoy doing crosswords will often be presented with place names, or even action scenes, which, when described, are clearly anagrams. For example, one person had a dream that focused on his work situation. This was evident when, in his dream, he described somebody as 'riding hard', which is an anagram of 'I grind hard'.

This play on words becomes evident when we consider just a few cases that the authors have encountered. Homophones, for instance, are similar-sounding words that have different meanings, e.g. son/sun, vane/vain.

Approximate homophones can also appear: wisteria/hysteria, Germans/ germs. Often, dream symbols can be summed up in a word, phrase, sentence, or even a metaphor. For example, Atlas might be seen supporting a globe. Immediately we can guess that the dreamer might be going around as if 'he had the weight of the world on his shoulders'.

Therefore, in message-bearing dreams, everything is linked by a simple law of least effort that uses visual- and verbal-associative pathways. Understanding these issues will make it much easier to recollect more of a dream's content than could be achieved by normal means. First, though, let us consider a few simple steps that can be taken to improve dream recall.

Changing the Mind-Set

Bearing in mind the power of the subconscious, if we utilize expectation to change the mind-set, remembering dreams becomes a simpler task. Just as expectation can be used to incubate dreams, so will it serve a purpose in dream recall.

First, you must send a message to your unconscious mind to the effect that you mean business. Your intentions can be declared by making a conscious effort to record your dreams in a dream diary, which can be as simple as a pencil and piece of paper next to your bed. Throughout the day, give the matter some thought and make a mental affirmation:

Tonight, or tomorrow morning, my unconscious mind will awaken me with a meaningful dream that I will be able to remember.

This can be incorporated into your dream-incubation chant.

Remembering Dreams

If you are sincere, you are almost certain to be woken with a message-bearing dream that can be recalled. However, some parts of dreams still have an annoying habit of remaining tantalizingly out of reach. It is unusual for the entire contents of a dream to be remembered. Nevertheless, by following a few simple rules, far more of a dream can be reclaimed from the unconscious recycling plant.

To begin with, upon waking, do not move around, but maintain your sleeping position in bed. Keep your eyes closed; external stimuli bombarding the senses are almost certain to cause a dream to evaporate. Bring to mind the part of the dream that caused you to wake up (the trigger effect), then start working backwards through the dream. Go over it time and again until it has become fixed in your mind.

Once you have recalled as much of the dream as possible, you may then open your eyes and record it in your dream diary. For years now, this method has been accepted as an efficient way of remembering dreams. However, because you now understand how dreams are structured, you have the advantage of being able to recollect dreams in far more detail than before.

Read your dream account and start looking for associative pathways. For example, your dream might read along the lines of this one, taken from our files:

> I woke up, startled, to see my son acting in a cannibalistic manner with an effigy of a child [the trigger mechanism]. This brought the dream back in frightening vividness. I remember seeing my son in a group of young men, who were dancing to some sombre music – they were gathered round a life-like human doll. I felt sad and it brought a tear to my eye.

This presents enough information to cause the dreamer to suspect that her son might be involved in some sort of duplicitous behaviour. However, if we now employ our knowledge of dream structure, more of the dream could be revealed. First, let us look for verbal-associative pathways. If we take the dreamer's emotional state into consideration, she mentions a tear in her eye. Thinking of homophones, we must ask if the word 'tear' could be hinting at 'tier'.

At this point, the dreamer might recall that, earlier in the dream, she had been standing in the front row (tier) of a dance hall. Next, using visual-associative pathways, she might recollect that there was a disco which, in turn, could help her to remember certain details, e.g. of her son's clothing.

By continuing her search for associative pathways, the dreamer might conclude that the dance being featured possibly symbolized that she was being led a merry dance. This again could serve to jog her memory that, earlier in the dream, she found herself in a darkened corner. This could be a metaphor: she was being kept in the dark.

By repeated study of the dream, combined with understanding of how it progresses, more and more of the dream's content will be unearthed until almost total recall is achieved. The dream then might read something like this:

> Unusually for me, I found myself at a loud, crowded disco, with flashing bright lights. Each time I went to join in on the dance floor, my son, who looked bonny in his kilt, pushed me back into a dark corner. He said that I wasn't allowed to see his next performance.
>
> The people at the disco congregated around the outside of the dance floor, while my son, becoming the centre of attraction, joined a group of others in the middle. Although I knew I wasn't meant to see what was going on, I pushed my

way through the crowd until I was in the front row. I couldn't believe my eyes as, in tune with some very depressing music, I watched my son slowly dancing around an effigy of a child. Then I was horrified as they began to dismember the dummy, while displaying cannibalistic behaviour. I woke up in a state of shock!

Use of Detail in Interpretation

The dream above was presented for interpretation by Claire, from Scotland, and illustrates perfectly how dreams sometimes present their messages by incorporating anagrams. Claire, mother of a 15-year-old boy, said that, at the time of the dream, she had nothing of particular importance on her mind.

It is widely acknowledged that the unconscious mind is on duty 24 hours a day and is ever vigilant. It is also generally accepted that it has the capacity to notice minute changes in the circumstances around us which we tend, on a conscious level, not to observe. Therefore, some seemingly precognitive dreams (premonitions) may be the result of the subconscious predicting an outcome from consciously unnoticed alterations in the surrounding environment. This appears to be the case here. Disturbingly, the consistent theme that permeates the dream is 'deception'.

First, Claire states that it was unusual for her to be at a loud disco. Accepting that this dream is precognitive, this suggests that she will soon find herself in an unusual situation. As we will discover, these events are likely to surround her son because he was the only one there whom she recognized.

The first clue to indicate that Claire's subconscious has identified something which her conscious mind has not recognized comes when her son pushes her into a dark corner (he continually keeps her in the dark). She was not supposed to see his performance. In this particular instance, the word 'performance' signifies misbehaviour of some kind.

Next, we come to the crux of the dream, and one that is pretty convincing. Her son, along with others (his peers), becomes the centre of attraction. This suggests that, whatever his performance is going to be (in real life), it is likely to be noticed by her eventually, and this is signified by her presence among the crowd of onlookers. Indeed, the dream suggests a certain amount of peer pressure could be involved.

The effigy of a child is a powerful symbol representing her son's naïveté. That he engages in its destruction points unerringly to the end of his innocence, mentally and perhaps physically.

Finally, the dream reflects precisely what it is that Claire's subconscious might have noticed which her conscious mind perhaps does not suspect. The fact that she mentioned his kilt is extremely relevant and helps us to identify her son. In addition, her choice of words in her description of the dream represents incredible odds if it is merely coincidence.

She states firmly that his behaviour was 'cannibalistic', which clearly breaks down into an anagram of two words: 'cannabis' and 'cilti' (kilty), the wearer of the kilt. It must be emphasized that the brain has limitations in its use of coded language, and cannabis might not be the issue. On the other hand, it could be, so she should be on the lookout for smoking, drinking, or anything else that teenagers are tempted to abuse nowadays.

When Claire saw the analysis, she admitted that her son had recently been displaying bouts of somewhat odd behaviour. She added that she would keep a closer eye on him. A few weeks later, she reported that he had been in some trouble at a dance, although she did not specify the nature.

~ ~ ~

Clearly, then, by using your understanding of dreams advantageously, much more detail can be uncovered which, in turn, will lead to a more accurate and fulfilling interpretation.

Individual Differences, Imagination and Symbolism

By understanding the scene-shift effect, we can see how, certainly in the West, dreams are individual to the dreamer; remember the black and white bullock grazing in a green field (p.81). However, our individuality also has other implications in the area of dream interpretation and firmly establishes that, unless a universal system of symbolism is previously learnt by subjects, then dream symbols have to be specific to the dreamer.

The Notion of Individual Differences (Unexplained Variance)

Dr Hearne recalls being on an expedition to Loch Ness in Scotland a few years ago. On a midsummer's evening, he sat on a cliff by the loch and was spellbound by the sight of a beautiful sunset appearing behind several ranges of mountains. The moon was shining brightly, and the mysterious loch was in black shadow. The scent of summer flowers pervaded the warm air.

To Hearne it was a unique and exquisite spiritual experience. He called to a colleague to come and witness the amazing sight. 'Oh yes, very nice,' was his response on taking a cursory view, and after a few seconds he went back into his camper vehicle to wash some dishes. What was unmissable and rapturous to Hearne was of no great shakes to his colleague – who no doubt saw beauty in other situations.

No two people experience the world in the same way. We have different physical/physiological thresholds to sensitivities, and we possess different abilities and interests. We vary in our attitudes to people and situations, on many levels and over time. These individual differences have long been recognized and were first studied by the ancient Greeks.

Individuals can vary in height from, say, between 4 and 8 feet (1.2 and 2.4 metres), but most are somewhere in the middle range of the normal (Gaussian), bell-shaped distribution curve. It is the same for many other physical, physiological, and measurable psychological aspects. Genetic factors and the effect of life events influence the very way we see the world and cope with life's vicissitudes or pleasures.

There was the interesting case of Mr Kinnebrook, who was dismissed by the Astronomer Royal at Greenwich in 1796 because his reaction times were too slow. Kinnebrook had to signal when a star crossed a measuring line, but his delays caused major problems in astronomical time-keeping. Perhaps his perception of the measuring of time was different.

Word-association tests – of the sort developed by Jung – also highlight individual differences. People answer according to their own sets of word-links and, indeed, sometimes cannot respond because a 'mental block' inhibits them. Some people cannot perform some of the psychological visual-figure tests, e.g. the cube which can be seen at different perspectives.

It follows that there is no such thing as a *standard stimulus* in psychology. A behaviouristic experimenter might assume that an electric shock to a person might be highly aversive. That might be true for some individuals, especially those who may have previously experienced shocks, but others may not be particularly bothered. Similarly, psychological stimuli, e.g. words such as 'pain', 'rape', 'tickle', 'accident', 'sex', will affect people individually. The 'settings' of our bodies and the current state of our mind – that intangible, unseeable component of organisms – affect everything we perceive. Everything, then, is relative. Reality is a variable.

In respect of dream interpretation, we need to be fully aware that, because we are all so different, we cannot ascribe definitive meanings to dream images and experiences. Dreams have to be interpreted from the perspective of the dreamer, no-one else – although an outsider can often see significant links as a result of the dreamer being somewhat defensive about their limitations.

Association

Much of proper dream interpretation is to do with seeking the dreamer's personal associations to key elements of the dream. Let us see, by way of a practical test, how individuals respond differently to the same words. Do the test opposite for yourself and, if possible, get a few others to do it as well.

As an example, someone might respond to the stimulus word *aircraft* in the following way:

Associations: Waiting, boredom, fear of flying, ears popping, turbulence, air sickness, queuing for toilets, possible crash.

Feeling: Negative.

Another person might give the following responses:

Associations: Excitement, love of technology, speed, talking to fellow passengers, view from the window, 'high-flying'.

Feeling: Positive.

Association Test

Write down your associations to each of the following stimulus words and indicate your feeling towards each word.

DOG
Associations: ....
Feeling: □ Very positive □ Positive □ Neutral □ Negative □ Very negative

WATER
Associations: ....
Feeling: □ Very positive □ Positive □ Neutral □ Negative □ Very negative

GUN
Associations: ....
Feeling: □ Very positive □ Positive □ Neutral □ Negative □ Very negative

MOUSE
Associations: ....
Feeling: □ Very positive □ Positive □ Neutral □ Negative □ Very negative

MY BODY
Associations: ....
Feeling: □ Very positive □ Positive □ Neutral □ Negative □ Very negative

BOSS
Associations: ....
Feeling: □ Very positive □ Positive □ Neutral □ Negative □ Very negative

SCHOOL
Associations: ....
Feeling: □ Very positive □ Positive □ Neutral □ Negative □ Very negative

FIRE
Associations: ....
Feeling: □ Very positive □ Positive □ Neutral □ Negative □ Very negative

HOSPITAL

Associations: ....

Feeling: □ Very positive □ Positive □ Neutral □ Negative □ Very negative

BABY

Associations: ....

Feeling: □ Very positive □ Positive □ Neutral □ Negative □ Very negative

Accepting that individuals can have widely varying associations to absolutely anything reflects on the inherent limitations of 'dream dictionaries', which provide fixed meanings for dream items but yet can differ greatly from publication to publication.

Imaging Modalities (Especially Visual Imagery)

For each of the sensory modalities, there is within us a system that enables us to synthesize (or imagine) some event so that we can 'experience' it as if it were actually happening. Thus, in the absence of real stimulation, it is possible to 'see' (visual imagery), 'hear' (auditory imagery), 'taste' (gustatory imagery), 'smell' (olfactory imagery), 'touch' (tactile or kinesthetic imagery), etc. The presence of these various types of internal imagery can be useful in recalling past events and in anticipating future ones.

The previously mentioned concept of individual differences can be demonstrated convincingly by considering the way in which we use imagination. It is so easy to fall into the trap of expecting everyone else to experience the world in exactly the same way as ourselves. But if you ask people, say, to visualize or 'image' a specific scene (e.g. their front door or an elephant), amazing disparities occur between individuals in their reported abilities. Some will instantly 'see' a vividly coloured scene and proceed to describe the minutest of details. Others will declare that they see nothing. Most will give an account somewhere between these two extremes.

Consider how we use the same symbolic language but can mean very different things for those words. To a nonvisualizer, the term 'day-dreaming' simply means thinking, with no visual component at all; words are simply registered in the mind. However, a good visualizer will view a scene virtually as if it were genuinely happening before their eyes. The two types of people can barely begin to comprehend what it is like for the other.

To some people 'seeing things' is often synonymous with having 'insane hallucinations', but evidence that it is not necessarily abnormal came from a paper written by Dewi-Rees, a general practitioner, in 1971. He interviewed 227 widows and 66 widowers and found that half had experienced some form of 'hallucination' of their dead spouse. 16.7 per cent of the widowers and 13.2 per cent of the widows had visual imagery of the spouse.

Some of the other manifestations of imagery are:

~ *After-images.* These occur after stimulation has ceased and are primarily physiological in origin.
~ *Eidetic imagery.* An almost photographic-quality reproduction of scenes is experienced by some people.
~ *Diagram forms.* This occurs to many proficient imagers. For instance, on hearing a number spoken, the person automatically sees it in a particular section of the visual field. Different numbers may occupy different positions, thus making up a diagram of increasing numbers.
~ *Synesthesia.* In this, the different imaging systems seem to be linked. A sudden noise can evoke, say, a flash of coloured light. A small minority of people experience this condition.
~ *Crystal imagery.* These images appear to some people on reflective or refractive surfaces. It is the basis of 'scrying' (seeing images of elsewhere, or of the future).
~ *Exaggerated perseveration.* Some people continue to see whatever they had been observing at great length previously in the day. This is not the same as an after-image.
~ *Micropsia* and *macropsia.* Some good imagers report that they can look at a person or object and make it apparently shrink or expand in size. It may happen at will, or it can happen spontaneously in an emotional situation, or when the person is fatigued. Some good imagers report that, when they are driving, the vehicle in front may appear to alter in size when its distance is really constant.
~ *Drug-induced imagery.* Mescaline, LSD, and toxic imagery is usually characterized by visual form constants, e.g. cobwebs, tunnels, spirals, latticework, etc. In the *delirium tremens* (DTs) of alcohol withdrawal, a common form of imagery involves seeing myriad small creatures, such as rats, spiders, mice, etc.
~ *Neurologic imagery.* Spontaneous and striking images may occur as a neurologic symptom in association with epilepsy, brain tumours, abscesses, and lesions. The temporal and visual-sensory areas of the brain are particularly affected. Multisensory imagery may form the 'aura' preceding a *grand mal* attack. Similarly, in the 'absences' of *petit mal*, visual imagery often occurs.

There is some experimental evidence for the existence of visual imagery. In 1910, Perky performed an experiment, in which he asked subjects to imagine objects (banana, book, leaf, etc.) while fixating on a screen. Simultaneously, a coloured shape, roughly that of the named object, was back-projected onto the screen in front of the subject and oscillated slightly to simulate a subjective image. The stimulus was gradually increased in brightness until well above threshold. Subjects assimilated the projected shape into their images and oriented the object accordingly. Significantly, they failed to realize that the image was, in fact, partly percept. In 1964, over half a century later, Segal and Nathan successfully replicated and elaborated Perky's work.

Those are situations of wakefulness. In dreams, however, there is a kind of equality. Even nonvisualizers see pictures in dreams, although, in wakefulness, such internally generated images are just out of their grasp. It is the same for the other sensory modalities: some people can 'hear' and 'feel' things well using imagination, while others find such tasks impossible.

Let us consider how individuals experience and perceive the world in their own unique way. Dreams are a form of imagery and people vary considerably in their ability to visualize in wakefulness.

Imaging Ability

Try the following test of visual imaging on yourself and, if possible, say, six other people. The idea is to discover for yourself the range of visual-imaging ability between people. Also try it for other high-imagery nouns, e.g. your front door. Then try out the other forms of imagery.

Tests of Imaging Ability

Visual Imagery
IMAGINE SEEING AN AIRCRAFT. To what extent (if at all) can you do this:
□ Not at all □ Slightly □ In between □ Quite well □ As clearly as the real thing

Auditory Imagery
IMAGINE HEARING A HORSE WALKING ON A STONE SURFACE. To what extent (if at all) can you do this:
□ Not at all □ Slightly □ In between □ Quite well □ As clearly as the real thing

Gustatory Imagery
IMAGINE THE TASTE OF A FRESH ORANGE. To what extent (if at all) can you do this:
□ Not at all □ Slightly □ In between □ Quite well □ As clearly as the real thing

Olfactory Imagery
IMAGINE THE SMELL OF A FRESH-BAKED CAKE. To what extent (if at all) can you do this:
□ Not at all □ Slightly □ In between □ Quite well □ As clearly as the real thing

Reflect now on which sensory modalities occur in your dreams. Are some of them lacking when you consider their presence as stimuli in everyday life? For your own information, which of the following sensory modalities can you recall having experienced in your dreams:

☐ Visual scenes ☐ Sounds ☐ Smells ☐ Tastes
☐ Touch ☐ Sexual stimulation ☐ Pain

Symbolism in Art, Life and Dreams

Symbols play a significant part in human psychology. Apart from our left-brain verbal-language system, profound communication also occurs in the right brain at a symbolic, largely visual level. It seems that, in sleep, left-brain thoughts become transformed into right-brain images. Symbols, then, are a language that dream interpreters need to know about.

In the last century, Silberer – an introspectionist who experienced copious hypnagogic (sleep-onset) imagery – was able to provide many examples of thoughts just before sleep becoming changed to representational visual images. For example, while trying to remember a name when dropping off to sleep, he developed an image of a tired-looking clerk looking through a filing system. This type of conversion of thought to an image, he termed the 'auto-symbolic phenomenon'.

In art, symbolism has been used for centuries, sometimes to evade censorship, but sometimes to provide more than meets the eye to the intelligent observer. A picture of a castle in a landscape, with peasants in the fields, could represent the status quo and social order of the nation, and more. Ancient constructions of man no doubt symbolized beliefs and wisdoms. The earth-mother figurines, standing stones, and pyramids of previous millennia were no doubt meant to convey important ideas to people who lived then.

It seems that the unconscious requires major symbolic events – or rituals – in order to reprogramme itself accordingly. Thus, weddings, funerals, christenings, graduations, etc. are all necessary events in that process. In psychotherapy and hypnotherapy, it is frequently observed that clients are often seeking some kind of finality concerning an unresolved issue. An imaginal revisitation to an early trauma can allow a dialogue between the parties, forgiveness, and a symbolic therapeutic ending.

6

The Interpretation Procedure

Essentially, the dream will have an underlying thought on a topic that may or may not be known consciously to the individual. The dream usually reflects a present or impending situation in a metaphoric way. Apart from the main metaphor of the dream, there are often verbal and visual puns present – sometimes repeatedly – which need to be identified because they often provide the key to understanding the dream.

Summary of the Melbourne Cross-reference Flowchart Interpretation Procedure

It is important in any real attempt at dream interpretation to acquire crucial background information about the dream and the dreamer. For that purpose we have designed the *Melbourne/Hearne Questionnaire* (MHQ) for dream interpretation, a shortened version of which is provided at the end of this book, together with a typical dream-report form.

The process of dream analysis must involve constant referral to that background information. The same dream experienced by two separate people could have widely differing meanings for them because of their individual lifestyles. Hence, the use of 'dream dictionaries', which give standard 'meanings', is a very unsatisfactory method of trying to understand the language of the dream. For instance, a dog seen in a dream may have a very different meaning for different people. The best approach to interpreting your own dreams is to imagine that they are someone else's. Try to be impartial and objective.

The questionnaire data are essential. Clearly, it is helpful to know which matters are currently on the dreamer's mind: whether a special event is anticipated, the thoughts before sleep, whether the events are possible and customary, the psychological state on waking, current stress, and all the other points raised in the questionnaire.

Read all the information several times. If it is someone else's dream and information, treat it absolutely confidentially. *Never* reveal information about the dreamer or the dream to another person without the full permission of the dreamer and keep your records in a secure place.

Get back to the dreamer to clarify any points. For instance, if a specific time period is stated in the dream account (e.g. 'I knew in the dream that the person had been dead for 3 months'), ask the dreamer what happened 3 months ago, or is due to happen in 3 months' time.

It is *not appropriate to interpret all dreams*. In lucid dreams, the dreamer is fully aware of being in a dream, and the dream scenery may be manipulated by mere thought. The automatic, subconscious DPP is displaced in such situations. Whereas in a lucid dream the imagery is produced as a result of conscious thought (although bodily asleep), in ordinary dreams the imagery arises from subconscious thoughts.

The *personal data are important* because, for instance, you will be searching for associations to keywords and symbols in the dream report, and those associations will depend a lot on the education, occupation, and interests of the dreamer.

The *emotional content* of the dream is of major importance in the analysis. It seems to be the feature most closely linked to the underlying subconscious thought and thus serves as the basis of an interpretation. However, the opposite of a reported emotion may occasionally be identified as the real key to the analysis.

It is best then to read the dream report aloud a few times and to listen very carefully to every word and group of words for *verbal puns*. *Homophones*, e.g. son/sun, frequently crop up in interpretations and approximate homophones, e.g. Germans/germs (i.e. infection) also appear (see also p.82).

Pay attention to the words rather than the apparent story. Ask yourself what other connotations each word and group of words may have. Thus, the words 'weight' and 'heavy-weather' may be present, with a reported waking feeling of dissatisfaction. This could refer to a dreamer's problem with *diet*, or it could mean frustration at having to *wait* for something.

The left-brain dream thought is represented in many ways by the right-brain symbolizing function. Look for links to establish the likely common theme. Constantly refer to the questionnaire data. The list of current problems stated in the report's questionnaire can often help to pinpoint the underlying topic.

Look also, especially in crossword fiends, for *anagrams* (e.g. the name of a station seen in a dream, *Akpinar*, triggered the next scene which was *in a park*) and even *acronyms* (a *Big Old Motor Bike*, written in a dream account, could represent a *bomb* – perhaps an emotional bombshell). These may not be the result of a disguising process; it is perhaps a more playful, recreational activity. Words may be presented backwards, e.g. 'Earth Om' was recognized to be a reference to the dreamer's mother. We cannot stress enough the significance of such play on words: it happens a lot in dreams.

Similarly, *visual puns* will be present, e.g. a horseman seen riding on the roofs of buildings could represent someone 'riding their high horse'. Is it the dreamer? The dreamer may be feeling a little guilty about being arrogant, hence the dream.

Often the *dream characters are aspects of the dreamer*, now or in the past, and perhaps in the future. Sometimes, subpersonalities, fixated at earlier ages when traumas (happy as well as sad) occurred, have their predictable say in the dream.

Seemingly *trivial items may be important*. A man may dream of a landau carriage with Princess Diana in it, but a 'lady-in-waiting' – also in the dream report (see p.126) – could be more significant to the dreamer. It might refer to someone with whom he is hoping to establish a relationship, i.e. a lady he is waiting for. In order to produce the image of a lady-in-waiting, the dream had to show the royalty image, but the presence of the Princess is actually irrelevant to the dream's basic thought.

In these circumstances, *the dream will probably produce a clue that the main image is a subterfuge*. A thought may occur, or someone in the dream will state (so overriding the visual presentation), perhaps, that 'It's not really her'. In those cases, shift your analysis to other persons or items in the same scene, no matter how inconspicuous they may seem at first.

The dream progresses along verbal- and visual-associative pathways connected to the basic subconscious thought. Therefore that underlying thought may be exposed by *tracing back the associations*. This is another major uncovering task in the process of interpreting the dream. What you are looking for is a common thread between items in the dream. Note down significant words in the dream, especially apparent symbols, and write down any reasonable associations, bearing in mind the dreamer's background. Also look for links in *settings*, *actions*, *dialogues*, and *emotions*.

Draw up flowcharts to look at associations. As an example, in the very important *symbols category*, Queen Elizabeth II might have appeared in the dream. Write down any associations that come to mind, such as the names Elizabeth, Anne, Mary, Cleopatra, Antoinette. Consider the dreamer's country of origin and general background in this task. Do any of these names correspond to the list of first names of people significant to the dreamer? Is there someone called Philip on the list of significant people? To an Englishman, the Queen could represent his wife. The word 'queen' also refers to a homosexual or a mother figure. Make as many connections as you can. What links might the dreamer make? (See flowcharts on pp.106 and 125.)

Refer constantly to the information given in the questionnaire. Eventually, links will be discovered, and suddenly everything will seem to fall into place. Do not impose an interpretation artificially. It will suggest itself quite naturally.

Remember that *there are inherent limitations in the DPP*, such as the light-switch effect (see p.33). These aspects do not lend themselves to interpretation. Most 'dream interpreters', including many professionals, are unaware of these discoveries.

Remember, too that the dream follows visual associations, and at scene-shifts it is common for the pictorial elements (including colours, persons, items, etc.) to be rearranged into the new picture. There will be strong links between the two scenes, even though the written account will describe two seemingly very different settings.

Always *look at simple explanations first*. A dream activity may simply reflect something that is happening in the dreamer's life. Check with the questionnaire for the list of topics currently on the dreamer's mind. Start every interpretation afresh, trying not to be influenced by, say, what a similar dream meant to someone else, or to you on occasion.

A person dreaming of looking over a house with a view to buy may have been doing just that in wakefulness anyway. The possible symbolism of the house representing the body may be inappropriate in that case, although bear in mind there may be a meaningful association between the two explanations.

The dream may be providing some kind of *warning to the dreamer*, perhaps of a faulty vehicle, or even an imminent illness. Subconsciously recognized symptoms can cause a prodromic dream, where the impending illness is symbolically portrayed in the dream.

Remember that, if a person is jolted out of a dream by a sudden unpleasant scene, that scene itself could have been a *waking ploy* by the subconscious (in total contrast to what Freud stated), perhaps as an 'internal alarm call', or to draw the dreamer's attention to something significant that happened earlier in the dream.

The anciently observed phenomenon of opposites in dreams still applies, e.g. a funeral can signify a birth or wedding. Again, it is not safe to assume that a devious disguising programme causes the discrepancy. The sequence of symbolic images is perfectly logical to the subconscious – operating within its limitations – and, curiously, the apparent opposite of the underlying thought may be presented occasionally.

Finally, look for an overall *metaphor* in the dream. As an example, if the overall theme is one of losing control (e.g. of a vehicle and then of a child), the dreamer may, in wakefulness, fear losing control in some other significant areas, e.g. financially or emotionally. Often a dream, or all the dreams of a night, can be summed up in a simple metaphor.

You will develop your own skills and insights in this art over time. It is important to get feedback from the dreamer about the accuracy or otherwise of your interpretation. Ask for an honest opinion from the dreamer each time.

If you are truly open-minded you will also look out for precognitive, telepathic, or clairvoyant information in the dream, especially if the individual has a history of experiencing such dreams.

Examples of Symbolism in Dreams

Example 1

I was ill with a bad chest infection. The day before the dream I had visited my doctor and was given a prescription for an antibiotic [*day residue* – things actually experienced that are carried over into the dream]. That night, I woke from a vivid dream. There were two large bare trees. I had been instructed to kill the 'bugs' in them with a spray device.

Dreamer's Associations and Comments

Bare trees strongly remind me of the arrangement of blood vessels in the lungs: an allusion to my chest infection. My task, to destroy the infestation of 'bugs', was a direct representation of my battle against the infection in my lungs.

Example 2

I was in a relationship with a woman, but it was going through problems. I consciously anticipated that the relationship would survive, but I was woken from a vivid dream in which the woman was riding away on a bicycle, waving at me. In reality the woman does not ride a bicycle.

Dreamer's Associations and Comments

'On your bike' is a well-known phrase in the UK, meaning 'go away'. The woman was leaving – and that is what happened in reality. Although I consciously thought that the relationship could be saved, my unconscious told me otherwise. It turned out to be right. The dream was in fact a visual pun.

Example 3

Mary came to England from the USA some 25 years ago. She is 52 years old, and has two sons and three daughters. She was rejected by her father, who, as a young man in the hungry 1930s in the USA, was homeless and had slept in warehouses on pallets. For several years she has suffered from depression, but did not seek medical help until early January 1997. She was prescribed an antidepressant. The day before this dream (18 March 1998), Mary went back to her doctor and told him she was beginning to feel very low again [a day residue]. Her dream was as follows:

> I went into the home of a Sikh woman. The woman had perhaps two boys and three girls. One of her sons slept on a pallet, which I was shown. She told me how her daughter woke the son early one morning. He was angry and threw the pallet.
>
> Then, my father's dead body (he actually died many years ago) was present in my house. My mother had sent it from the USA. He had been dead for 3½ months. I felt uncomfortable about it. It was covered by a white sheet and placed on a bed on my landing. I constantly had to walk by it. Slowly, the body began to come to life.
>
> Next, I was sitting at a nice desk in a cosy office. I was trying to phone my mother to tell her about the body coming back to life again, but a man was on the line. I wondered how to get my father back to the USA.
>
> He was walking around the house behaving as if he was alive. I woke up feeling very unhappy and distressed.

Dreamer's Associations

Woman with five children: Like me, the *dreamer*.
Pallet: My father slept on a pallet as a child during the Great *Depression*.
3½ months: Just 3½ months ago I went to doctor concerning my *depression*.
Cosy office: Like my *doctor's office*.
Coming back again: My *depression* returning.

Verbal Puns

Sikh/sick, i.e. ill.

Interpretation

Mary went to the doctor about her depression 3½ months (mentioned in the dream) before the dream. The homophone pun on the word Sikh (sick, i.e. ill), and the similarity between the numbers of children for the dreamer and the woman seen, indicate that the Sikh woman represents the dreamer.

The angry boy who slept on the pallet associates strongly with Mary's father at the time of the American *Depression*. The dream has cleverly linked the father with the concept of psychological depression. The scene shift (indicating a link) is from the angry boy to her adult father.

There is a change of scene to Mary's home, but there is a link in that the boy is now the dead father. Significantly, the dead body has been there $3^1/_2$ months, but begins to revive.

It seems that the underlying theme to the dream is Mary's worry that her depression appears to be returning, just as her father (who symbolizes the depression) was safely 'dead' but has 'come back'.

The dream does not provide information that was not known consciously by Mary, but it illustrates how a deep anxiety may be represented in a vivid and troubling way.

Technical Summary of the Interpretation
Underlying dream thought: 'I'm sick and the *depression* is returning.'
Person identifier: The projection of the dreamer onto a dream character and the homophone Sikh (= sick).
Topic identifiers:

a) Direct and specific identifier: Something that happened precisely $3^1/_2$ months ago.
b) Associative identifiers: The Great Depression; the dreamer's now dead father, who, as a child, slept in warehouses on pallets.

Current-situation identifier: A metaphor of something unwanted returning.
Basic emotion: Distress.
Whole: A symbolic representation of a matter of great concern to Mary: the apparent return of her depression.

Example 4
This dreamer is a very competent dentist, and likes to enjoy life and visiting places. She describes her dream thus:

> I was at an airport trying to get money from a cash machine. The card broke to pieces. I was shouting at a woman. How was I going to get enough money for my holiday? Then, I dreamt that I was working on a patient and a tooth broke to pieces. I felt very frustrated.

Dreamer's Associations
Cash machine: I am a bit short of *cash* at the moment.
Tooth breaking: I feel annoyed and *frustrated*.

Verbal Puns
Broke, i.e. short of money.

Interpretation
The keyword in this dream is 'broke'. It has a colloquial meaning, of course, of having little or no current financial resources. The woman at whom the dreamer is (uncharacteristically) shouting is herself. The part of her that is a little childish and too demanding takes over in the dream and reprimands her higher self.

Two symbolic representations of 'broke' are displayed: the broken cash card and the broken tooth. The dream has a clear message that the woman is overspending and behaving in a selfish manner. The woman could not see the connections until they were pointed out. It all then made perfect sense to her.

Technical Summary of the Interpretation
Underlying dream thought: 'I haven't got enough money for the things I want – I feel *broke*.'
Person identifier: A projection of the dreamer onto a dream character (the woman shouted at).
Topic identifiers:

a) Direct and specific identifier: Not being able to get cash from a machine.
b) Associative identifier: The significant word 'broke'.

Current-situation identifier: A metaphor for being short of money.
Basic emotions: Annoyance, frustration.
Whole: A metaphoric representation of a current state but also a warning of the presence of a demanding part of the dreamer's personality.

PART II

A Selection of Dreams for Interpretation

• • • •

This part of the book comprises numbered dreams for you to interpret. Those in the first section are fairly brief, and you should attempt to provide thumbnail interpretations of approximately 100 words. However, as you progress to the second section, the dreams will become increasingly more detailed and demand more in-depth analyses. In Part III, you will find the correspondingly numbered, correct interpretations. Once you have produced a written analysis, compare the two to see where you have gone wrong – if you have gone wrong.

Because of lack of space, it is impractical to incorporate each dreamer's completed questionnaire before each dream, so we have included important clues from the original MHQs, which have great bearing on the final interpretations. These clues appear in the introductory text before each dream. There are occasions, however, when no obvious clues can be gleaned, and this in itself is usually a clue. You should then look even more closely for visual- and verbal-associative pathways: homophones, puns, etc.

If, when analysing the earlier dreams, you find yourself stuck, take a quick glance at the accurate interpretations in Part III, then complete each task. However, as you progress – and certainly by the time you have reached the dreams in section 2, which require detailed analysis – you should attempt to complete the interpretations on your own. Even if your conclusions and the correct interpretations are not an exact match, the important issue is identifying the correct theme.

Finally, we have included a few dreams which, for various reasons, do not seem to fit the criteria of message-bearing dreams. See if you can spot them and then, as if you were providing an explanation for a client, give a written account of your conclusions. One dream in particular is so detailed that it appears to be contrived. However, assuming that it is still a product of the unconscious mind, attempt to provide an interpretation. Interestingly, whether it was contrived or not, the analysis in Part III was acknowledged as being accurate. Good luck!

Points to Remember

1 Nowadays, more and more dreams are proving to be spiritual in nature, therefore allow for the existence of the human soul. Remember that foreign countries can sometimes denote a spiritual realm or aspect to a dream, especially if there is some confusion as to which country is being featured.

2 Message-bearing dreams serve various purposes, among which are to offer reassurance and also to furnish warnings.

3 Nightmares rarely translate into something unpleasant. However, they often carry an important message.

4 Sometimes dreams that feature left-hand or right-hand places, events, etc. are alluding to the left (male = logical) and right (female = emotional) hemispheres of the brain.

5 Dream symbols can have dual or multiple meanings. A house, for example, can symbolize a house. It might also symbolize the dreamer. Dreams 27 and 28 provide good examples of this.

6 You may encounter so-called 'common dreams', but you should treat them individually. The theme may indeed be similar, but the message will be tailor-made to the individual. Older people commonly dream of being lost and in a struggle to reach home. However, we have included two dreams which, at first glance, appear to be very common but, upon closer inspection, reveal alternatives. Watch out for teeth falling out and wanting to use the toilet!

7 Be on the lookout for a metaphor that will sum up an entire dream. Watch out for the scene-shift, light-switch, and trigger effects.

8 Paths, roads, rivers, and even seas can sometimes represent the dreamer's path in life – but not always. They may simply symbolize exactly what they appear to be.

9 Above all, remember that dreams flow along verbal- and visual-associative pathways by a 'law of least effort'.

Section 1 Dreams for Thumbnail Interpretations

To give you a clearer idea of what you are required to do, the first dream is accompanied by an interpretation, then followed by further psychological observations and comments, each of which has been designed to make things easier for both you and the client to understand. After this, you are on your own!

Example

James, who regards himself as an introvert, is married with three teenaged children and says that, when troubles surface, he has a tendency to bury his head in the sand. He describes his dream thus:

I was driving my car along the road when, in my rear-view mirror, I noticed a police officer following me on a bicycle. For no apparent reason, I felt afraid. When I accelerated, I noticed that he was keeping up with me. No matter how fast I went, every time I checked the mirror, he was right behind me, yet he didn't seem to be pedalling fast.

Interpretation

This dream is all about responsibility. In your letter, you mention that you tend to bury your head in the sand, and this dream bears out that observation. The police officer represents authority, the establishment, and abiding by the rules. The fact that you were afraid and tried to escape reflects your tendency to avoid facing up to responsibilities until you have no other choice.

Clearly, the message behind the dream is that, no matter how tempted you may be to pretend these things do not exist, duty and responsibility are never far away (they have an unerring ability to catch up on us). Your subconscious is urging you to change your ways. It would seem that you would benefit by meeting these challenges head-on!

Further Comments

In psychological terms, the police officer represents your superego – the part of your personality that knows how you *ought* to behave. When, in your thoughts and subsequent behaviour, you ignore the presence of the superego (conscience), it will deliberately force its way into recognition by means of dreams or – in extreme cases – nightmares. Given that this is the case, it is a matter of pinpointing the specific area in which you think you may have been acting without consideration to others and then responding appropriately so as to maintain an inner harmony.

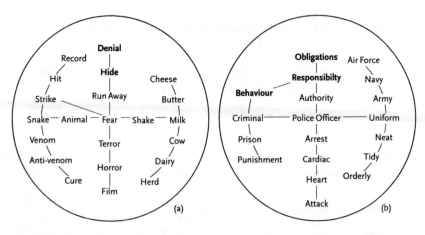

Figure 1. (a) Flowcharts are used to list possible associations suggested by images, characters, phrases, etc. which occur in dreams. (b) One dream dictionary states that dreaming about a police officer indicates that a friend is being untrue to you. The above example demonstrates that such a narrow interpretation would be artificial and unconvincing.

Dream 1

Carol is single, somewhat extrovert, works as a supermarket cashier, and says that, occasionally, she can be easily influenced by other people. In an accompanying letter, she expressed concern that her boyfriend and Barbara were holding hands, and stated that Barbara was a valued friend and always seemed to give good advice. This provided an important clue, which helped to decode the dream.

At work, sitting at my cash register, I saw Barbara, my best friend. wearing my favourite shoes. Suddenly, she was holding my boyfriend's hand, then they walked towards me. She paid for a Valentine card, which was in the shape of a heart. As I took her money, I noticed the card begin to shrivel. When they left, my boyfriend looked thoroughly miserable, and I felt angry.

Dream 2

Marylin has two grown-up children (one still at home), lives with her husband of 30 years, and considers herself to be neither extrovert nor introvert.

I was in a darkened room and, for fear of falling over unseen objects, was frightened to move. I could feel a light switch next to a door but considered whether the sudden brightness might damage my eyes. Instead of switching it on, I elected to fumble around in the dark. After a time, I found myself standing next to the light switch again. I was still apprehensive about turning it on.

Dream 3

Brian H., a 59-year-old store-owner, points out that he is experiencing difficulties running his business. The dream is recurring and unpleasant.

I find myself on an upper floor of an empty office block. I need to get down to the ground floor, but there is no way out. Set in the floor is an open platform, rather like an elevator, but with no controls, cables, or sides to it. I experience the feeling that it will start to fall away before I can get onto it, or it might begin to descend when I have only one foot on it.

Dream 4

The Reverend H. is retired and considers himself to be an introvert. Interestingly, in his questionnaire, he states that he wasn't sure in which country the dream was set, and that matters of spirituality are on his mind.

I entered a very large building from the road. I was enthralled. It was of enormous height and tapered away to a peak, rather like a church spire. It was transparent but sparkled with myriad jewel-like colours. A man came to talk to me and agreed that it presented a marvellous spectacle. I woke deeply impressed and felt that it was unlike any other dream that I have had.

Dream 5

Eileen, aged 65, is retired and states in her questionnaire that she is concerned about what her future might hold.

I was examining the inside of an eye with a bright green spotlight. Under extreme magnification, the internal structures of the eye appeared like very coarsely woven linen. But the eye was mine, and I was scanning it from the inside.

Dream 6

Caroline, aged 75, is a bit concerned about finances and illness in the family.

I was walking down a lonely lane in very thick fog. Unable to see my hand in front of me, I knew I should be feeling frightened, but was not. Suddenly, a large black dog appeared and approached me, followed by a man in dark clothing. He said, 'Don't be afraid, the dog is very gentle and will not hurt you.' I then stroked it and felt completely at ease. When I awoke, I felt a sense of relief and very happy.

Dream 7

Brian, aged 30, states that he is considering buying a house and making a long-term investment in an existing business.

While I was trying to push a straw, which had a blade of grass inside, into a massive dumpling without dislodging the grass, I could feel a heavy weight inside my mouth. No matter how many times I tried, I failed, and all the while there were three eggs with faces looking on. These eggs appeared to be dancing, and the expressions on their faces kept changing.

Dream 8

Here we have a recurring dream, which was sent in by Mandy, aged 24. Mandy points out that there are many changes which she is considering making to her life, so that she can stay abreast with the times.

Looking forward to a good night out, along with a group of friends, we are playing loud music, drinking alcohol, and are generally excited. Then, I notice that everybody is dressed up except for me. Although I have a full wardrobe, nothing seems suitable, or items of clothing that are suitable seem damaged in some way. I become anxious and begin to panic. I get the feeling that it might be New Year.

Dream 9

Kenneth, aged 70, used to be a successful sales representative. Although he has been retired for over 11 years, he has recurring dreams in which he finds himself back at work. He is financially secure and has no wish to return to employment.

I am at work experiencing some problems with my sales area. I know that I can retire when I wish, but, to help the company, I decide to stay on a bit longer. Then I wonder why I am putting up with the hassle of modern-day selling. I tell myself that I should pack it in and no longer push myself. Then I awaken, pause for a moment, and say to myself, 'You fool! You are retired. Relax.'

Dream 10

Judith, aged 59, is a midwife and has concerns about continuing work after the age of 60. She describes herself as introvert, serious in nature, and a bit of a worrier.

In my dreams I have always lost something, often my handbag, luggage, or even the address to which I am supposed to be going! Sometimes, I have lost my keys and cannot get in. Frequently, I wake up not knowing where I am, then rush downstairs to find my handbag.

Dream 11

Alison, aged 21, says that, after her boyfriend had an affair, to put her mind at rest, he promised that he would move in with her, but still hasn't done so.

In a restaurant, I was sitting with my family, some friends, and people who seemed familiar. After the main course, I went to the sweet trolley, where I saw a man to whom I was instantly attracted. He was a perfect gentleman. We talked about everything, until I saw my family leaving. I couldn't catch them up, so returned to find the man had gone. I asked around, but nobody knew of him, which made me feel that I wouldn't see him again. I woke up thinking that I had met the man of my dreams and wanted to find him.

Dream 12

Wendy, aged 48, is an extrovert and claims that she needs company.

Unlike usual dreams, everything was in darkness. A male voice stated, quite matter-of-factly, 'This life is not real, you are dreaming it all. When you wake up, you will find that you are Ruth Ellis (the last woman to be hanged for murder in the UK) waiting in the condemned cell for them to come and hang you!' Then I woke up. I don't know what time it was. I was too afraid to open my eyes and look. I reasoned that it had to have been a dream but, to reassure myself, I felt around for familiar objects – my pillow, the bed, the wall, etc. Eventually, I drifted back to sleep. However, when I awoke, I ran through the checks again before I dared to open my eyes.

Dream 13

Mary, aged 78, is a widow living alone, and she has a family problem on her mind.

Often, I dream about being lost in a crowd. There are people dashing about ignoring me. I want to find my way home, but nobody helps. I feel lonely.

Dream 14

This recurring dream concerns Betty, aged 63. In her questionnaire Betty lists many hobbies that she pursues and states that, apart from one, she and her husband have different interests.

I am always travelling somewhere, but never reach my destination. I'm running for buses, coaches, and trains, looking up timetables, and forever getting lost. I see numbers on the buses in London where I used to live. I used to miss the capital, but those feelings no longer apply. I have heard that you die when you reach your destination, but do not wish to know that!

Dream 15

Brian, aged 42, a machine-operator from Derbyshire, UK, had matters of finance on his mind.

It was a fine sunny day and I was standing in a field. In the distance, I could see a rainbow. I turned to say to somebody – although I'm not sure who – 'Look at that beautiful rainbow over there.' I noticed the rainbow moving across the sky then, suddenly, colours came cascading down onto me. I was then underneath the end of the rainbow. I was surrounded by the most radiant, shimmering colours. My feelings were of pure happiness and ecstasy.

Dream 16

Beatrice, aged 65, provides this recurring dream and describes herself as a mild person, with various concerns on her mind, including ageing, her family, and what the future might bring.

I am walking somewhere, although I have no idea where. The journey starts normally on a pavement but, after a short time, while other people ahead of me carry on unhindered, either my path turns into a grassy slope or I encounter a brick wall. To reach my destination, I have to overcome these obstacles, and the going is always tough. Then, I have to cross a road, but when I step onto it, the surface changes to a bog. Like stepping stones, I spy large grassy turfs, but as I jump, they move further away. The route then widens, the grass turns into reeds, the road becomes a river, and I'm petrified of water. I always wake up feeling depressed.

Dream 17

Here we have a fascinating dream from Dorothy, aged 74, who, at the time of the dream, was recovering from complications after undergoing successful treatment for cancer.

I heard the sound of a loud unusual engine, then I saw a huge silver disk – something like a flying saucer. The sky above it was frightening. It was raining blood from large red slashes which filled the sky. This faded and was replaced by three male winged angels, who were sitting around the disk. They had kindly faces, like Father Christmas. They were holding some kind of wand, and between them were three huge white owls. The engine was so loud and everything I saw appeared to be enormous.

Dream 18

Here we have a dreaming vision from Enid, aged 66, who is concerned about her health.

I was in bed and woke up? Ahead of me was a panoramic view of a grey, cloudy sky. High up and surrounded by blue sky was a circle with a pair of hands folded one inside the other. I sat up in bed to have a better look, and, as I did, the scene reverted back to a grey, cloudy sky. I sat up for a long time (awake now?) wondering whether I had had a dream or a vision.

Dream 19

Valerie, aged 48, sent in this dream, which has recurred since she remarried 10 years ago. Valerie often wonders if, when her children were young, she neglected them.

I am breast-feeding a very small, sickly baby. As the dream progresses, and although I love the infant, I forget to feed it and my milk begins to dry up. I know that if I want to maintain a good flow of milk I must continue feeding the child, yet, even though the baby is very hungry, I say, 'I'll feed you when I've done this job or that task.' Eventually, the baby becomes weaker, almost dying, then I force myself to stop being busy and feed it. At this point I wake up, saddened that I had neglected a tiny baby.

Dream 20

Here we have a recurring, enigmatic dream from Ella, aged 66, who states that she is emotional, trusting, and a bit of a worrier.

My son has asked me to do something for him: buy something, ring somebody, or collect something. In the knowledge that I haven't performed these tasks, I dream that I wake up and start looking in drawers and cupboards. It always ends in failure. As soon as I do wake up, I recall the dream and feel terrible.

Dream 21

This dream comes from Lesley J., aged 39. A few times Lesley has dreamt of being back in a house from which she moved 7 years ago. She states that she is content where she is living now.

Having a key to let myself in, I find myself back in our old house, looking around downstairs in the kitchen. My husband is with me, but not our children. At the time, it seems to be daylight. Somehow I know that the owners are due back and will find us there. We always go out the back door as they come in the front.

Dream 22

Margaret, aged 55, sent in this mysterious dream. Margaret is interested in healing and complementary therapy.

Clouds which were edged with gold, as if the sun were shining on them, opened up to reveal a patch of vivid blue sky, with a beautiful dolphin swimming around. My brother was with me but did not share my enthusiasm. I turned to gaze at it again, to find the scene had changed. This time there was a young mother, naked, with a baby in her arms, standing chest-high in water. Gently cradling it, she rocked the baby back and forth in the water.

Dream 23

Dorothy, aged 51, a secretary, says that this dream recurs occasionally. Dorothy is concerned about what the future might hold should her husband's job finish.

In each dream I find myself established somewhere and have settled down to stay, although I sense that I am really visiting. It is usually a large place (not my own home), and I think my husband is present. I settle down to sleep but decide to get up and go out of a door. I discover that I am unable to get out. I sense danger and fear that something might explode, or the door is locked. I feel very upset. I worry that I have no personal possessions with me: make-up, etc. When I wake up, I am surprised that I am able to open the door without anything bad happening.

Dream 24

Mrs S., aged 56, has a recurring dream which she finds stressful. Mrs S. used to be in charge of a school kitchen and was responsible for providing 400 meals a day on an ever-decreasing budget.

I am always in the school canteen, and the situation is invariably the same, although the details differ. The dinner bell has sounded, and the children are waiting to be served. Each time, I have either forgotten to cook a vital ingredient or cannot find the keys to the kitchen, while being aware that nothing has been cooked at all. I always panic, in a race against time. I awaken feeling very stressed, yet thankful that it was a dream, because I used to hate working there.

Dream 25

Frederick F., aged 58, sent in this dream, which he has had four times. Frederick has had heart trouble for the past 6 years.

I am standing at the entrance to a stone house, which has a black number nine on a white wall. I go through various doorless openings, past a hallway in which there are flowerpots, each filled with beautiful blooms. I find myself in the kitchen, which has a window on the opposite wall next to a door. I pass through the door and find myself in a small, unkempt garden which, again, has many flowers. Facing me is an embankment which houses a railway line. To my left is another house from which an old man is gazing at me. Then I wake up.

Dream 26
Colin S., aged 71, has had the same recurring dream since the age of 3 years until he was in his mid-50s. As a child, trying to seek an answer, he told his mother, and later his wife, about it, but to no avail.

I used to dream that I was lying in bed when a male lion walked into the bedroom. He stood by the side of the bed and just looked at me. He was not fierce but quite docile. I was not afraid and simply gazed back at him.

Dream 27
Anne, aged 45, a company director with four children, is concerned about financial affairs.

We are moving to a down-market house, reminiscent of our first marital home. I am very upset, but try to make the best of the situation. I know that we can't move back because somebody else has already moved into our nice house. I discover that the run-down house has large cracks between the walls and the floors. Instead of being able to walk from bedroom to bedroom, I have to crawl through narrow tunnels. I try to reassure my family, but feel a deep sense of loss. Downstairs there is a huge cellar which defies the size of the house, while the attic has some parts of the roof missing.

Dream 28
Sandra, aged 52, had this dream, which conjures up spectacular imagery. It occurred some time ago, but the memory of it still evokes sad feelings.

I was in a pub with my mother and aunt. To one side of the bar was a terrace overlooking the sea. The weather was calm, then an object resembling a meteorite landed in the sea, creating a hole which was surrounded by people, who were gazing down into it. Wanting to report the incident, I ran through the village trying to find a police station, but couldn't find one. Then I woke up, but I hadn't been frightened by the dream.

Dream 29
Donald, aged 73, sent in this dream, which he had about 8 years ago. Donald's wife suffers from Alzheimer's disease.

I was walking through a mountainous country (possibly Scotland or Wales). It was a sunshiny day, and I climbed a hill to a castle on the summit. High on the ramparts there were four maidens, clad in gold, silver, blue, and black, who were dancing in unison. The girl in black beckoned me to join in the dance. I did, and the steps came automatically. Leaving me behind, the girls danced away through the door of a wooden hut. After a while, I entered the hut, but there was no sign of them. Then I awoke.

Dream 30

Frances, aged 73, says that, although she counts her blessings, which she says are many, she had an unhappy life in her early years.

I am always trying very hard to clean up an extremely dirty house. I am surrounded by my parents and family, all of whom are dead (in real life). There is humdrum talk and laughter going on around me, but I am always ignored. Invariably, I wake up before I can succeed.

Dream 31

Helen, aged 30, who describes herself as a domestic manager, provided this dream. Helen says that, since starting an adult education course, she is beginning to realize her potential in life.

My husband and I visited an old house in which we used to live. In the dream, friends had bought it. It dawned on me that the kitchen was much larger than it used to be, as were all the other rooms. Then I realized that our friends had bought the house next door and knocked it through to make one big dwelling. It was all beautiful bare wood and antique furniture. We went upstairs to find a gorgeous four-poster bed in a room that was beautifully decorated – my dream come true. Finally, we were in the attic, which had lovely views, although it was bereft of furniture.

Dream 32

This dream is recurring and comes from Sylvia, aged 67. A widow with two adult daughters, Sylvia says that her dreams are peaceful.

I am in a market place where clothing is on sale. Then I have an urge to get home, but I don't know how to. I realize that I am lost. I find myself walking by the side of a very long brick wall, looking for bus stops. At other times the dream can be set in beautiful, serene surroundings, or even an industrial area. However, I am always looking for a way home.

Dream 33

Here we have a dream from Donna, aged 23, a nurse, who says that she is concerned about her relationship with her boyfriend: there is a breakdown of communication between them and she feels herself shut out.

I was at work preparing notes for outpatients. A colleague was trying to find my medical records, explaining that I had been added to the list to see the consultant. At this point all my ex-boyfriends and their partners started to come in to see how I was feeling. I knew who they were, but none of them seemed to look like they should. I was told that my boyfriend was too shy to see me and was at the main entrance. I went to see him and discovered that, as we were talking, his clothes kept changing. For some reason I didn't mention this to him.

Dream 34
This dream comes from Mrs S., aged 53, who is a part-time bank cashier and concerned about staff reductions.

My husband and I began to wade across a very clear, shallow river. The riverbed was made up of large, thinly sliced layers of granite. With my husband leading the way, we hadn't gone far when the head of an alligator appeared from my left. It was coming towards me and cutting me off from my husband, who was still wading. Knowing that I couldn't get back to the bank quickly enough, I saw another alligator wheel past my husband and approach me from the right. I stood still and cried out, repeatedly, 'I don't know what to do!'

Dream 35
Here we have a dream on a recurring theme from Vera, aged 74. Vera says that she has led a drab, often unremarkable life.

I was in a mansion, perhaps a girls' school. Lots of girls were going in and out of rooms and up and down a wide staircase. I could not seem to find where I ought to be. Twice, I was in a factory – different each time. At benches and machinery, there were lots of busy people. I tried to look busy but had nothing to do. In other dreams, I have found myself in strange, rambling houses with twisty corridors, and can never find a room for me. There are always lots of people, but I never ask for help.

Dream 36
This graphic dream was sent in by Robert, aged 68. Robert, a retired windsurfing instructor, who is very fit, has recently started a creative-writing course. Interestingly, just days before the dream, he saw a ballet on television in which a dancer pulled a red streamer out of the shirt of her male partner (which symbolized his heart).

I dreamt that Humphrey Bogart was in my house standing behind the settee. He threw a punch at Walter Brennan, who was standing next to him. Before the punch connected, Humphrey Bogart collapsed onto the settee, clasping his heart. I turned him over. Blood came from his shirt above his heart. I said that I would give him some of my tablets and take him to hospital.

Dream 37

Sheila, aged 69, who is frightened of flying, provided this extremely brief dream. Sheila says that she often worries about other people.

I look to the sky and see an aircraft. Suddenly it stops flying and plummets to the ground. I am always frightened that it might hit me.

Dream 38

Alyson, aged 89, supplied this recurring dream, from which she always awakens feeling anxious. Alyson says that the plot is always the same, but occasionally the venue changes.

I am in a huge block of offices. I am desperate to get out unseen. I go through floor after floor, up and down in lifts, always with a fear of something. I rush past doors either side in long corridors. Although I manage to negotiate my way from floor to floor, I never manage to find a way out. The other venue is at the top of a hill with rows of houses leading down to a town. I may find my way into the next street, but there is no way through.

Dream 39

Doreen, aged 66, supplied this rather unusual dietary dream. Curiously, a day or two after the dream, she was due to visit the Houses of Parliament in London, UK.

I had been invited to a meal at a large apartment in London. It was a Jewish home. When we were served, a guest enquired about the food. I said that it was moussaka, a Greek dish. Also on the plates were black cassette tapes. We all cut them up and proceeded to eat them. The crunchiness of the tapes was so awful that it woke me up.

Dream 40

Phyllis, aged 65, a retired ward nursing sister, provided this dream. Phyllis is a widow, who is troubled by widespread arthritis.

I was in the main corridor of a busy hospital when I fell to the floor. To my dismay, I found that I couldn't get up. There were lots of people in the vicinity, and I was confident that someone would soon help. Then I realized that I was being ignored. I managed to move a little, until I was almost blocking the entrance to a ward. I could hear voices discussing a very ill male patient. Again I thought that I would soon receive help, because I was then blocking the ward entrance. However, still nobody came, and I felt completely dejected – a total nonentity.

Dream 41
Margaret, aged 69, sent in this recurring dream and insists that it is not a nightmare.

> I am always on a building site, where none of the houses has been completed further than first-floor level. I dodge in and out of the structures, as a strange man pursues me with a gun. He shoots me at point-blank range. I feel no pain, but know that I have been fatally wounded. I fall to the ground, bleeding to death. The man has gone, and I know that I have just a few moments to live. I always wake up at this point feeling cheated that I have not been able to prolong the dream, so that I can actually see the 'other side'.

Dream 42
Sarah, aged 27, states that she is terrified of spiders.

> These dreams are so vivid that I believe I'm awake. I call them 'spider-mares' and 'cobweb-mares'. I dream that I turn over in bed and see lots of spiders on my pillow, on the floor, and hanging above my head. Sometimes I'm so convinced of the reality that, upon waking, I have found myself turning on the light, getting out of bed, and brushing them from my shoulders. During the cobweb-mares, I find myself crawling across the floor, in a room full of cobwebs. Again, I have to put on the light before I can go back to bed.

Dream 43
Dorothy, aged 57, lists a catalogue of things that are on her mind.

> I was in a large house with a grand staircase. I felt that I would like to decorate a triangular room, but it was too small. I found myself in another, oval-shaped, large room that needed redecorating. It had a lot of possibilities, especially with its large windows and French doors. Then I found myself in a bathroom, which also needed decorating. I felt that, left to my own devices, I could make something of it.

Dream 44
Daphne, aged 60, is worried about her son, who has cancer.

> Bathed in sunshine, I was walking along a street, overwhelmed at how beautiful the blue sky appeared. I drew level with a store, which had an aquarium in the window. I was overjoyed at how clean and sparkling the water was. I didn't think it was possible for water to be so pure. Then I noticed that the sand in the bottom of the tank was the most vivid yellow, far in excess of what one would imagine sand to be. As I resumed my journey, I was elated at what I was seeing – everything was so vivid. I felt as if I was somewhere really wonderful, somewhere abroad.

Dream 45

Doreen, aged 68, provides this fairly common dream and explains that it has recurred over the last 25 years.

I am usually in a hospital or hotel and urgently need a toilet. Although I know where the toilets are situated, each one I try is either disgustingly filthy or has no seat or door. Sometimes the toilet is an armchair. There are often men and women going in and out. There is never any privacy. I wake up in quite a state and find that I *do* need to go to the bathroom.

Dream 46

Renate, aged 32, is married with two children and says that this dream has recurred several times.

I am in a very dark room with a lot of people who are passing through – something like a station. Gently, I push myself up until, facing downward, I am floating waist-high. I am pleased that I am able to fly and glide from one room to another. To my surprise, the people take no notice of my extraordinary achievement. However, this reassures me, allowing me to test my flying skills in comfort and without fear of criticism. The rooms are totally bare – no furniture or windows.

Dream 47

Fay, aged 35, supplied this recurring dream, which she finds disturbing. Fay states that she had an unstable childhood, has been divorced for some years, and has borne the responsibility for her children's upbringing.

There are always big seas coming in, threatening to drown me and my three girls. I can never find my children. Desperately, I try to pack our things, but find that I can't. In fact, I don't seem to be able to do anything! Sometimes a war starts, and there are planes dropping bombs overhead, but I still can't find my girls. Often, a volcano begins to erupt, and I am searching desperately for my girls. Always, I start to panic, then wake up.

Dream 48

Maureen W. provides this extremely common dream which, she says, recurs and upsets her.

I always dream that my teeth become loose. I feel slight pain in my gums. My mouth waters and I swallow blood. I push the back of my teeth with my tongue and, one by one, they begin falling out. I swallow some and spit some out. My gums feel soggy. My mouth fills with liquid, which I spit out with more teeth. I scream for help, but none arrives. I wake up in a cold sweat, my pillow wet where I have been dribbling. My husband tells me that I grind my teeth a lot when I sleep.

Dream 49

Barbara, aged 59, says that this enigmatic dream has recurred throughout her life.

A man in a white gown leads me from a sandy place to a corridor where, before entering, I have to remove my shoes. I am taken to a classroom, where there are other men dressed in white robes. In the front of the class, similarly attired, is an older man, who hands me a scroll to read. Although I cannot understand the language in which it is written, I somehow manage to interpret it to the rest of the class. It conveys a message that is a beautiful, simple truth, which I know will be of benefit to mankind. Each time I wake up, the message slips from my memory, and I feel angry.

Dream 50

Erika, aged 38, says that, although she attends church, she has problems accepting some of the fantastic stories found in the Bible. In her questionnaire, Erica points out that the dream was set in unfamiliar surroundings abroad.

It was sunny, and from the top of an impressive, almost Biblical, rocky ravine, I descended some very rough steps that were hewn in the stone. About halfway down, to my left, I noticed a small grotto in which, on a pedestal, was a statue of a black Madonna with a child. It was well lit, and I wondered what it could mean. I then experienced strong feelings that I was looking at myself: that the Madonna was me! Then I woke up.

Dream 51

Mrs P., aged 38, says she is trying to move house and is under stress at work from associates.

On the deserted beach, I first came across a dog's ear, then its leg, and when I reached the water's edge I saw its head – floating. It was a Jack Russell. I realized that, if I wanted to swim, I needed a towel. I went to a hotel to look for my suitcase but couldn't find it. I looked out of the window and noticed it floating in the sea, which had turned into thick, green sludge, festooned with waterlily leaves, also covered in slime. Then, along with crowds of people, I found myself in a concrete basement waiting for a plane. Somehow I had my slimy suitcase with me.

Dream 52

Betty suffers from unpredictable bouts of ill health and experiences this dream frequently.

Although I haven't been consciously thinking about them, I often dream of seeing or being with family members who have passed on: my husband, father, grandmother, uncle, and former close friends. When I wake up I feel close to them for some time afterwards and regard it as a pleasant experience.

Dream 53

Mrs W. says that, since her early childhood, she has had a fear of vomiting and has been troubled by this dream since she was 7 years old.

As a child the dream used to focus on other children being sick in the playground. As an adult, people at work or on the street were vomiting. However, more recently, after watching a wildlife programme on television, my dream featured elephants, which had wandered down to a watering-hole and were suffering from sickness and diarrhoea.

Dream 54

Margaret, aged 62, had a dream at the age of 7 years, which was so powerful that it has stayed with her throughout her life. Margaret, now a teacher, says that she was brought up in relative poverty.

I was playing alone. I had over my shoulders an army greatcoat, which was like a tent to me: I could hide and be unseen in it. A beautiful, white-winged horse, which had been flying above me, descended and came under my coat.

I had feelings of pure happiness, something I have never experienced in real life. I seemed to be folded into his whiteness, as if wrapped in absolute joy. When he flew away, I can recall the wonderful blue sky which he disappeared into.

Dream 55

Deirdre says that she cannot recall any worries or fears at the time of this recurring dream.

I wake up in an unfamiliar bedroom, to the sound of a girl crying. At the foot of my bed, I can see a darkly dressed man, who is next to the fretting girl. She has long, flowing, golden tresses and is wearing a white lace dress. She points to the wardrobe and says, 'I'm afraid of ghosts'.

Although I know they are both dead, I feel peaceful. The girl climbs in bed next to me, and I comfort her. However, she withdraws and approaches the man, who takes her by the hand and says, 'It's time.' Both figures then depart.

Dream 56

Cynthia says that this dream has recurred about six times. She tends to be a risk-taker.

It's a warm, sunny day, and I am on the local beach. It's a typical holiday scene, with all sorts of people engaged in the usual activities. I decide to go for a paddle, until the water is just above my knees. However, when I turn round to come out of the sea, no matter how hard I try, I can't reach the shore. I don't drown, but wake up crying out.

Dream 57
Dorothy, aged 38, says that she is experiencing relationship problems.

I was walking in a field where there were two openings; each had a man leaning on a gate. I was drawn to the farthest one but, as I approached, I sensed danger. I ran towards the first opening, but somehow knew that the man who was leaning on the farthest gate was now chasing me. I can almost feel his breath on the back of my neck. As I reach the other man, the panic leaves me, I'm in a state of calm, and I seem to know that I'm safe. Then I wake up.

Dream 58
Mrs Johnson says that she is not a good sleeper and has had this dream on and off for the last few years.

I am always somewhere away from home, either on a trip by coach or in a car with friends and relations. Then I seem to become separated from them. No matter how hard I try I am unable to find my way back to them, or home. I can even awaken, go to the bathroom to wake myself up fully, and then go back into the same dream. Sometimes I think that I must wake myself up and not dream it again.

Dream 59
Gill is married, with three young children at school.

I am watching my husband dig the garden. He turns and smiles at me, and I notice that he is holding a bag of seed potatoes. Each time he kneels to plant one in the earth, potato chips, like in the advertisement on television, sprout from the previously planted potato. I watch in horror as they bounce their way towards me, but they are being eaten by huge maggots that also spring from the ground. Only a few make it safely to me, so that I can provide them with protection. I always wake up feeling upset.

Dream 60
Hazel, a convert to Islam, says that she still has some way to go on her spiritual journey.

I am looking at a map of Great Britain but, in bold letters, it has the word 'Alaska' written across it. This confuses me because, although I know the map portrays Britain, it somehow seems natural that it should be Alaska. I wake up feeling confused.

Dream 61

John, a builder and father of two children, says that he believes there is not enough discipline in society nowadays.

I was having a great time at a party, where there were nice people, plenty to eat and drink, and the most beautiful music I had ever heard. Then some tiny people dressed in white joined in but, although aware of them, nobody else seemed to be bothered. Not wanting to tread on them, I found myself continually looking down, but this hurt the back of my neck. Annoyed that they were ruining my fun, I left, feeling angry that they had spoiled the party for me.

Dream 62

Marion says that she dotes on her husband and two sons, and worries about this recurring dream.

Although the dream varies, the theme is always the same. I am going on holiday, a day trip, or just shopping with my husband and children. Despite knowing that we have recently eaten, I am concerned that they haven't had enough. Then I always see a café. It can look different in each dream, but the name is always the same: 'Café Tifon'. I urge my family to go in for a top-up, but they become annoyed at me and insist on continuing the journey. I wake up feeling hurt.

Dream 63

Michael, a farmer, says that he is pretty content with life and has no worries.

I was out walking through some of the most beautiful countryside I have seen – it was a warm, sunny day. However, I noticed a cloud hovering above two sturdy oak trees standing together. As I drew nearer, I saw that the leaves appeared to be wilting. Upon closer inspection, it was evident that both trees were infested with bugs, which made me feel low. Lacking in energy, I began to head for home, when I heard an aircraft in the distance. When I turned round, the plane made a low sweep and sprayed the trees. Now I felt happier, knowing that the proud oaks would survive, and awoke with a sense of relief.

Dream 64

This recurring nightmare comes from Melanie, a garden-centre worker, who says that, although she enjoys her work, her colleagues tend to pick on her.

Among a crowd of people, I find myself in the most beautiful walled garden imaginable – except that a part of it is cluttered. However, I soon become aware that something isn't right. Although the other people don't appear to be taking any notice of me, I sense hostility aimed at me from them. I look desperately for an exit, but can't find one. I try to hide behind a large mass of wisteria in coloured blossom. Nevertheless, someone approaches and points a purple Polaroid camera at me, which startles me awake, feeling scared.

Dream 65

Kelly, says that this dream began recurring around the time of a huge family upheaval. It usually repeats when times get tough.

I sense that I am in the USA during the big Depression. The streets are crowded with all sorts of people, who appear to be looking for work. The atmosphere is almost oppressive. I walk round a corner to see a woman digging a trench. Instinctively, the miserable look on her face tells me that she is excavating her own grave. I gaze into her tearful eyes, and we cry together. She sobs on my shoulder, almost as if she's crying for the rest of the world. A great sense of sadness comes over me, then I always wake up and have a good cry.

Dream 66

Brian, who works in research and development, says that he had this dream when, in an efficiency drive, his company recently began streamlining.

I was in a noisy battery-hen farm. My job was to collect eggs and inspect them for quality. Taking eggs randomly, I cracked them open to discover that they were empty. I was worried in case I was held responsible. Desperately, I started cracking all the eggs, but they were all the same. I heard a voice saying 'Not egg'. However, I seemed to become instinctively aware that there were some free-range chickens outside. I rushed out to find their eggs which, upon cracking, revealed brains within. Somehow I knew that I would be rewarded for this valuable find.

Section 2 Dreams for Detailed Analysis

By now, you will have a good idea of how to produce thumbnail interpretations. However, detailed analyses allow dreamers to see the methodology and exact breakdown of dreams. This will enable them to identify with the analyses and realize that you have not just plucked the answers out of the air. This allows people to relate to their own personal circumstances and to identify with the level of accuracy of the final analyses and broader explanations. If you think it would be helpful, in addition to the actual interpretations, include explanations of how dreams are structured and why you suspect what you do; put things in laymen's terms. If you like, give each analysis a title, which should describe the dream in the form of a metaphor.

The dreams in this section should be regarded as requiring detailed interpretations, say of approximately 300–500 words, or much longer if you feel they merit such treatment. As before, we start with an example.

Example

Euan describes himself as outgoing and has recently been promoted to area manager in a sales business.

I recall being in a crowd of people, possibly in a village hall. We seemed to be engaged in some sort of group bonding. At one point, five of us – myself and four girls – got on the floor and simulated rowing a boat (canoe). Rather bizarrely, as this was taking place, a few feet away, I espied the highly public figure of Richard Branson (of Virgin fame), who was in another group of four or five people engaged in the same activity. I recall that he had a worried look on his face, although I believe I was smiling, and my fellow rowers were very happy too. I then woke up.

Interpretation – A New Virgin Approach!

There are many varieties of message-bearing dreams, ranging from the inspirational and creative to those of warning, advice, and even reassurance. In this instance we have a dream of reassurance. Naturally, having been recently promoted, Euan is bound to be thinking of ways in which he can improve performance and create more sales. His subconscious, therefore, has provided him with a dream that underpins most of his ideas. Many people, after a night's sleep, wake up to discover that ideas with which they having been toying have crystallized into a firm plan for action.

Without a doubt, this dream concerns career and business affairs, and clearly points to the fact that Euan's subconscious has identified the best way to proceed. Interestingly, he mentions a 'village hall', which represents a place of community spirit. The next clue is discovered when we consider that the group with which he teamed up was female (co-workers). This suggests that, in order to 'go forward', a certain amount of right-brain thinking is called for, which is allied to emotion and intuition (sometimes a male will represent the left hemisphere of the brain and a female the right).

However, the interpretation all comes together with the appearance of Richard Branson. It is evident that Euan's subconscious has identified features in Richard Branson's approach to business that Euan himself would also benefit from employing. In this instance, Richard Branson is a representation of Euan. The fact that he wore a frown reflects Euan's real concerns about how to get the best out of his workers, so that the whole team can achieve a greater degree of success. Therefore, the message that Euan's subconscious is trying to impart is that, to skipper the ship successfully, Euan would do well to adopt a 'hands-on' approach. He will benefit by using more right-brain activity (following his instincts a little more) and involving himself directly with his workers, which is also a 'Richard Branson' trait.

His subconscious is suggesting that Euan has grasped this point already in conscious, waking life; hence the smiles. Therefore, it would seem that Euan's workforce have to prepare themselves for a new skipper who will pull together with them and perhaps steer a new course. If, as the dream suggests, he is already thinking about this new approach, his dream is providing reassurance. Following the advice of his own subconscious, Euan is bound to achieve these goals!

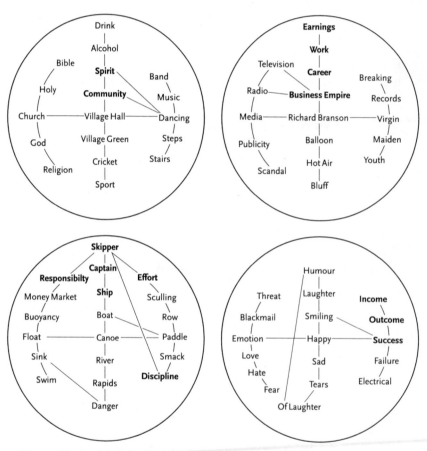

Figure 2. Viewing this dream in its entirety, as many flowcharts as necessary can be drawn up in order to reveal the consistent theme that links all aspects of the dream.

Dream 67

Isla, a nurse, states that she doesn't like to be made a fuss of and dislikes being in the limelight.

I found myself in a factory which I owned. I was walking through the shop-floor and was surrounded by lots of workers, some of whom were operating, or standing next to, machinery. I noticed that most of them were looking at me, which made me feel self-conscious and uncomfortable.

I went upstairs to an office in which my secretary was to be found – at first he was male, but, some time later, I noticed that the secretary had become female. Looking through a window, I could see down into the factory, where people were still gazing up at me.

My secretary suggested that we should leave. We went through a door and boarded some sort of train, then departed.

Dream 68

Betty is a designer in advertising and is always looking for fresh ways in which to attract new clientele.

I found myself pacing up and down a street, looking despairingly for my handbag. I felt lost without it. Then I noticed it sitting in a telephone kiosk. I ran over to it, and in my bag I found a lot of telephone cards. I tipped a whole pile of them out, only to discover that they were useless. Unlike real telephone cards, these were date-stamped and they had all expired. They were like rejects – clearly no good. Despite the fact that the values were all low denominations, they looked brand new and were all in new wrappers.

Dream 69

Morag states that, although she is introverted, she would like to pursue politics.

My husband, myself, and a few others were all in a park with a high chain-link fence. Having climbed up onto it, we began leaning back and then pushing forward again. I remember really getting into it, throwing my body back and forth, building up a fast rhythm, then feeling mesmerized and dizzy.

I lost conscious awareness of the world and found myself inside my own head. I was being drawn in, the pull was magnetic, and the sensation was exhilarating, almost hypnotic. I snapped out of it, looked up, and saw that my friends had long since climbed up into a tier of benches. Others were sitting there too, and everyone was regarding me strangely.

Dream 70

Margaret holds down a high-powered job, which she finds can be stressful. She states that her friend, Mary (in the dream), is a very conventional person.

I was in a shoe-store trying on shoes but I found nothing I liked. When I went to put on my old sandals I couldn't locate them (these were old, comfortable sandals I bought years ago). I searched but could not find them.

The sales assistants were helpful and offered me other shoes to buy, which I liked, but they were too big. It became clear that I would have to walk home in my stockinged feet.

I tried my friend's (Mary's) clogs, which seemed a good idea, but I had left the shoe-store then (so it was too late). Someone, maybe from the police, drove me all the way home to where I used to live as a child.

Dream 71

Maurice says that he was recently divorced.

Throughout the dream, I had a feeling of anticipation. I was at a big event, similar to the races, although it wasn't. There were lots of women and children present, who were seated. Despite the fact that it was pouring with rain, everybody was happy.

A landau came riding by, carrying Princess Diana and a lady-in-waiting. I found myself in the landau admiring the Princess, thinking how very sexy she looked in her mini-skirt. She seemed pleased to see the crowds of happy people. Then, somehow, it didn't seem to be the Princess.

Dream 72

Helen says that she has been concerned about her spiritual path in life and wonders if she pays too much attention to material gains.

I found myself near a house and stables in a serene country setting surrounded by trees at the edge of a forest. I entered the stables to discover a dirt floor, then a raised section made of shiny stones, some of which bore scars. It felt sacred. I picked up a loose pebble, and it fell in half. Inside, sitting in the lotus position meditating, was a small metallic statue of a guru. He looked like one of the three wise men. I felt really happy. The whole place had an air of expectancy, as if something major was about to happen.

Dream 73

Mary says that, despite a sort of unconscious awareness of her actions, she seems to have a knack of sabotaging romantic relationships.

I was walking along the street and came across a black dog. I was pleased to crouch down and talk to it. Suddenly I became aware that it had another (white) head, which was where its rear end should be. I said, 'Oh, you're a Siamese dog, I've never met one like you before.' I do remember in the dream trying not to show that I was in any way surprised or shocked at what I had seen. In spite of this I made a mental note that I did notice an abnormality.

Dream 74

Here we a have a recurring nightmare from Jan, aged 39. Jan, a single parent, says that this frightening dream began soon after she became involved in a new relationship, yet her partner, Steve, seems to be a kind, gentle person. She added that the dream always begins in pleasant surroundings, accompanied by feelings of well-being.

I find myself standing by a stream amid beautiful countryside. With me are various animals – a cat, dog, piglet, some baby chickens, and a lamb – all friendly and seemingly reliant on me for their care. I scatter some corn for the chickens and begin to prepare some porridge for the piglet. However, the lamb becomes distraught, as if I should feed it first. I tell it to wait its turn. I approach the stream to get water to blend with the porridge but, threateningly, the lamb forces itself between me and the flow. At this point I notice its eyes begin to glow red, somewhat like those of a werewolf. Its bleat is replaced by a dog-like growl, and the cat becomes aggressive, too. Then I always wake up feeling terrified.

Dream 75

Here we have a rather frightening dream on a recurring theme, from 38-year-old Ross, who is in advertising. In a relationship, Ross gives a comprehensive list of things that are on his mind, among which are concerns about his partner's commitment to him, his mother's health and his job.

I owned a strongly fortified castle. Standing in the courtyard, I felt elated as I scanned the ramparts, which were heavily manned with my soldiers. In response to a shout from an approaching messenger, who was exhausted after riding hard, the doors opened. He told us that an old, hooded man, who was blind, deaf, and dumb, would arrive at the castle at an unspecified time. His arrival would herald death, destruction, and chaos on a massive scale.

It was not the anticipated carnage that struck terror into me, but the thought of being face to face with the mysterious old man. It was the worst possible scenario I could imagine. In addition, something reminiscent of folklore reminded me that, a long time ago, his coming had previously brought disaster with it.

After refortifying the castle, and an interminable wait, suddenly four swordsmen appeared, killing my men before turning their attention on me. In view of their incredible skills in battle, I felt my strength draining away. I was powerless, at which point they claimed to be friends and to have been merely testing my defences. Although the forewarned destruction did happen, I couldn't recall seeing the old man. Incredibly, somehow I managed to survive, but the rest of the dream was spent with me being forced to flee and hide from the enemy. Then I woke up.

Dream 76

William, who is aged 62, wonders what sort of problems and crises life might throw at him next.

I was living in a flat, one I used to live in 20 years ago. Instead of being on the third floor of the block, this one was on the fifteenth. It was approached by a lift that was distinctly dangerous: there was a gap between it and the floor. When I got out I had to leap. The lift did not just go up vertically but did some horizontal travelling too.

The flat was a two-bedroom, kitchen, living-room, and bathroom type. I knew there were some extra rooms that I did not use, but then I decided I wanted to use them. I had put some spare furniture in store in them.

However, when I went in, they were occupied by a school, and the teacher, whom I insulted, threw me out. I told her that she was no lady, but a stuck-up bourgeois bitch who should get a proper job – or a husband – and stop messing about with children's minds with her teaching methods. After this, I returned to my flat, then rain started to come through the ceiling, except that it was not on the top floor.

Dream 77

Here we have an interesting three-part dream, which comes from Alexa, aged 71. What makes it so fascinating is that, at the time of the dream, Alexa was waiting for an appointment to have tests for a recently diagnosed heart problem.

Part 1: I was surprised to find that my husband had built a shiny flying-machine in the kitchen. With room enough for only one occupant, I could see a pretty blonde girl inside. There didn't seem to be any means of propulsion, and the girl appeared to be pedalling. Excitedly, my husband was reading off figures from outside the machine, which was stationary throughout. He told her to try harder, to pedal faster.

Part 2: As I was feeling tired, I decided to go away and sit down. However, the back door opened, and someone came in, arms full of clothes from the washing line. This shadowy figure deposited them on the table, then left.

I was taken aback at the huge pile, especially as I hadn't done any washing! I was quite exhausted and wanted to put my feet up, but felt that I couldn't leave it like that. I started smoothing out the clothes, folding them, and placing them in a basket ready for ironing.

Part 3: I glanced out of the window to see a small group of people who, looking quite lost, were in my garden. I assumed that they had missed their turning to the beach. I told them that they were on private property and gave them directions.

They thanked me, but one of the younger ones informed me that they had already been to the beach. Feeling puzzled as to why they had come into my garden, and wondering where they wanted to go, I watched them depart. I realized that my directions had been needless. Knowing that they would soon find their way, I wasn't concerned about them. Then I woke up feeling vastly amused at such a ridiculous dream!

Dream 78

Sue, a reflexologist, is divorced and often wonders about the future.

I was with someone (a man), sheltering in a doorway of a large building, watching and listening to two women. I recognized the building as an old library. One of the women (my aunt) was talking about a wedding connected with my cousin in New Zealand.

We went looking for the church where the wedding was to be held. We were in a hilly place. Then a strange man appeared to show us the way, but I couldn't find the church.

We were in the doorway again. An aircraft appeared overhead, carrying the father of the bride-to-be. Suddenly there was a lot of noise, smoke, and darkness; the plane had crashed, killing the father.

There was a small crypt outside, in which the man's coffin was held. There was fire (candles or torches?) surrounding the coffin. I said to the man, 'Why are some families so touched by tragedy?' He said that he didn't know.

We emerged from the same library. It was night-time, and we were on top of a grassy slope. On our way down to pay our respects, we encountered someone carrying a torch, who meant us harm. We ran back into the doorway, and the man, who was my ex-husband, pushed me through revolving doors and said, 'Go hide in there.'

I leapt into something similar to a sentry box. He leapt in after me, and we stood very still, hoping that we would be safe. I woke up hot and fearful.

Dream 79

Patricia, who works in the media, is married, sometimes works away from home, and expresses a desire to start a family.

My dream doesn't contain much action and isn't very long. However, I always wake up in distress and feel extremely embarrassed by it. It's always the same. I am detached from my body and can see myself. I have shoulder-length hair and am crying. Then my hair begins to fall out. Desperately, I try to cover it up. As more and more of it falls out, I notice that my scalp is bright red. Finally, all of it falls out, and I end up with a glowing, red head, which is very sore. It is so vivid that, when I wake up, it takes me a while to realize that it was a dream.

Dream 80

Moira, who describes herself as introverted, states that this dream has recurred since she was a child, and it is always identical in every respect.

I dream that I wake up in a hammock, which is swinging violently. Instinctively, I know that I am a young seaman on board a ship. There is a lot of noise, as a howling gale tosses us around like a cork. Panic is evident in the crew's voices, as they shout commands at each other and grab at the air in a desperate attempt to hang on to any immovable object.

I have a sensation of falling, until there is an enormous crash as the ship finds the bottom of a deep trench in the sea, at which point I am thrown out of the hammock. I hit the floor with a sickening 'crack', which reverberates throughout my body and echoes in my head. I am aware of tremendous pain in my shoulder, which is made much worse by the violent action of the ship.

Somehow, the coarse fabric of the strange top I'm wearing becomes entangled in something behind me – something I can't see. My inability to move makes me realize that I have broken my shoulder. Then water starts pouring in through a split in the timbers, and I know that it's every man for himself.

Nobody seems to be aware of my plight as the rest of the crew rush past me in a panic to get up on deck. In the half-light I am afraid. It occurs to me that I am alone, and the water is getting deeper by the second. In vain I try to call out for help, but my voice is drowned out by the intense noise of the sea and the cracking and twisting timbers.

At this point I always wake up – glad to be alive. Then it occurs to me that, in the dream, it had felt perfectly natural for me to have been a young man.

Dream 81
Maria states that her ex-boyfriend still works out in the same gym as her.

I was attending the wedding of my best friend, Sarah, which was being held in a gymnasium. I was surprised to notice that she wasn't wearing a wedding dress. A circle of girls, who were dancing with their hands linked, surrounded her. Then the bride's mother, wearing a long pink dress, pulled me on to the dance floor. 'Let's dance,' she smiled.

As I held hands with the others and began to dance, I noticed my ex-boyfriend out of the corner of my eye. He was wearing his gym shorts and appeared to be running on the spot. When I looked back at the bride, I observed that she didn't seem to be enjoying herself. I felt sad for her, then woke up.

Dream 82
John says that his girlfriend dumped him, but he cannot understand why.

I found myself in a long, narrow, almost tunnel-like art gallery, seemingly without end. Both sides, as far as the eye could see, were lined with portraits. The floor was paved with chequered, black-and-white floor tiles, and the entire place was dimly lit.

As I walked slowly along, studying each picture, it struck me that all the painted faces were familiar, although I couldn't identify them. Then it dawned on me that they were all paintings of the same subject: a man. However, in each, he was portrayed differently. In some, he had no eyes or ears; others revealed an enormous mouth; a few showed different hairstyles and tints. In many, he was wearing all sorts of different styles of clothing.

Nevertheless, without exception, they shared something in common. In each the man appeared to be standing in front of a mirror. I got the feeling that the person who posed for all these paintings used to worry continually about his appearance.

My journey seemed endless, as I peered at painting after painting, all portraying the same man in a different form. Then it occurred to me that there might not be an end to this art gallery, and I began to get worried. Was I going to spend the rest of eternity gazing at this same person? At that point, I woke up feeling quite disturbed.

Dream 83

Rosemary, aged 57, provides this fascinating recurring dream, which she has had since childhood.

I have had this dream hundreds of times. As a child I dreamt I was on a beach. I would turn round to see the tide racing in so fast that, as I struggled to reach the safety of the dunes, the waves overwhelmed me.

However, now I am middle-aged, I dream the tide is already fully in. I want to swim in the water, which seems warm and inviting. Nevertheless, when I move towards the sea, only wet sand remains and I am left high and dry. The latest variation (dreamt once) is that the sea has solidified and is impenetrable. When I touched the surface, it was like hardened papier-mâché.

Dream 84

Janet, a schoolteacher, provided this recurring dream, which has bothered her less and less over a 10-year period.

I find myself standing on a cliff-top. I know it's Blackpool [on the west coast of England] because I can see the tower. However, there are no other buildings or people. It is a beautiful day with a clear blue sky, brilliant sunshine, and a calm blue sea with the occasional white cap glinting in the sunshine. Behind me are miles and miles of beautifully kept fields, all marked by tidy hedgerows.

Then, some distance below me, I notice people, who are milling about on the beach. With the sea on my right, I begin walking down the cliff-path. The further down I go, the less vivid the colours become. When I reach the beach, the people have gone. As I walk along I notice that the cliffs have been replaced by a single step, which leads to a neglected esplanade. Nearby, there are shuttered wooden buildings, all with paint peeling off.

I look back in the direction of the sea and notice lots of stalls on the beach, rather like a fairground: a rifle range, roll-a-penny, hook-a-duck, candy floss, etc., but no people. I continue walking and become aware that now all the colour is gone – everything appears in shades of grey. Then the sea, which is still calm, gently comes up on the beach and washes all the stalls away. Then I wake up.

Dream 85

Margaret, aged 68, provides this fairly common dream, which she maintains has recurred over several years. Margaret lists a catalogue of things that are on her mind, among which are concerns about her recent hip replacement, her husband's health, her children, her ageing dog, and some money problems.

There are never any people whom I can recall. However, I know that somebody is chasing me. I am very scantily dressed in a long vest that keeps riding up. In a futile attempt to hide my embarrassment, I keep pulling it down.

I find myself travelling down a long, straight road, which looks rather grey. Then, quite suddenly, I take to the air, slowly flapping my arms – they feel quite heavy. I'm not very high and worry about coming down too heavily. I can see houses, and then wake up feeling quite exhausted.

Dream 86

Stuart, aged 27, an unemployed graduate, is recovering from alcoholism, which he says was triggered by dysfunctional relationships.

I found myself in a very familiar room, which was incorporated into a railway station. The room had just been redecorated in green and sky-blue (my favourite colours), and was much brighter than before. Leaning against a wall was a bicycle that I identified as mine. It, too, had been painted, cleaned, and polished, and looked brand new. I knew the bike was there for me to cycle home, but I was worried that I would fall off and damage it and myself.

Two women appeared in the room with me (in waking life I know both, and fancy one of them, but she is already in a relationship). In the dream both of them told me that, as I was young and fit, I shouldn't be scared, nor have any problems riding my bike home. While this was going on, there was lots of activity outside, yet I was too preoccupied to notice.

In real life, I recently attended a course with other people. They didn't appear to be in my dream, but I knew that they were close by. Then the project manager did actually come into the room and she, too, encouraged me.

I knew that I had to ride the bike home, so I walked out of the room and into the train station, which was full of strangers going about their business. I mounted my bike, but because I was still insecure and unsure of which direction to go, or whether I would reach my destination safely, I didn't actually ride it. I was also aware that I was perspiring with nerves. At this point, I woke up.

Dream 87

Here we are dealing with a fascinating recurring nightmare (over a number of years) from Patricia, aged 48. Now a writer of fiction, Patricia states that she had a neglected childhood and became an avid reader. During the 1980s, around the time of her father's death, she suffered a nervous breakdown. She also lost her mother and only brother before she was 18 and she now lives alone.

The plot varies, but the theme is always the same: in the past, I have murdered one or more people and secretly buried the bodies somewhere. I'm afraid the bodies will be discovered and I'll be found out. It's not the punishment I fear, but simply being found out. I'm also afraid of seeing the bodies, which I know will be an unpleasant sight. Sometimes they are buried in the basement of my house (in real life I don't own a house), while at other times they are in shallow graves outside – but they are always buried. Invariably, there are police officers who just happened to be digging in the same location, or have been tipped off. There is also a chance that they might not find anything.

I never know anyone in these dreams. It's always a secret that I have to face alone! Occasionally, for a moment, I may even be aware that I am dreaming a vision I have dreamt before.

Dream 88

Mrs W., aged 23, provides this intriguing recurring dream, in which things crop up that are associated with her past. Mrs W., who has a stepson, says that she would like to have a baby.

It's always hot and the sun is very bright. I find myself in the area where I was brought up, but not in a place I ever frequented. Laughing and smiling, I am running or cycling along a road at great speed through a village, when a nice, friendly-looking black Labrador dog stops me (I had a Labrador for 12 years). To keep people away from me, he growls at them. Then he turns on me and takes my hand into his mouth and starts pulling me – it's not the bite that hurts so much, but more the thought of him attacking me. Although he is pulling me, we don't seem to go anywhere, and his growls don't deter the people, who continue walking by, even though they are meant to. I feel afraid and trapped, then I usually wake up.

Dream 89

Mr K., aged 74, provides this dream, which has recurred over many years. After seeing active service in the British army during World War 2, Mr K.

was demobbed and took on a job as a salesman for a bread and confectionery company. For 6 days a week, he drove many miles, delivering produce to a number of small outlets. Mr K. explained that the job demanded punctuality and a high level of service, and his dreams reflect this in detail, even to the extent where many of his old customers and their names are recalled.

I am always back doing my old job. However, instead of the smooth-running successful business it used to be, these dreams reflect problems: running late, a lack of, or too much, stock, the van boy not turning up, lack of planning to give certain customers priority, etc. Often I have lost my van and find myself wandering the streets in a futile attempt to locate it. Completely lost, I look for somebody to help.

After a lot of confusion, I find someone who understands my plight. This individual drives me in another vehicle to where I should be, at which point I always wake up feeling relieved that it was all a dream. Please help!

Dream 90

Iain supplied an extremely long, well-structured dream which, for reasons of space, has had to be edited considerably. Nevertheless, as we will see, there is a consistent theme that runs throughout the entire dream. Iain has recently taken early retirement and wonders about his present situation.

I started by rushing around in a house into which I had recently moved; therefore everything took a bit longer to find. I was starting a new job and didn't want to be late. I took two dinner plates with me from which to eat my lunch. I didn't want to be seen carrying them around in my new place of work, so I looked for a bag. The bag I found contained compost, so I discarded it and headed back towards the kitchen. However, I encountered two old men who were dithering in the hallway, preventing me from passing.

As it was now five to nine, I rushed out of the house and into a car park. I was going to be late for my first day, but hoped it wouldn't be noticed. However, I could not find my old red Ford Sierra, nor could I recall where I had left it. I searched between intervening buildings, which belonged to this foreign hotel. I asked one of the hotel staff if he had seen my car, to which he replied, 'Oh yeah'. I was surprised he spoke English, because somehow I then knew that I was in a Spanish-speaking country.

Time was ticking by, and it was now well after nine. I felt frustrated and knew my new employers would be upset if I didn't phone them. With no phone nearby, I rushed back into the hotel and through a series of passageways. Then I realized that I was no longer in a hotel, but in a train instead.

Iain's dream continued along this theme, through trains, buses, streetcars, plus many diversions caused by individuals, who at first appear to be helping. The dream culminated in conflict with some youths, when Iain saw an official through a glass door. He was just about to ask where he was when he woke up.

Dream 91

Joan, aged 49, who is divorced, says that she is concerned about making ends meet, finding true love, reaching decisions concerning her career, and improving family relationships.

I was in a sort of holiday camp, where entertainment was taking place. The first act featured a woman, her teenage daughter, and four younger daughters. They were all wearing light blue dresses and performed songs surrounded by pictures of themselves on posters. Other entertainment was provided in the form of a man conducting guided tours through a series of green doors.

I joined a game of cards, using several differently decorated packs, which were all mixed together. I shuffled them and noticed that a quarter of one of the red-and-black patterned cards was torn off. I felt very embarrassed. Then lots of people began to show off their shoes to me, especially women wearing black ones.

Then I found myself camping outdoors, where I had fluffy pink blankets. I noticed sheep that had filthy grey blankets. I wondered whether to wash theirs, but considered the possibility that it might ruin the washing machine. Then I woke up.

Dream 92

David S., aged 22, sent in this most unusual dream that has recurred three times. David, a computer-operator, says that he is experiencing difficulty getting over his recent break-up with his girlfriend. He is also nervous about the possibility of being relocated in his job and is conscious that, when it comes to managing his finances, he lacks self-discipline.

I dreamt that I went back in time to 1984. All I had to do was walk towards my bank and, hey presto, I ended up in the past. Absolutely astounded, I went through a door and saw myself talking to my parents – my other self was 8 years old. I also saw my brother, when he was younger, in a nightclub. Then I went to a betting shop and placed a bet on Rangers to beat Celtic 2–0, in the [soccer] Cup Final, which was taking place the following day. Somehow, I knew the score and was guaranteed to win!

In another version of the dream, I went back to my old school in 1979. I recall seeing some of my old teachers, who were starting their first day of a new term. Then I came forward to the present time, to get a camera so that I could go back and take pictures of my old school and classmates. With the intention of returning to the present time, so that I could show my friends photographs of these old scenes, I travelled back to 1979 and took some snapshots. At that point, I woke up.

However, I slipped back into a similar dream and found myself travelling back to 1979 again. I entered a classroom full of faces which I didn't recognize. Then I noticed a sea of children running back and forth along the school corridors. Then I woke up again.

Dream 93

Margaret, who has written a novel, says that, more than anything else in the world, she would love to get it published.

I am walking along a long, straight road when I come across an enormous pond, about 300 feet by 100 feet. It is full of fish of different colours, shapes, and sizes. The pond is man-made and tiled in blue and white. There are several slip-roads leading in all directions from it, but they all go uphill. At the far end of the pond, I can see a bridge that joins up with the straight road again.

Despite the feeling that I should cross the bridge and follow the straight road, my curiosity sidetracks me. In different versions of this dream, I follow many of these slip-roads, but never seem to get anywhere, at which point, I always wake up. The dreams are colourful and pleasant, and I don't want to come out of them because I want to find out more.

Dream 94

Sarah, aged 23, experienced this dream shortly before deciding to pursue a career in theology. Sarah stressed that this is by far the most vivid dream she can remember.

Full of anticipation, I was on a walking holiday in an unfamiliar, rather exotic country. It was hot and sunny, and I was surrounded by rolling, wild-flower-laden green hills; the beautiful sweet scent was almost overwhelming. I came to a crossroads but didn't know which turning to take. Eventually, I felt compelled to turn left, although I seemed to know instinctively that, if I had turned right, I would have ended up at the same destination, albeit by a longer journey; in other words, the roads were circular. However, the route I took seemed to be the quickest.

Sure enough, as I rounded the first bend, I came across an old church that was brightly decorated with exotic blooms in hanging baskets. At that point, although the general ambience was still nice, it had lost something, and my feelings of anticipation were no longer present. Somehow, I sensed that, if I doubled back and took the other road, although my journey would take considerably longer, I would encounter some excitement along the way. It was then that the feelings of expectation returned, and I could pinpoint that the atmosphere surrounding me was one of love. At that point I woke up feeling happy and content.

Dream 95

Duncan, aged 34, furnishes this extremely revealing dream. Duncan says that he is ambitious and determined to reach the top of his profession. He works in sales.

I found myself crouching down in a thicket in a field in the countryside. Nearby, completely ignorant of my presence, there were people walking to and fro along bridle-paths. If I had wanted to, I could have surprised any of them. However, in the distance, some movement caught my eye.

Almost like a cat stalking its prey, I saw a fox advancing towards something in the distance; as it went, it took cover behind several oak trees. Then, as if looking through a zoom lens, I could see that it was stalking a lion, which seemed totally unaware of the fox. I didn't want to warn the lion but was enthralled as to the outcome. Then I woke up feeling disappointed that I didn't witness the upshot.

Dream 96

Barbara, aged 34, who is divorced, supplied this rather clear-cut dream to interpret. Barbara explained that she is somewhat possessive of Geoff, her new boyfriend.

Geoff and I were on holiday. Hand in hand, we were strolling along a strange beach, which had stretches of sand and areas of pebbles. We were on the sand. It was a sunshiny day, and we were laughing. In the distance, I noticed about four younger girls approaching, which made me feel uneasy. Somehow I knew that they wanted Geoff and presented a danger.

Geoff then tried to let go of my hand, but I strengthened my grip. We were then on the pebbles. Soon, the girls were within earshot, and I heard them making innuendoes, which I sensed were about Geoff's good looks. I was becoming enraged because, as we passed by, instead of continuing their journey, the girls turned round and began to follow us. I also noticed that, wearing a smile, Geoff kept looking round at them.

It was then that I gripped his hand even harder and tried hurrying him towards the end of the beach. However, he prised his hand away from mine and walked back to the girls and engaged them in flirty conversation. I woke up feeling devastated.

Dream 97

Helen, aged 45, who is in senior management, provides this thought-provoking dream, in which an unequivocal message stands out. Helen is considering a job offer that represents a step down in status (made by an up-and-coming rival company), although she says it will certainly be more of a challenge.

I was alone in a smoke-filled, dingy room, lit only by a single, old-fashioned light-bulb housed in a miserable, green-enamel shade. I sensed an atmosphere of uncertainty accompanied by a certain amount of excited anticipation. I was drawn towards a table and four rickety-looking chairs. As I approached, I saw a Monopoly board, on which a game had been deserted halfway through.

I sat at the position with the most money and began studying the state of play. I remember thinking that whoever occupied this seat had the advantage of power and was in possession of all the trump cards. At this point, a door creaked open, and two men and a woman appeared each taking their respective seats around the table. The atmosphere was now electric, as they all looked at me expectantly, as if I was to make the next play. I found myself picking up the dice and rolling them. However, when I looked up, my opponents appeared to have mutated into snakes. I experienced no fear, but a state of complexity instead. Apart from their forked tongues flicking in and out, I couldn't help noticing how their eyes glistened under the single pendent lamp. At that point, I woke up in a state of confusion.

Dream 98

Shona, aged 45, sent in this recurring dream, which reflects accurately the ongoing financial difficulties she is experiencing with her son David (not his real name), who is at university.

It's a bright day, the sun is beating down, and I am tending our fishpond in the garden. I notice that the sun has evaporated much of the water, so I rig up a hosepipe to replenish it. However, no matter how much water I pour into the pond, it seems to evaporate faster. As we have expensive Koi carp, I am worried that they will be left floundering on the bottom.

I turn round to ask my husband, who is lazing in a deckchair, to help, but notice that he is no longer around. In addition to the hosepipe, I double my efforts by filling buckets and ferrying them back and forth to the pond. Despite all this, the water is getting lower and lower, and the fish seem to be in some distress.

My son David appears, offering me a huge water-filled sponge, telling me that it will help. I grasp it with both hands and try squeezing the water from it into the pond. To my horror, the sponge increases in size, and I notice that, instead of adding water to the pond, it is absorbing even more. By this time the fish look at me with sorrowful eyes, and I know that unless I can get help I will lose them. I always wake up at this point feeling frustrated and helpless.

Dream 99

Brian, aged 30, is a manager of a transport company and says that he would like to set up his own business.

My wife was waiting outside my house in a white Rolls Royce, which I instinctively knew was there to take us to our son's wedding (I am not married in real life and have no children). There was an air of excitement and, when I got into the car, my wife seemed overjoyed to see me. She kissed me, then presented me with an Easter egg, telling me to open it before we set off. 'It's for the birth,' she said.

Without even trying to work out her remark, I gazed in amazement as the egg began to hatch. The two halves of the egg fell apart, revealing a miniature college professor dressed in a mortarboard and gown. He presented me with a scroll and announced, jubilantly, 'Congratulations, it's a bouncing baby boy!' I took the tiny, yellowish parchment from his tiny hand and, with incredulity, watched as he stepped back into the chocolate egg, which then sealed itself.

Suddenly, the scene changed, and I found myself dressed in a yellow suit, standing on a brown carpet in a church. However, instead of finding myself attending my son's wedding, a minister approached me and asked, 'Are you ready for your baptism?' Unsure, I hesitated for a moment. Then he added, 'There's nothing to worry about, everything will be fine.'

I walked forward, then a crowd of people appeared in front of me, and all yelled, 'Surprise!' They then threw confetti over me, and I found myself amid a party. At this point I woke up feeling highly amused at such a bizarre dream.

Dream 100

Maureen, who works in local government, provides this fascinating and telling recurring dream, which has run on a similar theme since her childhood. Maureen states that she is proud of her achievements in life, is aware of being psychic, but is still looking for more challenges and fulfilment.

As a child, my dreams would be superimposed on my real surroundings, which sometimes made them difficult to distinguish from reality. I am usually standing between two groups of people of equal numbers – normally three in each – two men and a woman. Although they all take human form, I am aware that one group comprises people who are alive, while the people in the other group are spiritual or heavenly. Instinctively, I know which is which.

Both groups pull me gently towards them. However, knowing that I'm in control, with a certain amount of mild irritation, I stand firm between the two. Then the two sides try to cajole me to join them with softly spoken words and a warm pulling sensation. I don't feel threatened, just slightly put out by all the attention.

Dream 101

This strong vocational dream comes from Valerie, a middle-aged widow, with two children who have recently flown the nest. Valerie is speculating about returning to work. However, she is at a loss as to which sort of occupation she should pursue.

It was a bright sunny day and, surrounded by beautiful wild flowers, I was walking in the countryside. The scene was extremely vivid and extraordinarily colourful. Children were playing happily and, as they passed by me, people acknowledged me with nods and smiles. Everybody was so friendly I felt overwhelmed and imagined that it was almost how I envisioned the Garden of Eden to be.

Then, in contrast, I noticed a huge marquee, which housed some sort of hospital beds, similar to those you see depicted in scenes from a battlefield in the last century. Instinctively, I walked towards two nurses, who told me that they had been waiting for me to give a hand. I approached one patient, who was an old man and seemed to be in some discomfort. As I laid my hand on his head, he smiled, got out of bed, and announced that he was cured, at which point I woke up rather startled.

Dream 102

Jean supplies this dream, which furnishes a warning of some sort of duplicity by a third party. Jean, who is married with three grown-up children (one of whom still lives at home), says that she often feels as though she is simply treading water in life and getting nowhere.

I found myself in my living room, which was in a state of darkness. Although I knew my way around, I could sense that somebody else, who was familiar, was in the room and, as if putting obstacles in front of me, was continually moving the furniture from one place to another. This had the effect of dulling my confidence, so that I was almost too afraid to find my way to the door.

Eventually, my lack of confidence turned into fear. I then fumbled my way towards where I sensed the door could be found. My intuition told me that whoever was in the room with me was now moving the furniture in order to block my way. In my panic, I tripped over once or twice, but eventually made it to the door. Nervously, I turned the handle and, thankfully, found myself in broad daylight. Then, with an intense feeling of relief, I woke up.

Dream 103

Cate is divorced and responsible for the upbringing of her children.

I found myself in a sort of village hall, which was packed with people. The cramped environment frightened me. I was relieved to see an old schoolfriend, who led me to a seat.

After an unnerving encounter with another old friend, I left the hall to discover a howling gale and blizzard outside. I was in a mini-car and, in hazardous conditions, drove along country roads, alone and very scared. I was aware that

I was approaching a cliff, and the road condition meant that I was going to career over the edge. I realized that the situation was bigger than I was, so I went with it.

After somersaulting down the cliff, undamaged, the car came to rest the right way up, with no injuries or harm done. The weather and scene had now changed dramatically: sunshine and beautiful green, rolling hills. Nearby, in their 50s, there were two figures in a cottage who welcomed and accepted me unconditionally. Inside this sunny room were trees laden with luscious fruits. I picked a pear and tasted the sweet juice. I had come home. I woke up.

Dream 104

Joan says that this strange dream about futuristic aircraft has recurred over more than 40 years. On her questionnaire, she lists the usual concerns in life that, from time to time, bother us all, which include money, house, and uncertainty about what the ageing process might bring.

In every dream I am watching the sky from the same place: the garden of the house where I grew up, and which my parents left many years ago. In the dream, I have no knowledge of how I happen to be there, nor of the date or time, and I'm always alone. I am not afraid, yet I am aware of a slight sense of menace, although it is never directed at me. The dreams are usually set in daylight, but occasionally in the dark.

Invariably, an aircraft flies low and comes slowly across the sky. Due to its low altitude, I always get an excellent view. The aircraft never come towards me, but pass me by, then disappear from sight. They are complicated in design, perhaps futuristic. However, they are never the same twice, and don't seem to come from an alien source.

Occasionally, when I see newsreels of modern Royal Air Force planes, they seem familiar, although I don't experience a sense of déjà vu, or precognition.

Dream 105

Carol supplies this recurring dream, which she says has bothered her for the last year or so. Carol runs her own shoe-store and is considering opening another.

In a tall office block, I find myself climbing seemingly endless stairs. As I reach a landing, I encounter several people who are sprawled across the floor, almost as if they are trying to block my way. Each time I reach another landing, I discover more obstacles placed in such a manner that, in order to avoid falling over and tumbling back down the stairs, I have to be extremely careful how I tread.

Finally, after an exhausting effort, I reach the top. However, now standing on a cluttered flat roof, I notice that there are no walls or handrails to stop me from falling over the edge. Nevertheless, I know instinctively that I should be standing on the tidy roof of the adjacent building. I am faced with two choices: I can either go all the way back downstairs and enter the other building by its main door, or jump the fairly narrow gap between the two buildings. I wake up scared at the thought of jumping, while, at the same time, frustrated at the idea of retracing my steps through the mire of obstacles.

Dream 106

James says that, as he does a lot of work for his local church, he is wondering if this dream has a significant connection.

I was in a gorgeous country setting surrounded by the most beautiful blooms imaginable – somewhere abroad, I believe. On the other side of a stream a meeting was being held. I knew instinctively that those attending were people of high-ranking authority. The weather was warm and, between exotic clouds tinged with pink, the sun shone brightly. As I gazed up at them, a sort of an elusive shadowy movement attracted my attention. I was fascinated as I tried to locate and bring it into focus.

Suddenly, the most resplendent, smiling, halo-decked face of an angel peeped over one of the clouds. Slowly the angel's entire form came into view, from its gossamer wings to its dainty, cherubic feet. I was filled with incredibly loving emotions. There was no action or dialogue, just a wonderful exchange of loving feelings. Then the angel pointed at something ahead of me, in the distance. I stared hard and was just able to make out a crystal city, nestled among trees, on the horizon. When I looked round, the angel had gone, leaving me with a strong sense of inner peace. I woke up and was in a jubilant mood for the rest of the day.

Dream 107

Rose states that, at the time of the dream, she was concerned about her daughter's relationship with her boyfriend. Furthermore, she wondered if the penguin in her dream could be a symbolic representation of her daughter.

My husband and I took a penguin for a walk in the park. The bird's beak resembled that of a toucan, and the bird kept biting or pecking people, including me. When we tried to escape from it, our way was blocked by security guards, who were policing the park because the Queen and Prince Philip were due to visit.

The scene then changed and I found myself walking with my husband along a street; we were going to call on someone. Then somebody mentioned a bump that had involved a vehicle, the description of which sounded like my daughter's car. We entered the house to find an older man lying on the floor, and I got the distinct impression that he was my daughter's boyfriend.

Next, her boyfriend was arguing with an unidentified person in the kitchen, where a Down's syndrome child lay asleep. I got the impression that this child was the penguin. I went through the door and, instead of being in my friend's house, I was in my daughter's kitchen, which was full of dirty dishes.

Dream 108

Fiona, who is a health-worker, says that, for many years, she has been troubled by dreams similar in nature, which always involve her childhood home. Some of these feature the house being attacked by Nazis, an enemy, and scenes of humiliation, always accompanied by an unpleasant atmosphere.

Set in my childhood home, I was preparing a meal for some of my present-day friends. As an additional treat, I went to an Indian restaurant to get some seafood delicacies, which I had to boil, to complement my home-made soup. I was impressed with myself at putting on such a delicious spread.

However, when I served it, some of my guests took a wee nibble and, from their reaction, I realized that there something dreadfully wrong with the food. I noticed that small, horrible, beetle-like beasties were crawling out of the pot and into the soup; they came from the Indian delicacies.

I was so mortified that I had served my friends with such a disgusting meal that I couldn't cope with the situation. In order to have them examined scientifically and identified, I was desperate to catch one of the creatures. They were similar in appearance to very large greenfly, but much more horrible. By then, they were jumping all over the place.

Aware that the seafood had cost me £150, I was determined to get my money back. Filled with anger and shame, I remember approaching one of my female friends and punching and shouting at her. I felt isolated, humiliated, and deeply ashamed. The more the pot, which was still on the cooker, boiled, the more creatures poured out over the rim.

PART III

Correct
Interpretations
of the Dreams

. . . .

In this part of the book, we include the original interpretations that were acknowledged by the dreamers to be accurate. You will notice that some of these analyses have been left in their original form. In other words, they are addressed directly to the dreamers. Others, however, refer to dreamers in the third person. The reason for this is to give you an idea of how to write a report for a third party – usually a doctor.

In the first section, the interpretations are accompanied by *Further Comments*, the objective being to drive certain points home, to add any recommendations on how dreamers can best act on dreams' messages, and sometimes to offer a slightly different opinion. You will also notice that, as you progress through these interpretations, some points are repeated. These points concern some of the most significant aspects of dream interpretation and so are worth repetition.

You will also encounter some very similar dreams. Instead of grouping them together, they have been included randomly. We hope that this will give you an added incentive to pick them out.

Section 1

Interpretation 1

This dream concerns affairs of the heart. In your letter, you expressed concern that Barbara and your boyfriend were holding hands, and stated that Barbara was a valued friend and always seemed to give good advice. This provided an important clue, which helped to decode the dream.

The dream implies that, where affairs of the heart are concerned, you shouldn't listen to what other people say ('If I were in your shoes!'). If you take well-meant advice from others about your boyfriend, the results are likely to lead to misery (represented by the shrivelling heart). The dream shows clearly where your romance will lead if you try to emulate the way Barbara would behave in a relationship. Instead, be guided by your own heart, and be yourself!

Further Comments: Dreams convey valuable information from the wise subconscious by way of visual and verbal symbols around a decodable theme. The shoes and shrivelling heart translate clearly around the main characteristics of Barbara as being an advice-giver. The strong emotion reinforces the importance of the message to you.

You may lack self-esteem and tend to be too open to the influence of others. Trust your own judgement and become more assertive and independent. The matter of your relationship is too precious to you to allow interference, and your subconscious is naturally trying to warn you.

Interpretation 2

This dream is highlighting a problem in your life that you haven't yet recognized, or that you do not wish to recognize (your concern about 'switching on'). You seem to be in a state of darkness concerning an issue going on around you. It is also likely that these circumstances have been present for some time (the obstacles were static). Perhaps you have been content to turn a blind eye (fumbling in the dark).

However, your subconscious is showing you a way out (represented by the door). It is significant that you were led back to the light switch again. The dream is telling you to *switch on* to what is going on around you. If you identify the problem, a door of opportunity is likely to present itself. Open your eyes!

Further Comments: There seems to be a distinct metaphor, or symbolic statement, in this dream. Normally dreams communicate by strong visual symbols, but here, the verbal pun – not seeing the light – predominates. We all possess defensive processes that can prevent us from seeing the truth about something, but through the truth comes freedom and greater self-insight. Overcome your reticence and seek illumination, whether what you have avoided concerns a situation around you or your own spiritual development.

Interpretation 3

The empty office block confirms your own suspicion in that it represents a work situation. The fact that it is empty reflects your feelings about your store (there is nothing left to try). The ground indicates that you need to 'earth' yourself. It also points to a place of stability, where the majority of people operate (employees in regular jobs). This dream is likely to recur until such time as you look for, and find, another way out of your troubles, or take the plunge and try a plan of action that you have considered (perhaps finding regular employment). Your subconscious is urging you to be brave and take the plunge!

Further Comments: Your knowledgeable and wise subconscious, operating in an unbiased way, is attempting to guide and protect you. The metaphoric message, produced here in the form of a verbal/visual pun, is for you to return to security, be more real, think the unthinkable, cut losses, start again at ground level if necessary. It is encouraging that, in the dream, you know that you need to descend, and indeed prepare to do so, but it is only the procedure that causes trepidation. It is a matter of being logical, decisive, and bold in order to return to basics.

Interpretation 4

Our own research has revealed that, when there is some confusion about the country in which a dream is set, *sometimes* this can be indicative of a spiritual realm. To confirm this, your subconscious has made it easy by presenting a transparent (crystal?) building in the shape of a church. The fact that it seems to be encrusted with glistening jewels tells us that this is a dream of reassurance. The message is unmistakably clear: you are beginning to 'see through' matters of spirituality to the truth. When your time comes, riches beyond anything in the material world await you in heaven.

Further Comments: This is an interesting dream because it provides a magnificent, inanimate representation of completion. Usually the dream produces coded messages concerning how to deal with ongoing and sometimes very difficult situations. Here we have a self-image of complete spiritual (peak) fulfilment – of preciousness, clarity, and permanence, and all the qualities we associate with priceless jewels. This is not an image that would appear to a person plagued by conflict. No action is required by the dreamer. The spectacular dream image conveys everything. The aged Reverend has had a wonderful glimpse of his own self-worth.

Interpretation 5

Here the subconscious has made excellent use of symbolism to put its message across. As you suspect, this dream is all about examining your situation in life. It is no mistake that it elected to demonstrate this by incorporating an eye (through which to see things). However, if you gaze through high magnification, instead of taking an overview, you will also notice the detailed areas, warts and all (a coarse web we weave in the fabric of life). As the green light indicates natural vibrations, or emotions, the message here suggests that you would do better to stand back and view things with a dispassionate eye. Don't get so close that you are unable to see the wood for the trees, but notice instead all the knots and imperfections, and don't be too self-critical.

Further Comments: Things that are currently on one's mind tend to persist during sleep and form the basis of many dreams. The dream thoughts are not so much disguised as simply using a different kind of language, with valuable comments from the subconscious on the situation. The verbal pun is recognized as a particularly frequent and significant feature in dream construction, and in this dream the eye is also a representation of 'I' – the dreamer.

Eileen needs to avoid excessive self-scrutiny and see things in perspective, without exaggerating any minor anxieties. She should not dwell on inconsequential matters.

Interpretation 6

This is a dream of reassurance. The lonely lane (your path in life) and thick fog suggest that you are feeling vulnerable and perhaps a bit *mys*tified about your future circumstances. Indeed, the large black dog and man in dark clothing represent your concerns about what may lie ahead.

However, because your subconscious has the gift of foresight, instead of being afraid, it is urging you to face these obstacles with a warm heart, for love begets love, and courage begets courage. Share your concerns with somebody close. Sometimes a problem shared can be halved (talk to the man and stroke the dog).

Further Comments: The dreamer is disoriented: a situation which can often proceed to a nightmare. It is a general fact about dreams that what you think, you then dream, so that a fearful thought usually brings about a frightening dream experience. But here, although the scene is set for unpleasantness, the *fog* is followed by a *dog*.

Such phonetic links often occur at crucial points in dreams and encapsulate the metaphor. Caroline has unexpected reserves that she can call on, and, although she is currently in an unclear position about something, she will find the strength from inner resources and perhaps from another person.

Interpretation 7

This is a dream that is likely to recur every time Brian feels that he is faced with the heavy responsibility of an important decision (the weight in his mouth). In his constant efforts to achieve perfect solutions to problems, he is bound to fail because perfection is rarely achieved (trying not to dislodge the blade of grass).

The eggs underpin this interpretation in that the changing expressions represent different problems, which he fears might result in him being led a merry dance, with egg on his face. His subconscious is urging him not to take life too seriously.

Further Comments: Often, the basis of dream interpretation consists of 'spot the well-known saying' in the dream report. If you simply look at the arrangement of words in the dream report, rather than reading to comprehend, keywords of a commonly used phrase may become obvious. Here, the link between egg and face instantly suggests such a metaphor, which then has to be linked carefully to the dreamer's present life-situation. The repeating nature of the dream shows its significance and the need to unravel the message. The dreamer may be too obsessive and needs to recognize and modify that aspect of his personality.

Interpretation 8

This dream reflects your concerns about keeping up with and staying abreast of life. You worry that opportunities might pass you by. The party-goers, all dressed up and ready to go, reflect your anxieties about being left behind. Nevertheless, your subconscious knows better. You should be happy with what you have and worry less about what others might think is right for you (the wardrobe). Slow down, think things through – be more patient! The fact that this dream is recurring suggests that your subconscious is trying hard to get the message across.

Further Comments: A person's current life-situation is so often represented in their dreams. There is no sense of stability, mastery, or control in this dream. Mandy is reacting and producing changes (of clothes) that are not suitable. This reflects the alterations she is considering making in her waking life. Even the year is changing. The sense of panic shows that the dream is giving her a warning about her behaviour. Her subconscious is telling her that she is excessively changeable – to a point where she is perhaps looking foolish to her friends. Mandy certainly needs to cool down, stop being so flighty, and make clear, sensible decisions.

Interpretation 9

Clearly, this dream tells us that, although you are retired, you still put yourself under too much pressure. It is evident that you have always been conscientious and put a lot of effort into what you do, and see things through – sometimes to the point of excess (you feel you ought to stay on to help the company). It seems that you haven't yet learnt how to 'let go' and relax sufficiently. Until you do, this dream is likely to recur. In fact, you state the message behind the dream very well: you are retired; try relaxing just a little more!

Further Comments: The dream of being back in time, e.g. in a house that one lived in years ago, or even being back at school, is often a replaying of anxieties associated with that time which have a relevance to a current situation. In this case there may be an area of anxiety in your present life which is being represented symbolically in this 'time-slip' fashion. You could try complementary medicine. There are many excellent forms of relaxation therapy available nowadays, which are beneficial to both body and mind. Your local alternative-health-store will give you lots of ideas.

Interpretation 10

The linking theme in these dreams is unmistakable: insecurity! The handbag, luggage, keys, and even the buildings you intend entering, are all allied to security. Here your dreams are reflecting that side of your personality to which your subconscious wants you to pay most attention. It does this by presenting you with situations which are almost palpable, to the degree that you feel the need to go downstairs to find your handbag. Resisting these urges will be the first step to overcoming your insecurity and is likely to result in lessening the frequency of these dreams.

Further Comments: The dreamer's insecurity is following her into her dreams and becoming exaggerated, just as some too-busy people continue doing monotonous work in their dreams. Using introspection, Judith should seek to uncover the reasons for her lack of faith in herself and set a programme of restructuring her self-image, using methods of positive thinking. In future, Judith might also be able to recognize that the situation of losing things is a dream and then convert the dream to a lucid type in which she will find that she can control the events to a positive outcome. That sense of mastery will then spill over into wakefulness and improve her self-esteem.

Interpretation 11

Family, friends, and people with whom you felt familiar represent a situation in your life to which you are accustomed. The dream then homes-in unerringly on the central focus: the perfect gentleman to whom you were attracted. He appeared immediately after the main course (emotional sustenance or reassurance from your family), and it is no mistake that you saw him while at the *sweet trolley*. If you follow your present path (the family leaving), as your feelings suggest when you awaken, you are likely to miss the 'right' man. Maintaining the status quo is not suiting you!

Further Comments: Despite what might be consciously thought by an individual about a given situation, the dream comes up with that person's real, deep, considered attitude based on many different factors. The unconscious will put forward its influential and knowledgeable view in the form of dreams, but these are presented in a special visual/verbal language which needs to be translated. The unconscious guides and protects the individual and suggests action that is in the person's best interest. This dream is not about Alison's current boyfriend and is urging her fairly strongly to look elsewhere and find a more suitable and caring partner.

Interpretation 12

This most unusual dream had to be identified as a message-bearer before an interpretation could be attempted. Clearly, it points to Wendy's fear of being alone, especially in the future. Indeed, if we picture the hapless Ruth Ellis in the condemned cell, awaiting death, the central theme of the dream becomes obvious: loneliness. There is also a play on words with the phrase 'hang you'. The word 'you' identifies Wendy. 'Hang' can be allied to time, as in hanging around, and this is where the message behind the dream is revealed: Wendy must devote less time to worrying about what may or may not happen in the future. *This is* her life and she should live more for today!

Further Comments: This dream was interesting because the initial and most obvious approach was not appropriate. Dreams frequently centre on verbal/phonetic play on words. It seemed at first sight that the key to the dream was that someone was being *Ruthless*, but a thorough dream-questionnaire analysis did not support this approach. The personal significance of Ruth Ellis to the dreamer was her final loneliness.

Another possibility was that Wendy experienced a false awakening (where you dream, very realistically, of having woken), but this too was a false lead. The dramatic form of the dream emphasizes the message from Wendy's subconscious mind that she should live a fuller life.

Interpretation 13

This is a fairly common dream, although each dream has a different meaning peculiar to the individual. This is where obtaining background information about the dreamer is crucial. In this respect the crowds of people are a representation of friends and family members. That they are ignoring Mary reflects the fact that these individuals can sometimes seem to be uncaring and too busy getting on with their own lives. In this instance, however, it seems likely to symbolize Mary's feelings and perhaps her reluctance to make the first move. This is the message behind the dream: communicate and ask the way home (metaphorically). Mary is likely to be pleasantly surprised by the response. As with so many dreams of a recurring nature, Mary is likely to experience it until she acknowledges the message from the subconscious and acts upon it!

Further Comments: Readers who submit dreams are sent a copy of the MHQ, which establishes background to the reported dreams, the dreamers, their current lifestyle and matters of their mind. A dream can then be seen in the full context of the individual. This is the only way to interpret a dream properly. Here, the questionnaire shows that the dream reflects a basic long-standing feeling of loss and abandonment. Mary has become rather isolated. However, there are various voluntary organizations that can help people in her situation.

Interpretation 14

This dream is reminding you of happy days when you used to live in London. However, it also serves the purpose of isolating the root cause of the regular, weekly, recurring nature of the dream. The fact that you never reach your destination suggests that, to a degree, as far as your relationship with your husband is concerned, you aren't sure in which direction you need to travel in order to bring you closer together. This is underpinned by the fact that you are looking up timetables and seeing numbers on buses (searching for alternatives). You will find that, if you are able to recapture and share a common interest from the past, these dreams will cease. It is also very important for readers to understand that you do not die if you reach your destination!

Further Comments: There is a constant anxiety on a single theme here, causing the same kind of recurring dream. The underlying problem results in you feeling as though you have lost your way. From the questionnaire data, the likelihood is that your relationship with your husband is the issue. You need to face the matter and discuss with him why you feel that you have lost direction; otherwise, your unconscious will keep presenting the dream. You clearly want a resolution because you are repeatedly trying to find the right 'route' in your dream.

The myth about dying if you reach your destination in a dream is as erroneous as the myth that dreaming of hitting the ground after a fall will result in death.

Interpretation 15

This dream is a classic case of wish fulfilment, but also carries a powerful message from your subconscious. It is no mistake that your dream elected to show you standing beneath the end of a rainbow (the site of the proverbial pot of gold). However, you were not alone: there was an anonymous presence, whose attention you were trying to attract (your subconscious). The fact that there was no reply to your observations indicates that this other representation of yourself was detached and disinterested, which suggests a clear message. Instead of wishing for material riches, be more appreciative of the assets which already exist in your life – the simple things that are a true gauge of one's wealth!

Further Comments: A rainbow has been documented as representing a wide variety of good and bad things in different cultures. In fact, the meaning of the rainbow is personal to the individual, but it seems here to be very positive and linked to joy and fulfilment. It moves across the sky and specifically seeks out *you* – as if you have won the lottery.

This is a clear desire, in view of your financial troubles, but it is a rather unrealistic way of viewing the situation. You can dream of financial salvation, but it will always be a different world when you wake up. Don't live too much in a dream.

Interpretation 16

The nature of this recurring dream echoes your concerns about everyday life: your husband, children, your house, and the fear of becoming a burden as you get older. The dream suggests that you tend to worry unnecessarily about things beyond your control (the grassy slope, the brick wall, the road changing its consistency, grass turfs moving further away, etc.). The fear of water reflects your concern about old age. This dream is likely to persist from time to time unless you stop worrying about events which are out of your control. What will be will be – and that is the message behind the dream.

Further Comments: Basically, in sleep, whatever you *think* you then automatically visualize in the form of a *dream*. Anxious people tend to find their worrying waking thoughts – which continue in sleep – expressed symbolically and graphically. One's progress through life is often, as here, represented by a journey of some kind. The simple, essential thought in this recurring dream is that 'things are becoming more difficult as I move on in life'. Naturally, things do become harder with increasing age, but usually in society compensations are made to assist. Your thoughts are too serious and negative. Actively seek to change your life in order to achieve more social interaction and enjoyment.

Interpretation 17

Unlike a prodromic dream (which gives a forewarning of future illness), this dream is one of comfort and reassurance in that it provides confirmation of a cure. It starts quite frighteningly, with slashes of red across the sky. The blood represents the traumas you have gone through on your way to a cure. However, the three winged angels, who appear like Father Christmas, and the wand and silver disk all represent the magical qualities of the doctors who treated you, and the technology which was used. Staying with that theme, the enormous owls represent the wisdom and knowledge employed by these same individuals. In that sense, this is a healing dream.

Further Comments: The unconscious monitors a vast amount of information about bodily processes and becomes aware of slight alterations from what is usual long before there are any noticeable physical symptoms. It has a problem, though, in communicating such knowledge to the consciousness. The dream is a possible means, but the message has to be recognized as prodromic and deciphered. The unconscious is also aware of reversals of illness, so that an improvement may similarly be detected and represented in a dream – as has happened here. Significant dreams can herald the onset of disease as well as its departure.

Interpretation 18

Here we have one of a variety of different kinds of false awakenings. Usually, it is unwise to attempt an interpretation because false awakenings can be contaminated by conscious thought. However, after close study, it is evident that Enid had no influence on the scene. As false awakenings sometimes have paranormal qualities, it would seem that Enid experienced a spiritual vision. In this instance, the grey sky represents everyday life and problems. However, the area of blue sky (clear sight), the disk (the circle of life), and the hands (comfort and security) all translate into positive omens of reassurance amid the grey. It would seem that Enid has a guardian angel looking after her.

Further Comments: Sometimes, dream imagery persists for a short while after waking (hypnopompic state). Another condition is the false awakening, where you *dream* that you have woken. In some false awakenings, the dreamer is convinced of being awake – everything in the bedroom is so perfectly real – but there are give-away clues, e.g. a bedside lamp which will not work (this is the universally reported light-switch effect), or floating down slowly if you jump off some steps. Interestingly, the level of critical consciousness and awareness matches that of wakefulness. Some people even report 'waking up' several times in succession!

Interpretation 19

This dream reflects the guilt you carry (perhaps unconsciously) that you had your children too early in life and might not have ministered enough to them. It is no mistake that it started after you found yourself in a stable relationship, and it reflects your thoughts that perhaps you were too busy to give enough time to your own offspring. However, the fact that, in your dream, you did force yourself to make time indicates that, when you were a young mother, you did your best under the circumstances. That is the message behind the dream: don't feel guilty! If you acknowledge and accept this message from your subconscious, the dream will stop bothering you.

Further Comments: The unconscious has its own visual-symbolic language, and its vocabulary is linked to the experiences of the individual. The symbolism here, though, is relatively straightforward to comprehend. The nourishment referred to is representative of emotional love, caring, attention, etc. concerning the family. Valerie's second marriage triggered unconscious thoughts and feelings that have continued trying to express themselves for years. Guilt is a strong motivator and has provided, here, the driving energy behind the recurring dream. Now that the dream theme is exposed, Valerie needs to think the matter through and indulge in a little self-forgiveness.

Interpretation 20

Your feelings of despair as you search in vain for things you cannot find, or are unable to identify, demonstrates that you are, indeed, a worrier. In addition, the fact that you feel accountable to a third party (symbolized by your son) suggests that you tend to be too anxious about what other people might think. This illustrates a degree of low self-esteem, as does feeling terrible over failure when you wake up.

Your dream is urging you to stop worrying over issues that don't really concern you (signified by missing objects that belong to somebody else). Clearly, it is time for you to pay more attention to yourself. Perhaps you could begin with a small treat, such as a hair-do.

Further Comments: Such recurring dreams are an annoyance consciously because they repeatedly put the dreamer through a discomforting experience. It may be purely illusory, but the dream, while it lasts, *is* reality, and so the accompanying emotions and thoughts tend to persist into wakefulness. The effects of a dream can last all day.

It has been discovered that there are certain predominant personality traits in individuals who have unpleasant dreams. These people tend, strangely, to be emotional, apprehensive, and tense. Here, the dreamer should work on the underlying problems of self-esteem and anxiety. Hypnotherapy can work wonders in such cases.

Interpretation 21

There are important keywords and metaphors in this dream which reveal that, to a certain extent, you miss the good old days. However, you possess the wherewithal (the key) to enjoy life more (the daylight). Your old house represents memories of happier times before your children were born (they are missing in the dream). You are alone with your husband in the kitchen, a place where sustenance (mental stimulation) is prepared. The fact that you are aware of the risk of being caught suggests daring. Therefore your subconscious is letting you know that you hold the key to a happier life. Be a little more daring – like you used to be.

Further Comments: When a particular dream crops up occasionally, the unconscious is dwelling on an unresolved issue in the dreamer's life. The theme of revisiting a place – which might be a former home, school, or workplace – points to a significant comparison being made between the present and the past by way of similarities or contrasts. Some event or thought in the day may stir the mental or emotional link, thus triggering the dream. Sometimes the dream regression looks longingly on a previous situation, and this seems to be the case with this subject.

Interpretation 22

Dolphins are often associated with psychic ability, specifically healing. The clouds tinged with gold, parting to reveal a vivid blue sky, represent a higher realm (your spiritual side). Your brother, who is not interested, symbolizes the masculine side (left hemisphere of the brain) of your personality, which is allied to cold calculation and logic. The dream is telling you that, to advance spiritually with healing, you must, to some extent, ignore logic and employ more right-brain thinking, associated with emotion, intuition, and following your heart. This will result in a new birth or advancement in your healing abilities, which is represented by the mother, baby, and the water (another spiritual association).

Further Comments: The language of the dream is pictorial. Changes of scene in dreams are very meaningful and indicate strong links between the before-and-after items in the imagery. These shifts can actually now be scientifically studied using hypnotic dreams. It has been discovered that the various pictorial elements simply become rearranged instead of being completely replaced, so that the dream progresses by a 'law of least effort'. Thus the dolphin image transforms into the mother, who is really a projection of the dreamer. The baby is a developing, spiritual part of the dreamer that should be carefully nurtured.

Interpretation 23

The contradiction of being established somewhere, yet just visiting, symbolizes a nonpermanent situation (your life circumstances). Your husband, whom you only think is there, reflects your uncertainty concerning the security of his job. The door, which is locked, or which you fear will trigger an explosion, represents a doorway to the future and perhaps another way of life. Having no make-up (material possessions) to take with you demonstrates the futility of worrying over your husband's position. Your subconscious is telling you to cross each bridge when you come to it. You might be pleasantly surprised.

Further Comments: Dreams mull over matters of concern or interest to the individual, but, in sleep, those thoughts which are verbal in nature become translated into a very different visual symbolic form because a separate part of the brain is used. The consequent images make sense to the unconscious but are not easily understood when the 'coded' version is recalled on waking. Dorothy's repeated dream thoughts, resulting in the same dream pictures, reflect a continuing condition of uncertainty and anxiety in her life. The conflict between being settled ('down to stay' or 'to sleep') and unsettled (emotionally and 'visiting') generates the dream circumstances.

Interpretation 24

Your subconscious has cleverly used a former work environment which you disliked to enable the dream to be identified with an ongoing situation in your life. It is evident that you feel responsible for somebody who is close to you, which is symbolized by the children waiting to be served dinner (drawing sustenance, or energy, from you). This person seems to be relying on you to the point where he/she takes you for granted. Unless you stop pandering to the needs of others, life will pass you by (the race against time). Make more time to enjoy yourself.

Further Comments: People in stressful jobs often spend hours in their dreams being hard at work and under great pressure. The dream is reality while it lasts, so it causes even more stress, undermines the quality of sleep, and is unpaid!

Mrs S. is still working in her dreams long after she has actually left her employment, but the original stressful circumstances no longer exist. Therefore it seems likely that she feels similarly stressed but in different present circumstances. The dream calls for action from her to remove pressures in her life. It's a pity she cannot claim overtime!

Interpretation 25

In dreams, a house sometimes symbolizes a house, while at other times it can symbolize the dreamer. The presence of the number nine (a mystical number) suggests that we are indeed dealing with a symbolic representation of Frederick. This is underpinned by the appearance of a railway line, which, in this instance, symbolizes Frederick's journey through life and beyond. The flowers suggest the rewards Frederick has gained through his life (as we sow, so shall we reap). The old man gazing at Frederick represents the dreamer himself. Therefore the message behind the dream is that Frederick should concentrate on what he has already achieved and try to cultivate those accomplishments rather more.

Further Comments: At times when one's mortality is considered, the introspection often results in such a spiritual self-assessment dream. The number nine probably represents the dreamer's name, which also has nine letters.

The dreamer explores the house (which does not belong to him) without feeling that he has to seek permission because it is indeed a visual model of his own psyche. There is a certain solidity or steadfastness (the stone material), and the place is modest, but there are many beautiful and positive aspects in the dreamer's soul – even though an amount of disorganization or preparedness exists.

Interpretation 26

If you look back over your life, it is pretty certain that this dream would have occurred just before a landmark event, e.g. starting school, puberty, marriage, retirement. In fact, it is also likely to have visited you at times when you were faced with a significant challenge. The lion (king of the jungle) sometimes represents savagery and power. However, the fact that, in this instance, it appeared to be friendly and docile symbolizes inner strength and courage.

Therefore, each time you had this dream, it constituted a message from your subconscious, underpinning your will and determination to meet head-on, and overcome, any significant hazard or challenge that you found yourself facing.

Further Comments: In wakefulness, as well as in dreams, many people hold an auto-symbolic image which may appear from time to time and seems to be a visual analogy signifying their basic frame of mind. A visual image, say, of Concorde soaring into the sky, may occasionally represent itself to a 'high-flying' individual, particularly when things are going well. Colin's image of a lion appeared even as a small child and perhaps reflects an innate temperament. It did not frighten him because it was recognized as an aspect of himself.

Interpretation 27

In this instance, the house serves two distinct purposes: it symbolizes an actual house (security), while at the same time being a reflection of Anne's unconscious thoughts about her life circumstances. The narrow tunnels, being in the upper part of the house, reflect a certain amount of narrow thinking with regard to security. The disproportionately large cellar suggests hidden dreams that are not realistic.

The fact that Anne put on a brave face indicates that she feels trapped in a rut. Therefore the message behind the dream is for her to be more open-minded in recognizing the blessings she already has and to have a more positive attitude towards the future.

Further Comments: Questionnaire information has highlighted the particular topics of present concern for the dreamer. Financial problems can undermine our security considerably, and those anxious thoughts of wakefulness continue during sleep. In dreams, they are transformed into the right-brain language of images; hence this disturbing construction. The dream has probably greatly exaggerated the matter, describing the 'worst-case' scenario, graphically and worryingly, in order for the dreamer to realize that things in her life are not really as bad as they seem.

Interpretation 28

If Sandra looks back to the time when she had the dream, it is likely to have occurred around the period of a family upheaval, in which she was hurt fairly deeply. The pub represents a place of social gathering, and the presence of her mother and aunt ties it down to a family situation. The sea symbolizes Sandra's life situation, which had been calm. The sudden arrival of the meteor (like a bolt from the blue) created a large hole (in her life) into which people were gazing (various aspects of Sandra's own psyche). The search for a police station suggests that Sandra sought comfort from an authority figure, but to no avail. The message here is that there is a need to forgive so that healing can take place.

Further Comments: It may be that an interesting verbal pun directed the events in this dream. An observing part of the mind notices the arrangement of people and objects in dreams, so, when considering the seating positions in the pub, relative to her mother and aunt, the internal thought could have been 'me to your right' (sounding like 'meteorite'). That phonetic link would have acted as an instruction to her mind to produce such a scene. The event then dramatically depicted an upheaval in the dreamer's life, centring on her mother or aunt, with the help of a verbal trick.

Interpretation 29

Our own research has revealed that confusion about which country is featured can sometimes indicate spiritual connotations. A mere glance at the dream's entire content confirms this to be the case here. At the time of the dream, it is likely that Donald's health was threatened. The dancing maidens, particularly the one in black, were telling him that his time had not yet come. He would be needed to continue unfinished business in this life – perhaps caring for his wife. Nevertheless, the dream also demonstrates that a loving environment awaits him when he dies.

Further Comments: The imagery of elevation – mountains, a castle, and its ramparts – here symbolizes achievement and higher developments of the soul. And Donald knew the steps of the dance of life.

Interpretation 30

This dream is taking you back to the more unhappy times of your life. It is apparent that you often give thought to those days and have regrets. However, there is a positive message behind your dream. Your subconscious is trying to tell you not to dwell in the past. What is done is done! The fact that you find yourself trying to clean a dirty house suggests that you are trying to find ways in which to put life's house in order. The presence of deceased family members unmistakably symbolizes past upsets. However, they are ignoring your efforts, which suggests that what you are doing is not the important thing. You can't go back, so there is no house *to* put in order. The fact that they were laughing indicates that forgiving and healing has taken place, so don't worry about the past.

Further Comments: A recurring dream is restating a thought that constantly protrudes into consciousness and is portrayed visually – not to disguise and deceive, but simply because the language of dreams is visual. The imagery is often based on a simple verbal word or phrase. 'I need to put my house in order' seems to be the underlying thought here, but the message needs to get through to Frances that the past is the past. The early years have a profound effect on us, and in dreams it is still childhood, or any other time in which we find ourselves. Frances can cut free now.

Interpretation 31

First, the beautiful furniture and decor represent the appreciation of material wealth and possessions. You were admiring the way in which your friends had improved your old house. This suggests that, in waking life, you are now beginning to develop a desire to obtain such things. However, this dream comes with a warning! If you link the fact that the attic (symbolizing your mind) was devoid of furniture (material wealth) with your newfound confidence in your potential, it becomes clear that you should not be too eager too soon. However, the dream shows that, if you are patient and follow your present course, the rewards (lovely views) will come.

Further Comments: A house in a dream can have several possible meanings. Here it is referring to the body/mind of the dreamer. The dream has cleverly manoeuvred the story so that Helen can 'revisit', or review, herself. The dream is on the theme of enrichment – although the enlarged kitchen may refer to a physical increase in size. The attic (mind) has a good prospect, but requires more content, i.e. information. Through various courses, Helen will advance her own 'domestic (i.e. personal) management'.

Interpretation 32

The clue here is that you find your dreams peaceful because they have elements that most people would find frightening: being lost and away from home. Your subconscious is telling you that there is a need in your life for some sort of feeling of completion. The market place, bus stops, the beautiful scene, and the industrial area each represent periods of your life that had significance; the brick wall symbolizes your life itself (steady and reliable). The need to get home reflects a desire finally to establish your position in life. The message is clear: look back in fond remembrance and realize that, perhaps in subtle ways, you most certainly *have* made your mark. The peaceful manner in which these dreams are perceived reflects your serene heart.

Further Comments: A dream is often a metaphor, commenting, in visual form, on some aspect of the dreamer's life that is unresolved. The resulting production may seem a little odd because the dream has to convert a verbal thought into a symbolic, observable form. The other main consideration about dreams is the accompanying emotion or feeling, which does not have to be 'converted' and so is a good indicator of the basic nature of the dream. Here, the feeling of peace is positive, and the seeking is for personal wholeness – but in fact much has been achieved.

Interpretation 33

Your subconscious has cleverly elected to include your work situation in order to alert you to a relationship problem you already suspect. There is a definite link between your ex-boyfriends and your current partner (they didn't look like they should have, and your boyfriend's clothes kept changing). These deceptive appearances suggest a common theme which could involve some sort of duplicity. In other words, your dream is confirming that you are indeed being shut out, or kept in the dark. You should seek advice from a reliable third party (the consultant).

Further Comments: Technically, the analysis looked at the progression of ideas which here are clearly based on the word 'out' – (patients) leading on to the *out-* or ex-boyfriends. But here the dreamer herself has been added to the list of patients, strongly indicating her own sense of being excluded. The dreamer may have finished too many relationships in the past for no real reason. The ex-boyfriends were essentially saying, 'Now how do you feel, being outside?' The current boyfriend's changing clothing shows that he is too changeable – something the dreamer has tried not to see in the past. These are not good signs for the relationship.

Interpretation 34

This dream definitely reflects your concerns about employment. First, you leave the safety of the 'bank' (you work in a bank) to wade across a river (a possible hazard or new path in life). The alligators merely represent your fears of not keeping up with your husband as regards doing your bit. Also you were worried that you wouldn't be able to get back to the 'bank' (or place of security). However, your subconscious is bringing you a positive message: don't worry, because no matter what happens, you are on solid ground (the granite riverbed), and you are not in 'deep water'. Things bode well for the future.

Further Comments: The absolute necessity to have background information concerning the dreamer's life is illustrated here. That is why people who submit dreams are given the unique and specially designed comprehensive MHQ to complete and return before an interpretation is attempted. 'Leaving the bank' is the crucial metaphor in this case, based on the supplied information about the dreamer's employment. The dreamer's mind is, in sleep, running a 'translated' pictorial dramatization of a situation that could arise. Leaving the reassuring routine of a job can create anxiety in people. Words said in dreams are particularly significant, and the final exclamation here is directly applicable to the dreamer's waking concern.

Interpretation 35

Sometimes, buildings in a dream can be a representation of ourselves. In this instance, the staircase, large rooms, and twisty corridors symbolize Vera's path through life. The factory benches and machinery represent tasks that have to be performed along the way. The fact that there are always lots of people – often girls – who seem to belong, whereas Vera feels left out, provides a valuable clue. This suggests that Vera looks back on her life with regret, perhaps envying what other people have achieved. The message behind the dream is hidden in Vera's final remark: she should confide in a trustworthy person about her regrets. She is then likely to count her blessings.

Further Comments: This is a dream that is urging change in the dreamer. The buildings themselves are large and spacious, representing a generally comfortable situation in life, but the dreamer feels she has not been involved enough in life and has merely 'wandered around'. This is an unresolved matter that needs addressing. Counselling would enable Vera to express and come to terms with her regrets. She may then decide to become more involved, e.g. by helping others. Certainly, she should start to look at the greater perspective beyond the material world and concentrate on her spiritual development.

Interpretation 36

Here we have a connection between ballet dancers and a film star, all of whom have performed in works of fiction. If we now link both scenes, a further association concerning 'the heart' is established, and this ties in neatly with Robert's recent interest in creative writing (fiction). The message, therefore, is that, for Robert to succeed in this field, he must resist the temptation to write in an aggressive style (the thrown punch). Instead, he would do better to concentrate on trying to write with emotion (from the heart).

Further Comments: Verbal links predominate in the construction of dreams, especially the first letters of words. The surnames of the two actors seen in the dream correspond to Robert's surname, indicating that they reflect two different aspects of the dreamer: 'in my house' (i.e. body). The topic uppermost in Robert's mind at the time – his writing – is reflected in the appearance of well-known persons on the 'set' (settee), and the recent day residue of having seen the ballet on stage has influenced the dream's production. Robert's unconscious is giving advice on how he should progress in his newfound interest.

Interpretation 37

It is fascinating to observe how Sheila's dream has cleverly used her fear of flying to alert her to a powerful message from her subconscious. We all know that flying is perhaps the safest means of transport. Therefore the fear of flying is irrational. In addition, the chances of an aircraft falling from the sky and hitting somebody are extremely remote – another irrational fear. So we are dealing with perhaps two irrational fears that Sheila has in her life, which we can help to pinpoint. As she was detached from the dream situation, she must look for a third party, someone who regards him/herself as a bit of a high-flyer, or has a 'top-of-the-pile' attitude; somebody, too, whom Sheila suspects is in for a fall. It would seem that she has an irrational fear of being caught up in the fall-out. The message is clear: don't worry, the chances of that happening are remote, get on with life as usual.

Further Comments: Many people dream of seeing plane crashes, but these dreams are only rarely premonitions. The key to the basis of this dream is the amount of shock and anguish felt by witnessing the events. The emotions have been 'lifted' from the dreamer's recent life experiences, but the symbolism metaphorically concerns someone else (usually close) who is going to 'crash' in some way. This could mean a 'fall from grace', say, or the consequence of the breakdown of a relationship. Certainly the event would be upsetting to the dreamer. But here, like a plane crash, the event is actually unlikely to happen.

Interpretation 38

It would seem that Alyson has borne much responsibility in her life. Sometimes buildings can represent the dreamer, but in this instance the block of offices and the streets of houses symbolize arduous responsibilities. It appears as if Alyson has spent much of her life solving one problem after another – more than usual. Her desire to be free from responsibility and worry is clearly evident. And that is the message behind the dream: she would benefit greatly if she learnt to let go of the past and relax. In doing so, she could finally find her way through and attain the feeling of freedom for which she craves.

Further Comments: People with recurring dreams have a great opportunity to recognize that the situation is in fact a dream and can then alter the dream – simply by thought – to a pleasant outcome. Alyson should tell herself before sleep that, if she finds herself in the 'office' dream, she will immediately stop, become calm, and remember that it is only a dream. At that point she should become 'lucid', i.e. aware of being in a dream. Dreams can then be easily controlled – what you think you will then dream – so, if she 'closes' her (dream) eyes and 'wishes' herself to a lovely location, she will find herself there!

Interpretation 39

Ingeniously, to put its message across, Doreen's dream played on her anticipation of visiting London. The large apartment and guests suggest a degree of pleasant social interaction. This is confirmed by a play on words, in that it was a Jewish home: *'Je'* meaning 'I' plus 'wish'. The theme continues with the appearance of moussaka, which is usually a communal dish. Greece, too, is renowned for its close-knit social gatherings. All these elements point to a desire to mix and form new friendships. This suggests that Doreen is somewhat lonely. The appearance of the cassettes, which are eaten as if they are a bitter pill to swallow, symbolizes past relationships that have dwindled away (a record of Doreen's life). Her subconscious is urging her to make new contacts with whom she will be able to fraternize.

Further Comments: Dreams often look forward to forthcoming events. The impending visit to London was on Doreen's mind and provided the setting. The unconscious mind then came up with its own flow of associations concerning that trip. As we know, dreams build on subtle verbal connections which point to meaningful links that need to be recognized in the interpretation. The word 'moussaka' was important because it was spoken by the dreamer. It is similar, phonetically, to the word 'music', which perhaps was represented by the tapes and could here relate to significant past social situations. The dream touched on Doreen's concern about becoming isolated.

Interpretation 40

In this instance, the hospital symbolizes two things: a busy hospital and your present life-situation (people around you always seem to be engaged in their own lives). The fact that you were unable to get up and could only move slowly reflects your arthritic condition. Your feeling of dejection suggests that, after being in a caring profession most of your life, perhaps you now feel that the system has let you down. However, the introduction of the very ill patient is to remind you of the priorities which the British health service has to consider at the present moment. Keep your chin up!

Further Comments: Dreams present scenarios which are right-brain metaphors or puns based on left-brain thoughts. If a message needs to get across to consciousness, the events are more exaggerated and unlikely. The emotional elements of the dream's communication, though, are real and unchanged. Here, the dejection and sense of being ignored are genuine and establish the key to the dream's meaning. The metaphor appears of 'lacking support' (probably emotional), resulting in the dreamer falling. The dreamer's unconscious is indicating an anxiety, but one which can be acted on. Practically, Phyllis should make efforts to have more involvement with people, perhaps the disadvantaged.

Interpretation 41

This dream appears to serve two distinct purposes: to provide reassurance and to foretell the future. Occasionally, we all consider the issue of death, more so as we get older. Here, it is evident that Margaret also speculates about it. However, the state of the houses on the building site clearly suggests that she still has many years ahead of her (there is much business yet to be completed). Nevertheless, when her time does come, it is likely to be quick and painless.

Further Comments: Most people pursued by a gunman in a dream or reality would be frantic, but Margaret almost revels in this repeated pain-free, play-acting simulation. The dream is 'prospective' – anticipating the final event in the dreamer's life – and the nature of the dream reveals that Margaret has an inquisitive and positive attitude toward death. Nevertheless, she is rather too concerned with such eventualities. The here-and-now needs to be addressed. Margaret should make attempts to be more involved in living life now. She is ahead of herself.

Interpretation 42

Assuming that the subconscious is our friend during REM sleep, this sort of nightmare becomes easier to understand. Nightmares serve a variety of purposes, among which are to give warnings, to bring powerful messages, and to confront pain. In psychology it is sometimes acknowledged that confronting one's pain can be used as a healing tool. In this instance, it seems likely that Sarah's subconscious continually brings her these dreams in order to somewhat desensitize her.

Further Comments: These dreams are false awakenings – where the setting seems totally realistic. Images of masses of small creatures are a form constant which is also seen in the DTs!

Since the problem is recurring and seems to be linked with Sarah's phobia, she should perhaps consult a hypnotherapist who can uncover the source of her problem concerning spiders and cobwebs. Once the link is established, and the original situation, with its emotions, has been processed, the fear will have been exorcized. If Sarah can tell herself in the dream that seeing spiders means that she is dreaming, then that opens the door to her enjoying controllable, lucid dreams.

Interpretation 43

The large house symbolizes your life, each room having its own significance. The grand staircase represents an uphill struggle through life. The triangular room suggests family concerns (eternal triangle). The bathroom indicates your feelings about yourself, both mental and physical. The oval room, with its large windows, is a symbol of your psyche; each window represents a different outlook on life. In other words, your dream is telling you that these areas are in need of a make-over, and you have the knowledge of how to go about it.

Further Comments: Ideas and images in dreams progress along pathways by associations. Here, the mention of different sizes (small, large) and shapes (triangular to oval) links to the general concept of 'sizing up' the dreamer's life situations.

The overall feeling of a dream is the main indicator of its message. Here, the final attitude is a positive one: of being confident of improving things. Dorothy is recognizing the changes that need to be made in her life, and her unconscious is showing her that she has the necessary motivation and resources.

Interpretation 44

Our research has revealed that, when there is confusion about the country in which a dream is set, this can sometimes be indicative of a spiritual realm. And here we have a classic case, which addresses Daphne's concerns about life.

In short, this dream is serving the purpose of providing reassurance. Daphne's subconscious is telling her that, whatever happens in life, another, much nicer place awaits us.

Further Comments: A good dream can really make your day, and this beautiful creation of Daphne's unconscious was meant to be encouraging. The complementary colours of blue and yellow, and the sparkling pure water, provided a wonderful sense of well-being and joy, probably contrasting strongly with Daphne's current waking state of mind concerning her son. The dream is actually providing a perspective for the dreamer. The mood engendered by the dream serves to show that there is great happiness, both in life and beyond.

Interpretation 45

This is a common dream, and different schools of thought place a variety of so-called 'universal meanings' on it. For example, a Freudian analyst would have a field-day claiming that there is some sort of repressed desire on the part of these dreamers to expose themselves in public. A Jungian would probably suggest that the subject has a basic need that should be fulfilled. A Gestalt workshop would look at it from the viewpoint that a toilet represents the dreamer herself! In reality, they would be wrong because, in the Western world, dreams are specific to the individual. In this particular instance, it is clear that Doreen's subconscious is cleverly alerting her to the fact that she does indeed need to use the toilet and is acting like an alarm clock. However, it does so in such a way as to prevent her from having an unfortunate accident in bed.

Further Comments: Freud said that the purpose of the dream was to keep you asleep, but he was wrong. Dreams like this, and message-bearing dreams, deliberately wake you up, either to alert you to a physical discomfort or to try to present a significant dream that needs to be decoded.

Doreen's unconscious mind, which protects her, woke her in the only way it could: by deliberately engineering a state of agitation that would automatically rouse her. Similarly, when the bedcovers have slipped off and your body becomes cold, you may have a bad dream designed to awaken you.

Interpretation 46

To begin with, the dark rooms represent different aspects of Renate's life (her station in life), and the people passing through symbolize individuals whom she has encountered. That the rooms have no windows and are in relative darkness suggests that Renate doesn't believe that her outlook is bright – she feels in a rut! In this instance, her ability to fly reflects her desire to free herself and perhaps explore the world outside. Her response of feeling reassured at not being noticed suggests that she has hidden depths. The rooms being void of furniture echo her present feeling of being in a rut (void of worth). She has the know-how and potential to put the wheels in motion to achieve her goals – almost without being noticed.

Further Comments: Dreams reflect our personalities. This is not the dream of an extrovert, outgoing person; the dreamer is sensitive to criticism and practises things before displaying them. Renate probably has an embryonic project in the back of her mind, such as a course of study. It is 'in the dark' at the moment, but her unconscious, which guides her, from time to time attempts to prod her into action. There is a message here because of the dream's repeating nature. Renate should introspect carefully and allow the wise advice from within to emerge.

Interpretation 47

The big seas threatening to overwhelm you symbolize life with all its challenges. Similarly, war breaking out represents upheaval in your life. The bombers suggest that, at the time these dreams occur, there is nowhere to run and hide from certain issues. The erupting volcano continues the theme and possibly mirrors your feelings over certain issues concerned with the upbringing of your children. This is underpinned because, in each dream, although you try to get packed (get your life organized) and find your children (on a mental level), you are unable to do this. It seems that the message behind these dreams is for you to slow down, calm down, and take stock during periods of uncertainty. You will then be more likely to find a way forward (find your children and get packed).

Further Comments: A repeating dream is a re-going-over of significant and usually worrying thoughts that are on the mind of the dreamer. It is dealing with unresolved business. The emotions present – here a general anxiety – tend to come through unaltered by the symbolization procedure in dreams. Fay has taken her responsibility for bringing up her three girls very seriously, but she is still fixated in the past. It would help if she were to indulge in complementary-medicine relaxation techniques.

Interpretation 48

This common dream can have myriad meanings specific to each individual, from not being able to get one's teeth into a project, losing face, or fear of going to the dentist to losing one's will to deal with a problem and even losing one's grip. The interpretations are almost endless. However, in this instance, when linked with Maureen's remarks about bruxism (teeth-grinding) – which occurs during SWS – it seems likely that it is connected. Therefore it would be unwise to attempt a detailed interpretation. Suffice it to suggest that Maureen might be harbouring some hidden aggression or anxiety.

Further Comments: There are two distinct and alternating states in sleep: SWS, in which muscular activity is possible (including teeth-grinding), and REM, or dreaming, sleep, in which the body is completely paralysed (except for breathing, which is automatic). We suggest that dreams of losing teeth are sometimes a direct representation in dreaming sleep of the bruxism of SWS, but, of course, in REM sleep no grinding actually occurs. Usually, teeth-grinding is associated with suppressed anger, frustration, and worry. In this case we would recommend hypno-analysis to uncover the personal cause of this distressing, recurring dream.

Interpretation 49

The clue here comes from the fact that this dream has stayed with Barbara since childhood and has a 'holy' feel about it. In this instance, the sandy place symbolizes the sands of time (her journey through life). The corridor and classroom represent a place of spiritual learning (she has to remove her shoes). This is reinforced by the way in which the men are clothed. The fact that the scroll is in a foreign tongue underpins a spiritual element and suggests that, because she is able to interpret it, Barbara has hidden depths of spirituality, and perhaps deep understanding and intuition. The dream is reassuring Barbara that life is eternal, and humanity still has much to learn.

Further Comments: Close to being a universal symbol, an as yet unvisited, or foreign, place is – to the unconscious – the existence beyond death. At a deep level, there is a knowledge that we are here on earth but that an inevitable transition to that place will one day occur. Hence, symbolically, foreignness in dreams, and in art, can often refer to that 'other' location and our personal belief system around it. The men present probably allude to the concept of mankind, but the older man may represent someone close and of high status to the dreamer – perhaps her deceased father, who is already in the foreign place.

Interpretation 50

Again we are dealing with a spiritual dream. The uncertainty of the dream's foreign location is the first clue. The Biblical-looking ravine, the sunshine, and the well-lit statue of the black Madonna and child reinforce this analysis. The fact that Erika sensed that she was the Madonna is very significant indeed. It is thought that black Madonnas, which are surprisingly common, are the true representation of spirituality; white Madonnas appeared much later. The powerful message of reassurance behind the dream is that each one of us encompasses part of God and that life is eternal!

Further Comments: A significant thought in a dream – usually the 'message' or underlying theme – often causes immediate waking because the unconscious is deliberately attempting to communicate (in one of the few ways it can) to the consciousness. The dream, though, is speaking another language – an ancient visual and symbolic form of communication – so it needs to be deciphered. A deep spiritual realization has been understood and accepted by Erika's unconscious, and it will affect her greatly. It needed to break through into her consciousness.

Interpretation 51

In this instance, the beach represents your present standing in life. However, the sea symbolizes your life in the past. The dismembered Jack Russell terrier points to upheaval in the present (ear and leg on the beach), caused by a past event (the dog's head in the water). Wanting to swim in a warm, calm sea reflects a desire to get back to a pleasant status quo. However, you find yourself in a basement (feeling low) with crowds of people (associates?) and your slimy suitcase (troubles from the past), waiting for a plane (new opportunity). The dream is telling you that, to move on successfully, you must leave the baggage of the past behind and go forward with a fresh approach, using new ideas.

Further Comments: Dream construction is very deliberate and uses devices such as associations, puns, and metaphors. This life-review dream is cleverly alluding to unpleasant past situations in which the dreamer may have 'lost her head'. There are links between the dreamer, the dead dog, and the contents of the suitcase. But the consequence is that the sea (or what you 'see') is now contaminated. The slimy 'luggage' is clearly something which needs to be discarded. The future can be better, given a new attitude.

Interpretation 52

Message-bearing dreams serve many purposes, among which are to provide warnings, reminders, guidance, and, as in this case, reassurance. In this instance, Betty's dream does not require detailed study because a consistent theme is easily identified. In effect, the dream is saying, 'Don't worry about the consequences of ill health. Whatever happens, life continues after death, where you will be reunited with friends and loved ones.'

Further Comments: Dreams can be so real and vivid that they can have the same effect as if the events actually happened – and they can influence the dreamer strongly throughout the day. They are the products of our own, superb, built-in 'virtual-reality' system. Dreams like Betty's have a powerful comforting and healing effect. They occur universally and help us cope with the prospect of physical extinction and other unpleasant thoughts. Such dreams also happen after a death, when the deceased person is often seen in the dreams of family and friends, healthy and happy in the next place after earthly life.

Interpretation 53

Dreams are specific to each dreamer and so is symbolism. However, the symbolic meaning of sickness and feces comes extremely close to having universal meanings – and this seems to be the case here. The senses that are affected by witnessing these scenes – taste, smell, sound, and sight – often make the dreamer wince with feelings of disgust, which are usually rooted in the past. If Mrs W. can cast her mind back to an unpleasant, perhaps traumatic, experience in her childhood and can confront the pain of the memory, these dreams are likely to cease and stop bothering her.

Further Comments: When a trauma happens, part of our mind remains 'trapped in time' at that day and may even influence us decades later. In therapy, that original event can sometimes be 'uncovered', and a healing may then occur. If the event cannot be recalled, one simple technique is to sit quietly, with palms upwards, and imagine the problem (disgust, in this instance) in one hand and the mind's (unknown) solution in the other. Gradually, perhaps over minutes, the hands will come together as an unconscious and automatic healing process begins to take place. Readers, please let us know of your success with this method.

Interpretation 54

At the time, this was a precognitive dream (foretelling the future). In this instance, the Pegasus-like creature symbolized speed of advancement, strength, and nobility. The fact that you could hide in your greatcoat suggests a place of safety. Add to that the horse entering your secure domain and wrapping you in his whiteness (purity and joy), and your feeling of happiness, and we can see that this was a dream of reassurance for the future.

Further Comments: A good dream can 'make your day', but some dreams – like this one – affect the dreamer for life. Here, it provided a symbolic 'self-image', which many of us have – manifesting in daydreams and dreams. Nowadays the image may be, say, a positive one of a high-flying plane. In this case it was a more traditional image of strength and spirituality.

Interpretation 55

The crying girl symbolizes Deirdre when she was younger and more innocent (the golden hair and white dress). This is confirmed because she is dead – Deirdre has lost that naïveté, which is characteristic of many younger women. The fact that she points to the wardrobe and mentions her fear of ghosts suggests that Deirdre, like many of us, has a skeleton in her closet that is never far away. However, the fact that she feels at peace indicates that this skeleton was not of her own making. The message, therefore, is that she needs to share her secret with a sympathetic ear.

Further Comments: Seeming to wake up in a realistic bedroom setting, i.e. a false awakening, is often accompanied by figures seen at the foot of the bed and forms the basis of many ghost stories. There may conceivably be a paranormal element, but dream figures are often symbolic representations of the dreamer and other people significant to the dreamer. 'Aliens' (i.e. alien, or split-off, aspects of the dreamer's personality) tend to be seen more nowadays. Sometimes the dreamer experiences real paralysis, but this simply reflects the natural bodily paralysis of REM, or dreaming, sleep.

Interpretation 56

Dreams often play on words, and this is a good example. The warm, sunny day and beach scene tell us that we are dealing with something appealing – perhaps a pursuit that you have considered taking up that carries a risk? You can see (sea) the sense in meeting the challenge (you test the water). However, there are doubts, symbolized by the fact that you cannot reach the shore: you are unsure ('un'-shore). It would appear that your subconscious is cautioning you not to get into deep water!

Further Comments: A recurring dream is like a persistent reminder letter: it needs dealing with. This is effectively a warning dream, and your unconscious feels that the matter is significant enough to alert you to its visual dramatization by causing you to wake. The metaphor contains the message. The fact that you are on the nearby beach indicates that the topic which needs a solution concerns you and a local situation. It seems that you feel you need help to extricate yourself from something that was enjoyable at first, but which you now realize is becoming decidedly unpleasant.

Interpretation 57

This dream clearly points to two choices in your life, both on a romantic theme. The field symbolizes your present position, and the man at the nearest opening represents your present relationship. The presence of the man at the farthest opening (opportunity) suggests that you have the chance of a new relationship. However, it would seem that your subconscious has identified an unacceptable risk if you follow that path. Return to your present partner and get things between you sorted out.

Further Comments: When it comes to making decisions, it is sensible to take the advice of your unconscious, which attempts to guide you. It has access to much more information than is available consciously. The problem is how to convey that knowledge to your awareness. Dreams are the main vehicle, but the underlying thoughts cannot be transferred directly because they use a different 'language' – representational imagery – which requires decoding. Here, the solution to a personal dilemma is simply and dramatically illustrated.

Interpretation 58

In this instance, the word 'home' symbolizes the end of your journey through life. The coaches and cars represent your drive and purpose in life, and in this particular instance, the friends and family represent exactly that: friends and family who have become part of your life along the way. The fact that you are unable to find them, or your way home, signifies that these particular people have already passed on (they have gone without you). Therefore, although it is nice to bring them to mind occasionally, try not to dwell in the past too much. Look for new challenges.

Further Comments: In any dream where there is a recurring situation, the dreamer can actually learn to recognize the repeating theme and at that point change the dream by mere thought. It is a basic fact of dreams that what you think in the dream you will then see and experience. The dreamer should, before sleep, tell herself, 'If that dream of separation comes up again, I shall notice it, and then alter the dream so that I'm at a place that I really like (be specific), feeling happy.' The unconscious mind will then take the thought as an instruction and present imagery corresponding to the named location.

Interpretation 59

Your spouse digging the garden symbolizes your husband making love to you, the seed potatoes signify his seed, and the bag represents his scrotum. Each time he plants his seed, potato chips, which mean children (chips off the old block), sprout from the earth. The earth symbolizes you (mother earth). The predatory maggots represent less savoury people around you (low-lifers). That some chips make it to you safely suggests that your children will grow up relatively unscathed. You are worrying too much!

Further Comments: This dream includes examples of both ancient and modern symbolism. Tilling and sowing – and their variations – have, in all cultures, been observed to be sexual representations for millennia, long before Freud. Artemidorus, a Roman dream expert, wrote about what were, even then, reliable old truths concerning those same images.

The phonetic play on the word 'chip' is meaningful only to modern English-speaking cultures, but the pun-association is apparent. The emotional element, which gives the clue to the dream's significance to the dreamer, points to a recurring worry, which is basically unnecessary.

Interpretation 60

Again, this underpins our research which reveals that, when there is confusion about countries, this can sometimes be indicative of a spiritual realm, and this is the case here. The map of the UK symbolizes the UK and reflects the many different – sometimes conflicting and confusing – creeds and cultures that make up that society. In this particular instance, the word 'Alaska' is extremely relevant; it is an anagram of 'ask Ala' (Allah). Therefore, no matter what faith you follow, you are being urged to ask God for the answers you seek.

Further Comments: Readers will be aware how verbal rearrangements of key items in dreams (as indeed in ordinary waking speech) give the clue to a hidden, unconscious, agenda in the communication. Hazel is still in a state of transition in her religious conversion, and the basis of the dream is that, as a modern woman, she is still seeking clarification of certain matters of belief. The dream has skilfully illustrated her cultural transformation and sense of bewilderment, while indicating that the answer is to be found in a spiritual quest rather than a dry, academic approach.

Interpretation 61

The party, nice people, etc. suggest wish fulfilment: how you would like your life to be (to make beautiful music). However, the tiny people in white (innocent), who symbolize your children, join in and are accepted by others (nobody else minds). However, 'looking out' for them gives you a 'pain in the neck' (you find them tiresome). Your subconscious is urging you to view your children in the same way as the other party-goers do, to lighten up, relax a little, and enjoy life more.

Further Comments: This dream is trying to get across an important topic of concern for the dreamer. There is almost a resentment that the 'little people' (children) are requiring so much attention from him. It is becoming a real problem with John. He needs to discuss the matter with his partner. Is it a selfishness on his part, or is he being put-upon too much? Such issues, if left unresolved, can cause great marital disharmony and stress. Now is the time to talk and come to an accommodation.

Interpretation 62

The holiday, day out, or shopping trip represents your journey through life with your family. As we will see, in this particular instance, food represents love, namely the love you pour out on your family. Despite knowing that they have recently eaten, you feel they need a top-up (more love).

Dreams often play on words in the form of anagrams, and it is the name of the café that gives the game away. 'Café Tifon' is an anagram of 'affection'. Therefore, Marion, you should be careful not to smother your family with too much of it.

Further Comments: Puns are very frequent in dreams, and their identification accelerates cracking the code. They often seem to result from mischievous word-play in the DPP, pointing out a personal fault, say, but occasionally they may represent an unconscious disguise to hide an unpalatable truth. Marion may well be excessively attentive to her children, which could be an overcompensation for a lack of love when she was a child. She should look at the matter clearly and change her behaviour so that her children do not become greatly resentful. Treat them with respect, listen to their point of view, give them appropriate independence, and show your undoubted love in manageable quantities.

Interpretation 63

It seems likely that we are dealing with a precognitive, prodromic dream (forewarning of illness). The pleasant setting reflects Michael's present circumstances. In this instance, the shape of two oak trees, standing side by side, imitates effectively the human lungs. The strongest clue comes in Michael's reaction to the realization of the trees' plight (they had caught a bug): he was lacking energy and felt low.

However, the dream indicates that all will be well; the aircraft suggests successful treatment (perhaps antibiotics). Michael should be alert to a chest infection.

Further Comments: The ancient Greeks and Romans were well aware of some dream symbolism indicating future illness and believed it to be communicated by the gods. Today, it is conceptualized that the all-knowing unconscious mind can be aware of imperceptible changes in the body's physiology and give advance knowledge in one of the limited ways of communication at its disposal: dreams. The message, though, is automatically 'encoded' and requires a conscious effort at translation. Thus, dreaming of blocked pipes may in some cases refer to vascular problems. The detailed study of dreams may, in the future, be used to prevent illness.

Interpretation 64

In this particular instance, the walled garden symbolizes your place of work, and the crowd of people your colleagues. Your unconscious then mirrors your concerns about your co-workers by introducing your feelings of mistrust. However, these people weren't taking any notice, which suggests that, in real life, they aren't as hostile as you imagine. This is confirmed by the way in which dreams often play on words. Could 'wisteria' and 'Polaroid' be the only way your subconscious can communicate the words 'hysteria' and 'paranoid'? Try looking on the bright side, and don't be too self-conscious.

Further Comments: The walled garden is a place of safety but it is also the dreamer's workplace – where she feels rather unhappy. The dichotomy is indicated by its two distinct areas.

Dreams progress along both verbal- and visual-associative pathways, and there is a good example here of a visual scene-shift effect in that the purple wisteria flowers transform into the purple Polaroid camera, indicating a conceptual link. The keywords are being cleverly altered so that they sound similar, yet refer to more disturbing words thought unconsciously in the dream.

Melanie's workplace is actually very healing for her, but she needs to work on the 'cluttered' part: her relationship with colleagues.

Interpretation 65

The single theme that links all aspects of this dream is 'depression'. You find yourself in the time of a national depression. The people looking for work (motivation) engender an oppressive atmosphere, and they represent troubled people around you. At times of stress, you dig yourself into a hole (become entrenched) and take everyone's problems on your shoulders (cry for the rest of the world). You have the capacity to empathize, but it is unwise to bear the burden alone. You, too, need a shoulder to cry on, or else you will lose motivation and risk being drawn into a state of depression.

Further Comments: It has become apparent that dreams have several useful functions, one of which is actually to release accumulated generalized emotions, a process known as *catharsis*. Here the dreamer's unhappiness builds up to a point where it spills into a symbolic dream scenario related to waking tensions and worries. In each of us, the unconscious is our caring friend and guide.

In this case, it is looking after Kelly's mental welfare by actively exaggerating and dramatizing her periodic state of depression to a level where the therapeutic release of 'emotional toxins' occurs. Her unconscious is being a therapist to her.

Interpretation 66

Linking this dream to your employment makes wonderful sense. The battery-hen farm symbolizes your company before it began streamlining: it was noisy, overcrowded, and hatching empty ideas. The free-range environment represents a new, efficient, more relaxed atmosphere, where there is less pressure to perform. This is confirmed by the appearance of eggs containing brains (new ideas). Your subconscious is telling you that your fears about streamlining are unfounded.

Further Comments: In recent years it has been discovered, amazingly, that our unconscious mind can surreptitiously communicate with that of others by 'reverse-speech' messages hidden in ordinary language; this is probably the basis of much 'intuition'. Reverse messages happen in dreams, too. Spoken information in dreams is usually significant and, here, the words 'not egg' become 'get on' when reversed. The message revealed backs up the main interpretation: for the dreamer not to be concerned about changing events at work, but to take things in his stride and proceed normally.

Section 2

Interpretation 67 The Logical Thing To Do

To begin with, you find yourself in a factory which you own (responsibility for others). Next, you are walking through the shop-floor (involved). Although the factory represents responsibility, it goes deeper. You own this factory, which suggests that, in this case, the responsibility is for the welfare of people outside your family (in a work situation or work environment).

It is then that you notice people are watching you, and you feel self-conscious and uncomfortable. In addition to your dislike of being scrutinized, this also implies that you feel everything depends on you (the smooth running of the factory). This points to a specific situation in your life where you found yourself in the unenviable position of having others relying on you to do something which you might have felt was beyond your capabilities (in the dream you feel the need to escape their glare).

However, the fact that you go upstairs to an office, where you find your secretary – who is male, signals that, ultimately, you rose to the occasion by employing the left side of your brain, which is allied to cold calculation and logic. The fact that you are in an elevated vantage point, seeing the workers, who are still looking at you, indicates that you succeeded in the situation in which you found yourself, daunting though it was (the workers are now looking up at you, which suggests admiration). It is around this time that you notice your secretary is now female (right brain). She suggests that you should leave by another exit (your dislike of attention). You then depart on a sort of train (you leave on the tracks, in power, feeling safe in the privacy).

The dream reflects a time in your life when you found yourself in a particular position in which you felt a responsibility to perform efficiently in order not to let others down. You rose to the occasion and succeeded by employing the left, logically calculating side of your brain.

However, once the task was complete (when the workers were looking up to you), you engaged the right brain, which is allied to your creative, emotional, and psychic aspects (your natural self). The dream certainly reflects your dislike of being made a fuss of. Once the task had been completed, which necessitated you employing a character trait that you did not feel comfortable with, you soon reverted to your natural self and withdrew (discreetly).

The message behind the dream indicates that, in future, to deal successfully with similar situations, you might need to use your capacity for left-brain thinking. Perhaps your subconscious has identified a similar challenge looming on the horizon?

Interpretation 68 Go for a Face-Lift!

Dreams can often appear to be nothing more than an illogical sequence of nonsensical events. However, if they awaken the dreamer (the trigger mechanism) and are vivid enough to be easily remembered, they are invariably message-bearing dreams that are demanding to be decoded. On the surface, Betty's dream looks uncomplicated, but we have to delve deep to reveal the complexities in the way the subconscious sometimes tries to communicate with the conscious mind. First, Betty finds herself pacing up and down a street (path in life). She has lost her handbag, which we will see symbolizes a receptacle for ideas (her creative thinking). She discovers her bag in a public telephone booth (her place of work, where communication is facilitated). Next, she notices her bag filled with telephone cards, which indicates a means of facilitating communication by way of ideas (telephone cards store information). So far, the dream reflects Betty's desire to come up with fresh techniques for successful marketing. However, the cards were date-stamped and had expired. This suggests that Betty feels she is running out of options. In other words, the telephone cards represent hackneyed ideas.

Nevertheless, if we probe a bit further, we see that these telephone cards were of low denomination (seeds). Accepting that each low-denomination phone card symbolizes an idea for a way in which Betty can improve her chances of success, and that the telephone represents the opportunity to have her ideas considered by prospective clients, we find a further clue in that the cards looked brand new and were in new wrappers. It is at this point that we discover the crux of the message behind the dream.

Clearly, Betty's subconscious is urging her to stop trying too hard to come up with new marketing ploys – they may be finite. Instead, the dream wants her to consider taking old techniques back to the drawing-board and starting with the basic idea again (the small denomination or seed). Then she should consider ways in which she can rebuild and repackage them to look like new, original ideas, approach them from a different angle, and give them a face-lift.

(Interestingly, some years ago, we encountered a dream from a different source that was almost identical. Although the interpretations were different, the theme was essentially the same.)

Interpretation 69 Bucking the System

In this instance, it becomes clear that a park represents freedom, as you will see later, and, more specifically, freedom of thought. To begin with, we are dealing with your mind and thoughts (you went inside yourself). So the dream uses this experience to communicate a message which concerns your thoughts, feelings, and concerns about the outside world.

Your husband is a representation of the (left-brain) male side of your character, allied to cold calculation – which we all possess. As no description is given of the other people's identity, they parallel different facets of your own psyche.

The chain-link fence represents a boundary of established thinking, which separates the park (free thinking) from the outside world. Its strength is solely reliant on the fact that each strand of wire is interlinked with its neighbour. In this sense, the establishment understands well that, if its own rules and parameters are not held together and maintained, its doctrines will collapse. The fact that you were rocking back and forth would be an accepted way to weaken and eventually bring down the fence. In other words, you were trying to remove the obstacle which separates established thinking from free thinking.

Next, you found yourself inside your head (you couldn't get through to the outside world). However, you enjoyed the experience: it was exhilarating, almost hypnotic. This seems to suggest that, although, on occasion, you fail to break through, you are happy to explore your own thoughts (the exhilaration).

Now we come to the crux of the dream. You looked up and found your friends (your own character traits) had long since climbed up into the seats (become established). But they were not alone; there were now others sitting there as well (new ideas), even though they looked at you strangely.

The dream indicates that your thoughts and ideas at the time of the dream were not ready to be accepted by the outside world. This suggests that there was a time when people whom you perhaps thought would welcome your new ideas were not really listening and may even have disagreed with you.

So, your subconscious is clearly telling you that, to achieve your goal (get your message across), you have to be somewhat clever in your tactics. Initially, gain people's interest with conventional ideas; then, when you have a captive audience, hit them with your free-thinking theories. At first, you would do well to use the calculating (left) side of your brain to appeal to the conventional thinkers.

Interpretation 70 A New Direction in Life

Primarily this dream concerns earthly decision-making, the results of which could lead to a new direction in life. To begin with, you find yourself in a shoe-store. In this instance, a shoe-store represents a place with access to the wherewithal to enable you to tread various paths in life (the various types of shoe which are available).

However, there are no shoes that you like, which suggests that you are at some sort of crossroads in life and are not sure which path to choose. Next, when you go to put on your sandals, you cannot find them (signifying that you might feel you have lost your way somewhere along the line). You state that they were not elegant but practical. These sandals represent the path in life you have been treading for many years. Then you search but cannot come across them (that path is no longer viable). The sales assistants are helpful and offer you other shoes to buy. The fact that you like the shoes, despite their being too big, appears to suggest that you have considered taking other directions in life, but have wondered whether these new avenues would represent taking too big a step – could you fill the shoes?

It becomes clear to you that you will have to walk home in your stockinged feet. This indicates that, to embark on your journey home (new way of life), you are going to have to strip away the barriers between you and your natural vibrations, so that you will be better able to 'feel' your way. To a certain extent, this could involve exposing a vulnerable aspect of your personality.

Next, you try Mary's clogs, which seems a good idea. But it is too late, you have left the store (already begun your journey). In your questionnaire, you point out that Mary is very conventional, which seems to suggest that you have contemplated these matters from a customary standpoint, but have now come too far along the road to turn back to that perspective.

The police officers drive you home, to where you lived as a child. This signifies that, to find your new way, you have to adopt a more innocent, perhaps more naïve approach to these issues. This message is being driven home in the dream. In other words, open your heart and perhaps resist the urge to view things too objectively (or in too adult a fashion).

Pulling it all together then, it would appear that you have lost your way somewhat and are undecided as to which route to take in life. Maybe your career is involved to some extent. However, you are too far along the road to return to conventionalism (too late for Mary's clogs). Follow your heart!

Interpretation 71 A Lady-in-waiting

Our research has revealed that, when a dream is accompanied by feelings of anticipation, this can *sometimes* be indicative of a premonition. Viewing this dream in its entirety, and bearing in mind the fact that you had a feeling of anticipation, we suspect strongly that we have an example of a pre-cognitive dream (foretelling the future).

In this instance, the women represent the female (gentle) side to your character and the children signify innocence and naïveté. But why should they be happy in the rain? The rain falling on them symbolizes that they become wet (they were 'wets', in other words). So the scene is set: we are dealing with the gentle, innocent, and naïve part of your character – the part which might be regarded as 'a wet', which, incidentally, we all have to varying degrees.

You find yourself in the landau, ogling the Princess. It would appear that she appealed to the gentle, innocent, and naïve within you. So we are looking for a woman (in the future) who invokes these character traits.

The Princess also seemed happy to see the crowds (there was a period of harmony). However, just before you awoke, the Princess seemed to change (she somehow wasn't the same). This indicates that there was some deception there (she wasn't who she appeared to be). She had deceived the side of your character which is gentle, innocent, and naïve.

However, remembering that the dream was accompanied by a feeling of anticipation, we have to ask why. And this is where the lady-in-waiting comes in. This dream clearly points to affairs of the heart (you were in awe of the Princess, only to discover that she wasn't whom you had originally thought she was). Therefore, the lady-in-waiting represents exactly that! She is the next lady in your life.

The dream cleverly leads us through an event, from start to finish and beyond. It points to a situation in your life that, initially, you will be happy to go along with (the period of harmony). It concerns a lady. This lady appeals to, and brings out the gentle, innocent, and naïve side of you. However, something happens which alerts you to a deception within her (she changes and isn't what she seems).

The feeling of anticipation suggests that there is indeed a lady who is waiting to fill a gap in your life. She may even have a name that is linked to royalty, perhaps Elizabeth or Margaret.

However, it seems likely that the relationship is not going to last. It could transpire that this lady will deceive you in some way, so stay alert!

Interpretation 72 Spiritual Birth!

Dreams that reflect spirituality in some way can come in an amazing variety, from a vision of an angel to seemingly bizarre settings and, like this one, serene surroundings and feelings. However, each dream has to be studied in its entirety before such a decision can be made.

After looking for a common theme that runs throughout the dream, and linking all the elements, including the guru, there remains little doubt that we are dealing with matters of spirituality. The feeling of anticipation suggests an element of precognition as well. So we are looking at a dream that relates to Helen's future spiritual development.

To begin with, Helen found herself in a tranquil place on the edge of a forest (strength of purpose, longevity, and life). The unfamiliar stables represent a place of discovery. Accepting the Biblical references, the stables also symbolize a place of birth. This is confirmed by the dirt on the floor (mother earth).

The raised section signifies a beneficial advancement. As we are dealing with a birth, this suggests new discoveries and developments. Putting it together, then, we are dealing with Helen's spiritual birth and growth.

Helen's description of the shiny stones indicates her future development (polished). The fact that some bore scars symbolizes the scars that she has acquired throughout her life (experience). More important, however, is the fact that the area in which she was standing felt sacred, which underpins the interpretation so far.

There were some loose pebbles (parts of the whole). Helen picked up one (a specific avenue of thought). As she picked it up, it fell in half, which reflects Helen's misgivings about her spiritual development (she feels somewhat torn between two different paths in life). Nevertheless, in one of the halves was a small, metallic (strong) statue of a guru, who was meditating (trying to attain spiritual awareness), which again symbolizes Helen's confusion.

The fact that the guru resembled one of the three wise men suggests strongly that he holds the answers to Helen's quandary. If, then, we consider that the stone represents Helen through her thoughts, the message becomes even clearer: the answer she seeks lies within herself through the process of meditation. Then, and only then, will the two halves come together again to make the whole complete person.

Bearing in mind Helen's feelings of anticipation, it seems likely that she is on the edge of spiritual discovery and awareness – in the near future. In addition, the guru might have been a representation of the Zen faith, in which case the interpretation is sealed. Zen followers believe that the the truth does not lie in writings but in each individual's heart.

Interpretation 73 Use Common Sense!

To begin with, we find you walking along a street (your path in life). You come across a dog, which you crouch down to talk to (an initial encounter) and which is normal for you, because you feel comfortable when being friendly and warm. However, you try not to show your surprise (denial).

So the scene is set: we are dealing with a situation in your life which, at first, feels normal to you (possibly a romantic encounter). However, you notice that the dog has two heads (two outlooks). The fact that one is black and the other is white suggests conflict. It is interesting that the creature's second head is placed where its backside should be, instead of side-by-side with the first.

There is little doubt that the dog is a representation of the animal or basic side to your personality, which, incidentally, we all possess, and this provides us with the next valuable clue. If we now view this dream from the standpoint of raw emotion, relationships, and instinct, then it all begins to make wonderful sense. In fact, the dream pieces itself back together quite naturally.

In your questionnaire, you state that your relationships are never stable, and it was this that put us on the scent. It would appear that, as far as relationships are concerned, you use two approaches: one which is the commonsense way and then, later in a relationship, the other, which is emotional and over which you have little control (the head at the rear end). The phrase 'Talking out of one's backside' springs readily to mind.

This is a very powerful message-bearing dream and says much about you. Indeed, it doesn't surprise us that it still preys on your mind for in it is hidden a way forward for you in future relationships. However, we sense *very strongly* that it is something which you already suspect (you say that you made a mental note about the abnormality).

Try to identify a consistent emotional character trait in your make-up, which appears to grow slowly and then to predominate in a romance. It would seem that you often start a relationship by following common sense or your intelligence. However, it is apparent that there is an overemotional side to your character (the head at the rear end).

The message therefore, is that, in affairs of the heart, you should employ more intellectual thinking. Don't give in to emotional feelings or irrational suspicions. Indeed, if you allow that side of your character to manifest itself, it is likely to provoke conflict. In other words, as far as relationships are concerned, you would do better to follow common sense rather than unfounded mistrust, which, you already sense, is at the bottom of your problems. Try to avoid digging too deep; accept and trust in love and happiness.

Interpretation 74 A Wolf in Sheep's Clothing?

Nightmares are invariably the most powerful of message-bearing dreams, and when they are as striking as this one they are usually fairly easy to interpret; the subconscious tries to impart its message in the simplest possible terms. This is particularly evident when the dreamer is left with strong emotions long after awakening, as in this case. As a rule of thumb, the more powerful the dream, then the more important the message that lies behind it!

Interestingly, instead of following an illogical sequence of events – sometimes found in other message-bearing dreams – nightmares often start pleasantly, appear to be well structured, then lead to a fearful, emotional climax, at which point subjects will always awaken, to find themselves repeatedly reflecting on the dream.

To begin with, the pleasant country surroundings reflect your previous life-situation, suggesting that, until the nightmares began, you were happy with the status quo. The friendly animals, which are dependent upon you, represent family members and close friends, and the baby chickens symbolize your children (they are babies, and you fed them first).

However, right from the outset, the lamb protests at the lack of attention, as if it is jealous of your other loved ones. The stream represents the flow of your love to your family. You mix it with the porridge (your physical behaviour) to provide sustenance (generally looking after the welfare of those who are close to you).

The fact that the cat becomes aggressive and the lamb growls like a dog demonstrates that these two animals also represent you and your partner (couples can fight like cat and dog). And this leads us to the crux of the dream: the word 'werewolf'. Dreams often play on words, and here the connection is obvious. Added to the fact that these nightmares began around the same time as your relationship with Steve, and there is no doubt whatsoever.

However, bearing in mind your conscious remarks about Steve, the message behind the dream is not a warning about him, but it is cautioning you; nightmares rarely translate into a frightening message. Nevertheless, it is a message that needs to be heeded.

Your subconscious is alerting you to the possibility that your relationship with Steve could be put under some strain unless you show the same level of commitment to him as you do to your own family members. The dream is not telling you to spoil him, but sometimes to put him first. It is likely that you will readily identify these occasions.

Interpretation 75 Meet the Challenge Head-on!

Like so many bad dreams, this one begins quite pleasantly. Ross found himself in a fortified castle, which he owned (the life-situation with which he feels most secure – the castle was heavily defended and he felt elated). However, as he knows, life just isn't like that all the time, and to demonstrate this Ross's subconscious elected to provide the first clue in the form of an anagram (these often surface in dream analysis).

To begin with, a good character trait is evident and points straight away to a work situation – hard work. The messenger was exhausted through 'riding hard' which, when unscrambled, translates as 'I grind hard'. Clearly then, the messenger represents Ross's subconscious.

In this dream, as in many, it is not unusual for more than one person to be a representation of different character traits of the dreamer. In this instance, Ross's subconscious has brilliantly encompassed much of his personality in one go. The hooded old man also symbolizes him. Like the three wise monkeys, he has a tendency to see no evil, hear no evil, and speak no evil – except, in this instance, we are not dealing necessarily with evil but with challenges in the workplace.

The swordsmen who were testing him (the cut and thrust of challenges) represent a work environment – they were very skilled. However, after killing his soldiers (bringing down Ross's defences), they declared their friendship. This clearly indicates that certain challenges at work are wearing Ross down (he felt his strength draining away).

The message, then, is clear: in order to overcome difficulties and avoid the upheaval that is threatened in the workplace, Ross has to meet challenges head-on and resist the urge to become detached – see, hear, and speak no evil – or let matters wash over his head (the folklore suggests that this character trait has brought problems in the past). He is then likely to discover that certain colleagues are friendlier towards him, and the recurring nature of the dream will cease!

Interpretation 76 Trust Your Intuition!

Sometimes, when we dream of a place in which we used to live, it can alert us to something that occurred in the past. In this instance, though, William's old flat symbolizes a way of life that has been established for years.

William revisiting it indicates that his subconscious is taking stock of his life and preparing him for a change – including a change of outlook (the flat was at a higher location than before).

The dream seems even more significant because William is approaching the age of retirement. He will have to make a leap of faith, as indicated by the gap between the elevator and the floor. The fact that the lift travels horizontally as well as vertically is very meaningful indeed. This is a strong clue implying that William would do well to employ some lateral thinking – but about what?

The next clue surfaces when we consider that the flat serves another purpose. It personifies William himself. The two bedrooms represent affairs of the heart, the kitchen practical matters, the living room material issues, etc. Therefore, the extra rooms that he hasn't yet used symbolize new areas in life which he has perhaps begun to consider for the future.

William discovers a school (a place of learning). It is interesting to note that the teacher is female. She throws him out. This suggests that William could be in conflict with his female side, which is allied to intuition, creativity, and a certain amount of risk-taking (the gap between lift and floor).

The fact that he was abusive to her is a strong pointer that, until now, William has rejected that side of his psyche. However, lately, he has contemplated viewing things from a different stance, perhaps because he realizes that some of his beliefs no longer hold water (the rain seeping through the ceiling – or mind). And this is what the dream is all about: a new outlook on life.

Therefore, if he is to succeed and make a smooth transition to new ideas, he is going to have to trust his intuition more than usual, take a plunge (risk), use lateral thinking, and go for it! In view of this analysis, William is likely to recognize opportunities for change when he encounters them.

Interpretation 77 Avoid Stress!

This dream is quite remarkable because it is prodromic (advising in some way about illness). As the analysis progresses, we will see how brilliantly Alexa's subconscious has constructed the dream in order to highlight a natural – perhaps unconscious – character trait which, if she ignores it, could cause her problems.

First, her husband symbolizes two things: the left (male) hemisphere of Alexa's thought processes and the heart specialist (taking readings and providing a demonstration). The left brain is allied to, among other things, a tendency to drive oneself or judge one's performances too hard. The girl inside the flying-machine represents Alexa herself. Here, the message is clear: to stay on the ground (not risk leaving this earth), Alexa must resist the advice of her (left brain) and pedal less hard.

Next, the shadowy figure, who symbolizes Alexa's psyche, alerts us to a character trait which can cause problems by creating frustration and stress. It is evident that, in spite of her exhaustion, Alexa's natural personality prevented her from ignoring the pile of washing; in smoothing, folding, and stowing the clothes she was overdoing it.

Then, the group of people whom Alexa believed were lost and needed her assistance – they weren't lost at all – provide the final clue, which reinforces the entire interpretation. Alexa realized that her directions (assistance) had been needless. In other words, whether she drives or judges herself too hard or not, the world will still go round. Therefore, to avoid becoming airborne (to stay on earth), she must, to a certain degree, change her ways. 'Don't be too hard on yourself or do today what can be put off till tomorrow!' Try to avoid frustration and stress.

Interpretation 78 Make the First Move!

The man who is with you represents your alter ego, and the library symbolizes a place of learning. Therefore we are dealing with a learning situation. Your aunt represents the left (female) hemisphere of your brain which, among other things, is allied to emotion and spontaneity.

Next, we observe that she was talking about the forthcoming wedding of your cousin. In this instance, the wedding signifies a new beginning connected to a family situation (your cousin). When we tie the two together, it is evident that we are dealing with a new learning curve, which has something to do with 'family'. Furthermore, it is related to an event of the past (you haven't seen your cousin for a long time).

The church suggests a spiritual connection. This indicates that the lesson to be learnt involves some sort of spiritual development. The plane carrying the 'father' (God) of the bride (new beginning) reinforces this. The fact that you found yourself back in the doorway of the library leaves little doubt (again, a place of learning).

The death of the father (God) represents the death of a past situation. However, the fire or candles (light) around the crypt tell us that you will find the answer with God. This is confirmed by your quest to pay your respects (search for the truth).

The fact that both you and your alter ego cannot understand why people are so touched by tragedy suggests that, until now, you have turned away from the pain of this past event.

Finally, the entire interpretation slots neatly into place and reveals the message behind the dream. It was night-time on the grassy slope (a state of darkness confirms a certain amount of denial). The approach of your ex-husband, who was carrying a torch, and your fear home in precisely on the dream's message. He pushed you through a revolving door (life) and into a sentry box (a place of safety), where you were hoping that you would *both* be safe.

In other words, to effect a certain amount of reconciliation with your ex-husband, you would do well to put your trust in God, overcome your fear, and make the first move towards your ex. The fact that he was carrying a torch (for you?) indicates that he will probably accept your advance gladly. If he doesn't, however, then you will have the comfort of knowing that your conscience is clear.

Interpretation 79

First, we must consider why you perceived yourself to be as existing detached from your body, and we don't have to look far to find the answer. In your questionnaire you stated that, sometimes, you work away from home. Immediately, we see that your desire to start a family conflicts with your career (sometimes you are detached from an environment conducive to that need). Therefore this dream has a direct bearing on issues of career and motherhood.

Next, we observe that your shoulder-length hair begins to fall out. In this instance, your hair symbolizes your femininity. If we then consider that, nowadays, women are under a certain amount of pressure to compete in what used to be regarded as a 'man's world', it becomes apparent that there is disharmony in your life. You feel the need to succeed in your career, but at the same time, you want to have a baby – can you do both?

The next clue appears when all your hair falls out. You are embarrassed and try to cover it up. This suggests that, in your work environment, although you are competing successfully, you feel that it necessary to employ a male character trait that goes against your personality (your head was red and sore).

In this instance, then, your dream is bringing you a powerful message that should be adhered to: it rarely pays to operate under a façade. Be your true self, follow your heart, and you will instinctively know what is right for you. Your subconscious is underlining the fact that then you are likely to discover that you will still be accepted at work – for who you really are – and you might even be able to satisfy both needs.

Interpretation 80

In the 1960s, Evans and Newman stated that dreams were merely a way in which the brain processed and discarded useless information from the previous day's activities, in a similar way to a computer taking data off line. Apart from lucid dreams (in which the dreamer becomes conscious within the dream), false awakenings (dreaming of waking up), sleep paralysis (dreaming of being paralysed), and the fact that dreams can be contaminated by external stimuli (e.g. a sound), this dream proves that Evans and Newman were greatly mistaken! Dreams come in an amazing variety and serve various purposes.

Here it is obvious that we are dealing with a violent dream that is set in another time, perhaps long ago. How, then, does this reflect the brain discarding useless information from the previous day's activities? In short, it doesn't.

Over many years of analysing dreams, we sometimes encounter dreams which share the same theme as this one. Invariably they contain three consistent elements and, sometimes, a fourth element:

1 Such dreamers don't recognize their bodies as their own in waking life.
2 Their clothing is from another time.
3 There is always great emotion involved.
4 Sometimes, as in this case, these dreams have recurred throughout the dreamer's life.

When David Melbourne interviewed Dr Brian Weiss, author of *Only Love is Real* (a book about reincarnation), Jenny Cockell, author of *Yesterday's Children* (on the same topic), and Dr Keith Hearne, who is the Principal of the College of Past Life Regression Studies, in London, UK, he discovered that these same features were present in the dreams of people who claimed to have recalled a past life.

Therefore, we don't believe that this dream is conducive to interpretation. Instead, our advice to Moira is to seek the assistance of a qualified and reputable past-life regressionist. She is likely to never look back again!

Interpretation 81 A Lighter Heart

In this instance, the best friend is a representation of Maria. A wedding can sometimes symbolize a new beginning. In these circumstances, however, it symbolizes a marriage of ideas. In order to understand what these ideas could be, we have to investigate why the events are situated in a gymnasium. In view of Maria's comments concerning her ex-boyfriend 'working-out' at the gym which she attends, we are able to make a connection. Therefore, it would seem that this marriage of ideas is connected to both Maria and her ex-boyfriend.

The next clue appears when we ask why dancing girls, who symbolize different aspects of Maria's psyche, encircle the bride. These girls appear to be happy, which indicates that Maria would be happy to be married.

Next, the bride's mother (a symbol of authority), who represents the more serious side to Maria's personality, asks her to dance. This suggests that Maria should loosen up a little and leave her more rigid ideas behind her.

Now we come to the crux of the dream. Maria sees her ex out of the corner of her eye. This demonstrates that, although they are no longer together, there is still a corner in her mind's eye in which he is never far away. He is running on the spot (getting nowhere) or, more to the point, not running away!

The fact that the bride doesn't seem to be enjoying herself points to Maria's conscious state of awareness. She does not enjoy being parted from him. The fact that, at this point in the dream, her subconscious elected to awaken her is very significant indeed.

Therefore, the dream is pointing out to Maria a way in which she might be able to rekindle the flames of romance. In order to wed her ideas to those of her ex-boyfriend, she has to let go of some of her more rigid notions of the past and view matters with a lighter heart.

Interpretation 82 A Warning in Vain?

Unfortunately, the consistent linking theme in this dream points to a somewhat selfish personality and issues a warning to the dreamer! However, because John has sought to find out what it means, there might be light at the end of the tunnel for him, provided he acts on the message from his subconscious.

In this instance, the long, narrow art gallery symbolizes more than one thing. First, it suggests a certain amount of narrow-mindedness. Second, it seems to indicate that, unless John changes certain views, he is likely to tread this path throughout his entire life (he was worried that his journey would last an eternity). The fact that the gallery was dimly lit (a state of darkness or ignorance) and had a chequered floor (life) reinforces the interpretation so far.

The interpretation leaves little doubt when we consider that it is extremely likely that the subject of each painting was a representation of John himself (all the painted faces were familiar). The mere phrase 'painted face' suggests both deception and vanity.

However, when we link this to the appearance of each one, further obvious clues emerge. The meaning of the enormous mouths is self-evident. The lack of eyes and ears symbolizes not seeing and not listening. Finally, the different hairstyles and fashions in clothing confirm the entire analysis.

It would seem that John suffers from vanity, in addition to placing material rewards above spiritual needs (the different hairstyles and clothing). However, in order to hammer the point home yet more, his subconscious puts each subject in front of a mirror and enables John to empathize with feelings of concern over appearance.

In a nutshell, unless John changes his ways, he is likely to continue through life being ignorant, self-centred, and perhaps lonely as well. The mere fact that he has sought to find out the meaning behind his dream suggests otherwise, however, and bodes well for the future. It is essential, though, that John changes his perception of himself.

Interpretation 83 Personal Growth

To begin with, in this instance, the beach represents Rosemary's standing in life at the time of the dream. The sea, however, symbolizes life itself and all the challenges that come with it.

As a child, it is not surprising that Rosemary always dreamt of the sea rushing in, because it was full of challenging issues which threatened her with an encounter she would prefer to avoid. Like many children, at times she felt daunted and tried to escape these undertakings (a form of denial). In fact, it would seem that sometimes she felt overwhelmed. In other words, if she looks back to her childhood, Rosemary might remember certain instances where she tended to turn her back on challenges that appeared 'too much' for her to take on.

Now she is middle-aged, though, it is evident that she has grown in strength and confidence. The tide is already in, and to Rosemary it looks warm and inviting. Straight away, it becomes obvious that nowadays she is prepared to face up to issues in her life that she once would have avoided.

However, Rosemary's last dream demonstrates a natural progression: the sea has become impenetrable. This suggests that other people who present Rosemary with challenges have identified her tenacious side and are trying to shut her out. It is they who are now in denial.

Therefore, the message behind Rosemary's dream seems to be that she might make more headway in these areas if she changed tack. Instead of meeting certain challenges head-on, it might benefit her to adopt a more subtle approach.

Her dream suggests that, sometimes, Rosemary can appear to be formidable to others, although she might not be aware of this herself. In this sense, to paraphrase an old Italian proverb, 'She might catch more flies with honey than with vinegar!'

Interpretation 84 Look Back In Happiness

Janet stated that this dream began to recur about 10 years ago and, although she still has it, it is far less frequent. Therefore this dream concerns something that happened in her life at that time – something quite important.

In this instance, looking out to sea from a cliff-top symbolizes reviewing one's life – possibly trying to see where mistakes have been made. The appearance of Blackpool tower – with the absence of people and buildings – suggests that, until this dream, Janet possibly regarded herself as 'a tower of strength', perhaps the mainstay of her family. The beautiful day represents how she regarded her life until this unknown event occurred 10 years ago. Miles and miles of beautiful fields marked by well-kept hedgerows (neat boundaries encapsulating an orderly lifestyle) underpin this.

However, as she began to go down (feel let down) the cliff-path, she noticed that the vivid colours began to fade. This indicates that, whatever this important event was, it had a profound effect on Janet: she felt that the colour in her life was draining away. The people who appeared on the beach indicate that, about 10 years ago, Janet considered taking her mind off things by engaging herself in some activity that involved other people. The fact that they disappeared seems to suggest that this alternative didn't work out.

The cliffs being replaced by the neglected esplanade and the dishevelled wooden buildings represent the fact that the status quo had been altered for good. To support this interpretation, Janet's subconscious presents her with fairground stalls, all of which symbolize the fun in her life before the important event occurred. That they were washed away by the sea is another indication of the permanence of this change.

Therefore the message behind the dream becomes obvious. Once Janet is able to link the dream to a life-changing event which occurred about 10 years ago, she will be able to see that there was nothing she could have done to prevent it. Just as the tide of life ebbs and flows, it was destined to happen. Moreover, if she accepts that fact and begins to look back over her life, concentrating on the happy memories, this dream will cease to recur.

Interpretation 85 Sit Back and Relax

Dreams of being pursued are fairly widespread, as are dreams of flying. However, it is futile to attempt to give a universal meaning to such images; they are specific to each dreamer. For example, people who feel under pressure at work might dream of being chased. Perhaps those who feel an obligation to sign an agreement, or who owe money, could have a similar dream.

People who see themselves as 'high-flyers' might dream of flying, while others who believe they are stuck in a rut could, by way of wish fulfilment, dream of soaring into the air – in other words, seeking freedom.

Dreams often reflect our life situation, ongoing anxieties, feelings of aggression, and sometimes a lack of self-worth or certain character traits that need attention. This demonstrates that, to achieve an accurate analysis, it is crucial for the interpreter to know a few facts about the dreamer's circumstances, thoughts, worries, fears, etc.

In this instance, Margaret's dream begins with a pursuit. However, when we link this to the way she was scantily clad, a clue emerges that begins to put us on the scent. In this regard, vulnerability is suggested and becomes the one consistent theme throughout the entire dream.

We see that, when she took to the air, her arms felt heavy, and she was worried about landing – or coming back down to earth – too hard (with a bump). Again, this symbolizes vulnerability.

If we now connect this dream with the surroundings in which it was set, other relevant factors begin to emerge, which steer the interpretation quite naturally to a conclusion. The long, straight road that looked rather grey reflects Margaret's journey through life. The fact that it didn't incorporate any twists or turns suggests that she has followed conventional rules and hasn't taken too many risks in her time. This is reinforced by the fact that it was grey (dull).

In this instance, the pursuit represents the pressures that Margaret has had to endure throughout her life: financial commitment, the responsibility of bringing up a family, worrying about her husband – in short, matters related to accountability and to her feeling somewhat vulnerable.

However, dreams can sometimes incorporate elements of precognition (foreknowledge), which appears to be the case here, and it bodes well for Margaret's future. At the end of her dream, she saw houses, then woke feeling exhausted. The houses represent stability, security, and financial gain. The fact that she woke exhausted reflects the way many people can feel after the bulk of life's struggles has been addressed.

Therefore the message behind the dream is that Margaret need not worry. Towards the end of her days, after the toil has finished, she will be able to sit back and relax in relatively carefree circumstances.

Interpretation 86 Pedal Like Mad!

This is a classic dream of encouragement and reassurance. To begin with, Stuart finds himself in a room set in a railway station. In this instance, the railway symbolizes Stuart's path or track in life. The room, however, represents a resting place where he has stopped to take stock, recover, and get his affairs in order. The fact that it has been redecorated in his favourite colours is very significant and suggests that much healing has taken place in his life.

The reconditioned bicycle (his drive) underpins this point and indicates that it is now time for him to move on and continue his journey through life – to reach home (his final resting place). Interestingly, three women appear, each offering encouragement. This fits in perfectly with the interpretation, in that they represent Stuart's right brain (female hemisphere) which, essentially, is responsible for drink problems and alcoholism. In effect, they serve the purpose of reassuring Stuart that all is now well, and that it is time for him to move on. The fact that he is able to link them to an educational course (learning experience) is also a powerful indicator that underpins the dream's message.

However, it is evident that, while Stuart has been taking time out to heal, he has lost some of his self-confidence with regard to both his career and relationships (he was nervous and didn't know which way to go). The entire dream pivots on this point. Therefore the message is crystal clear: Stuart has to overcome his fear, try to believe in his ability a little more, decide on a goal (direction in life), and go for it! The time is now right for him to make advances in career matters and relationships. Get on the bike, Stuart, and pedal like mad. You can do it!

Interpretation 87 A Trouble Shared!

When a dream recurs in the form of a nightmare, it is trying to put across an important message. It is only when the dreamer works out that message (perhaps unconsciously in the form of intuition) and, in this particular instance, acts upon it, that these bad dreams will cease. The subconscious will then have no reason to persist because it will have achieved its purpose.

Therefore there is every reason for Patricia to 'see' the message behind this dream; if she does, it will stop bothering her. The fact that the theme remains consistent in each episode indicates that Patricia has a negative character trait that has been in action for many years.

To begin with, specific to this dream, the murder victims represent distasteful events in Patricia's life – events she prefers not to recognize. Therefore she has murdered and buried them – a case of out of sight, out of mind. Nevertheless, they are never far away, and there is always the threat of them being discovered (unearthed) by the police who, in this instance, symbolize Patricia's conscious mind.

If we accept that the house is a representation of Patricia, the interpretation begins to make yet more sense. The basement suggests a hidden place, where things can be buried in secrecy fairly successfully. In other words, it symbolizes the far – almost hidden – reaches of Patricia's consciousness. This inference is underpinned by her statement that she has to face alone the threat of her secret being discovered.

Taken together, all these clues suggest that the negative character trait is Patricia's inability to share with others her concerns regarding unpleasant occurrences in her life. Instead, it would seem that she has developed a capacity for denial: she will put these issues to the back of her mind, then try to forget them.

However, because these things remain just under the surface (in shallow graves), they are never far away and are always threatening to reappear. Under these circumstances, the message behind the dream emerges quite naturally: these matters will never go away, therefore Patricia has to confront the pain of seeing them again before, once and for all, she can bury them deep. She needs to share her troubles with others instead of bearing the burden of life on her own! In this case, a trouble shared really can be a trouble halved.

Interpretation 88 Unjustified Fear

To begin with, the dream cleverly places us in your past: you were in the area in which you grew up. The fact that it is not a road (life path) you ever frequented tells us that we are dealing with an alternative track that you elected not to follow – but why?

That you are laughing and happy in the dream determines that, initially, we are dealing with your childhood. This is underpinned by the speed at which you travelled the road (children grow up almost too quickly). Your subconscious cleverly introduces the black Labrador, which serves two purposes. Again, it points firmly to your past, but it also symbolizes something else: a crossroads in your life and a time of mental conflict (it growls).

Next, we have to work out why your unconscious mind is alerting us to this particular symbolism, and we don't have to look far to find the answer: the dog was behaving covetously towards you – it wanted you to itself, so it was trying to pull you away from people. This jealous aspect is confirmed by the spiteful way in which it went about the task. As we know, jealousy rarely leads to anything constructive, just like in your dream, nor does it impress others (the undeterred people).

When dreams are linked so strongly to the past, they can be signalling an event looming on the horizon, which could bear a resemblance to a previous occurrence, thus providing a warning or reminder. In other words, they could be precognitive. Therefore, in this instance, we have to examine what prospective elements in your life could invoke the negative emotion of jealousy. Straight away, we see that you have a stepson, and you would also like to have a child of your own.

In this respect, it would seem that we are dealing with a definite warning about this negative character trait that, until now, you have buried in the past. In other words, your subconscious is imploring you not to allow it to manifest itself again; it is negative, it won't lead you to a constructive conclusion, and people will not be impressed by it. Maintain your even keel and stay on the path you have been treading since you learnt to overcome this negative emotion.

Interpretation 89 Share Your Concerns

Like so many people of your generation, this type of dream is fairly common – but why? To begin with, the first clue emerges when we take a look at your life. Unlike the British youth of today, who enjoy the benefits of peace in comparatively carefree surroundings, you had the cruel realities of life thrust upon you at an early age. Simply put, instead of the luxury of a naturally easy-going development, you had to grow up suddenly and take life seriously.

Your army training and wartime experiences would have taught you discipline, that you should not complain, and that you should get on with the job. Indeed, knowing no alternative, these reactions followed you into civilian life, and your responsible approach towards your job as a salesman bears this out. Little wonder then that your subconscious reflects this responsible attitude and manifests in dreams of anxiety.

However, it would seem that, if you had not been faced with the nature of war at such an early age, anxiety would not have become one of your natural character traits. And this is precisely the point your subconscious has been battling all these years to communicate to you. When we consider the repeating elements in your dreams– lateness, correct amount of stock, concerns with clients, etc. – a persistent theme emerges: 'bearing responsibility alone'.

It is because these dreams have followed you into retirement that there is no doubt of the interpretation. Until now, your subconscious has, unsuccessfully, been trying to alert you to the fact that your natural character – which has been hidden beneath a bushel all these years – would normally lean towards a more carefree attitude.

In other words, instead of bearing the brunt of responsibility alone, you should endeavour to share your concerns with others and allow them to carry some of the burden. This point is symbolized in your dream by the appearance of a third party who knows the way back to your van (your drive or natural self).

If you now acknowledge this message and act on it, you are not likely to be troubled by these dreams again!

Interpretation 90 Don't Be Too Anxious

Dreams often put their message across by association with past experiences. In addition, they can use time as a reference, either as a play on words or to give an indication of a present or future situation which has developed or is developing – as in this case.

To begin with, Iain finds himself in a new house. In this instance, the house symbolizes Iain's new situation in life: his recent retirement. That is why he states that it takes longer to find his way around (to find his feet).

Next we see him taking two (empty) plates for his lunch. In this situation, the plates represent things that carry food or, more appropriately, fuel. If we then link this to the two old men (dithering, or lacking drive) and the missing car, which again suggests a lack of drive, then we are starting to crack the code of this dream. Furthermore, if we recognize that the consistent theme that links all elements of the dream is anxiety, a clear picture begins to emerge.

The train, bus, diversions, etc. each represent Iain's journey through life. The fact that the dream finishes in a state of conflict with the youths reflects Iain's mental comparisons between how he used to be and how he is now. Therefore the message here seems to be that Iain should stop worrying so much about what the future might hold – this can only lead to anxiety. Instead, he needs to slow down and take stock. Then, and only then, is a solution likely to appear. Lighten up a bit, Iain, and stop worrying about getting older.

Interpretation 91 Be Yourself!

Dreams that bear messages try to put those messages across in the simplest possible way. However, for unknown reasons, the subconscious seems to be limited in the way it utilizes the brain to produce imagery; otherwise dreams would not be in code and would not require interpretation – the messages would be self-evident. Nevertheless, we do know that dreams flow along visual- and auditory-associative pathways. Furthermore, metaphors can often be seen at a glance. Understanding these facts made this dream relatively simple to interpret because it meets most of the criteria mentioned.

To begin with, the holiday camp symbolizes a period in Joan's life where she is taking time out, perhaps to take stock. However, her subconscious has brilliantly utilized the entertainment to put some of its message across. In this respect, if we bear in mind Joan's remark about finding true love, it is no mistake that the singers are all female (each representing a different facet of Joan's personality) and the guide is male.

Now, if we link the two, we are able to see how the subconscious uses associative pathways. At the age of 49, Joan will be very familiar with a song entitled 'Behind the Green Door'. The lyric contained the words 'They play it hot behind the green door'. This is a wonderful example of how easy dreams can be to interpret. Not only does the dream follow an associative pathway, but it contains an unmistakable metaphor.

Now we know what the dream is focusing on: Joan's desire to find true love. If we then make a similar connection with the game of cards (a game of chance) and the women showing off black footwear in particular, we can see that love is a game of chance that most of us hazard at one time or another. It is a shame that Joan cannot remember more clearly the card that was broken. We wouldn't mind betting that it was a heart! The shoes represent a mode of treading life's path. That they were black, in this instance, reflects hard experiences along the path of love.

Finally, we come to the crux of the dream – the powerful message behind it. It seems that, as far as affairs of the heart are concerned, Joan is considering leaving her individuality behind – symbolized by the fluffy pink blankets – and, like a sheep, following methods practised in this area by other women (the sheep). The message behind the dream, therefore, is that Joan should not sacrifice her standards because, if she does, she is likely to feel tainted (the ruined washing machine). No, Joan, by being yourself, you are far more likely to find what you are seeking!

Interpretation 92 Growing Up!

First we must consider the reasons why your subconscious elected to take you back in time. Immediately, it strikes us that you were shown an image of yourself as a child – but why? The first clue comes when we look deeper into the method of your time travel: you simply walked towards your bank. This ties in neatly with your concern over your finances: when you were a child, you didn't have the problems of knowing where the next penny was coming from.

The next clue is irrefutable and directs the interpretation quite naturally: you saw your brother at a nightclub. In this instance, your brother is a representation of yourself. It is likely that he has a character trait to which your subconscious wants to draw your attention (generally, youth and nightclubs equal a hole in one's pocket). So far, then, we have three elements to study: the bank, childhood, and your waking concern about money.

However, the next part of your dream seals the analysis and leaves little doubt: you entered a betting shop and placed a bet. Somehow, you knew you were guaranteed to win – don't most gamblers believe that?

Even more convincing is the content of the subsequent dreams, as if underpinning the entire interpretation. You saw old teachers and wanted to bring back proof by returning to the present bearing photographs of how things used to be. The teachers symbolize a lesson that needs to be learnt. The lesson is simple: in order for you to manage your financial affairs more prudently, you must go back and retrieve the more innocent outlook of your childhood, get rid of the attitude towards money that developed in your youth, and learn to be more thrifty.

Interpretation 93 Focus Your Mind

To begin with, we find Margaret travelling a long, straight road (her path in life). Then she comes across a pond that is full of fish, of different colours, shapes, and sizes. In this instance, the pond and fish represent life and all its distractions going on around Margaret. The fact that the fish are all shapes, colours, and sizes symbolizes people of different backgrounds and races (the different colours). To seal this part of the interpretation, Margaret makes a point of saying that the pond is man-made.

Next, she discovers several slip-roads that lead in many directions, but all are uphill. It is no mistake that the words 'slip' and 'uphill' are used. These roads represent alternative distractions from Margaret's route; they are distractions that lead her nowhere. Indeed, she makes a point of saying that she is sidetracked. And this is the point: each slip-road she follows in life (alternative distractions) prevents her from achieving her destiny (the long, straight road).

This becomes clear when we consider that Margaret adds that she had a feeling that she should cross the bridge, which would have put her back on the straight road (back on track). However, her remarks about the dreams being pleasant and colourful, to the point where she doesn't want to wake up but instead wants to find out more, presents Margaret with a problem. These comments suggest that Margaret enjoys these distractions from her main goal.

Now let's put it all together, and we can see that a clear message from Margaret's subconscious emerges. If we link this dream to her desire to see her book in print, the answer becomes obvious. Any successful author will tell us that to get a book published requires a concentrated effort, single-mindedness, a certain amount of thick skin – to ride the rejections – and determination. Distractions from that goal usually prove to be disastrous.

In this sense, then, the bridge symbolizes a point of no return. To stand any chance of getting her book published, Margaret has to make that her one and only target, then keep it in her sights for as long as it takes. She has to get back on the straight and narrow!

Interpretation 94 Follow Your Heart!

This was a lovely dream to interpret, and it delivers a beautiful message. To begin with, our research has revealed that, when we dream of foreign climes, and there is some confusion as to exactly which country we are in, this *sometimes* symbolizes a spiritual realm. Immediately, if we connect this to Sarah's chosen career and the timing of her decision to pursue theology, we have our first strong clue as to where the interpretation might lead. This point is reinforced by Sarah's description of the landscape and her emotion (anticipation).

The road she was travelling represents her chosen path in life. The crossroads suggest a time when Sarah had to decide which direction to take. The fact that she describes the roads as circular indicates that, at some future period, they will both rejoin her path in life. Therefore, they truly represent an alternative that she was not obliged to take.

Now we come to the crux of the dream, and one which leaves little doubt as to the final analysis – especially if it is connected with her chosen career. For a while, Sarah was in doubt as to which road she should take. In this instance, the left turning definitely represents the corresponding hemisphere of the brain, which is allied to cold calculation, study, and a measured approach. The right turning symbolizes the right hemisphere, allied to emotion, intuition, and following one's heart.

There is little doubt that the road of study will be shorter if Sarah employs the disciplined approach of left-brain thinking. However, understanding and empathy rarely accompany it. This fact is reflected in Sarah's dream by the lack of atmosphere (something was missing).

However, if she pursues her ambition by following her heart and employing intuition, the road will be longer. Nevertheless, her rewards will be more substantial: she will gain hands-on experience, which naturally leads to understanding and empathy. In short, she will conclude her journey as a more complete person.

Therefore, if Sarah follows her heart in her chosen profession, she will develop her spiritual side and avoid being efficient at the cost of understanding. You must follow your heart, Sarah!

Interpretation 95 A Sneaky Approach!

The first clue comes when we consider the setting of the dream and Duncan's place within it. The field in the countryside and the people represent life going on around Duncan. However, these people are walking along bridle-paths ('bridle', which sounds exactly like 'bridal', symbolizes new beginnings and opportunities, and 'paths' represent various options to follow in life to achieve one's goals).

Next, we see that Duncan is hidden in a thicket, aware that he could surprise the passers-by. This suggests that he is either hiding something and/or lying in ambush! If we now bear in mind Duncan's remarks about his ambition and determination to rise to the top of his profession, we begin to see a clear picture emerging.

The next part of the dream galvanizes the interpretation and almost casts it in stone. Immediately, it becomes obvious that there are incontrovertible similarities between Duncan's stance and the stance of the fox; in effect, there is no difference in their behaviour. It is this point which demonstrates that the fox is a representation of Duncan himself: a primitive, animal side, which encompasses cunning and preying on others.

Finally, the interpretation is underpinned by the appearance of the lion and demonstrates that symbolism within dreams is far from being universal. In this instance, if we look for the obvious, the meaning becomes transparent: the lion has long since been regarded as the king of the jungle, and it is as simple as that! In other words, industry and life itself are often regarded as a 'jungle'. The king, or lion, points to the head of, in this case, the sales industry.

Pulling it all together, then, we can see that Duncan could be behaving in a less than honourable way in order to achieve his ambitions. However, as already stated, it seems likely that he is unaware of this and perhaps finds justification for his conduct. We all possess this tendency. Nevertheless, Duncan's unconscious – which is ever vigilant and on duty 24 hours a day – knows better, or else it wouldn't have presented him with this dream in a way that spurred him awake (the trigger effect).

The message is clear: Duncan should take an honest look at himself and address these issues. There is nothing wrong with ambition, as long as it is not pursued to the detriment of everything else!

Interpretation 96 Give Him Some Slack!

To begin with, the holiday, the sunshiny day, and laughter symbolize your present situation in life and how you feel about Geoff: you are happy in the relationship. However, this dream brings a warning, which is confirmed by your unconscious remarks on your questionnaire – remarks concerning being possessive where Geoff is concerned.

The stretches of sandy beach represent easy going, but the areas of pebbles mean rough times. That the dream begins with you on the sand underpins the point that you are pleased with the status quo. However, your unconscious mind has identified a risk that could lie ahead, should you choose to ignore the message behind your dream.

In this particular instance, the four girls, instead of symbolizing different facets of your own personality, represent exactly who they appear to be: other females who, from time to time, Geoff encounters. The fact that you felt they presented a danger, and you strengthened your grip (your hold on Geoff) and tried to hurry him towards the end of the beach (rush your relationship to a conclusion of your choice) reflects clearly your tendency towards possessiveness in these circumstances.

The next clue, and perhaps the most significant of all, is your dismay when Geoff tried to let go of your hand (free himself from your grip). This is reinforced by your anger when the girls turned to follow you and clearly echoes your feelings of insecurity. This explanation is backed up by Geoff's actions: he smiled at them. At this point, the entire interpretation is corroborated by the fact that you then found yourself standing on the pebbles (hard going).

Now, we can see that the message behind your dream is obvious. If you continue to be so overly possessive of Geoff and tighten your hold on him, you risk losing him (he freed himself and joined the girls in flirty conversation). Therefore, Barbara, you must overcome this negative character trait and learn to trust him. In this sense, you must understand that there are risks in every relationship, and there are no guarantees. However, if you carry on the way you are, you are almost certainly going to lose him. Give him some slack!

Interpretation 97 Life is not a Game of Monopoly

Here we have a dream that gives a firm warning! To begin with, it is relevant that the room in which you found yourself was dingy and dimly lit. Essentially, it reflects your feelings about your present employment: stale and fairly miserable, hence your desire for a change.

The excited anticipation symbolizes your deliberations about the new job offer: you are keen to move on. The table and rickety chairs, however, suggest a rocky position on a seat, perhaps an unsteady position – and this is the first hint of a warning.

Next, the Monopoly board points fairly convincingly to a game of chance allied to taking a gamble. The fact that you elected to sit at the position with the most money is relevant. It reflects your current situation of security and power (you held the trump cards). So far, then, the dream is a perfect reflection of your present situation: you are in a position of power, hold the trump cards, and are contemplating a move.

If we now accept that the people who enter the room represent those in the rival company, everything becomes chillingly clear. They are relying on you to make your move; they want you to be a winner for them. That they mutate into snakes is a clear warning that suggests they are not who they claim to be. Your observation of the forked tongues reinforces this point.

What really seals the entire interpretation is your comments about their eyes. This is a strong indicator that tells us, if you do decide to throw the dice and make this move, you are likely to throw 'snake-eyes!' (double one). That being the case, it seems likely that you will 'crap out' (as in the game of craps).

If you feel that you have to leave your present employment, your dream is urging you to take a closer look at prospective opportunities. Take this dream seriously!

Interpretation 98

The brain, during REM sleep, is limited in the way it produces dreams. Therefore, they tend to progress by a sort of 'law of least effort'. It is because of these limitations, assisted by the ebb and flow of chemicals at the base of the brain, that dreams are presented in the form of symbols which have to be decoded. This appears to have something to do with the fact that they also flow along visual- and verbal-associative pathways and often play on word puns, anagrams, cryptic clues, and homophones – and this is a good example.

In this instance the word 'sun' represents your 'son', David. If we then acknowledge that the pond symbolizes a bank, the fish reflect your savings, and water indicates your income, the dream begins to make sense. To begin with, your first observation is that the sun (son) was beating down and evaporating the water (your income) from the pond (bank), endangering the fish (savings). Having acknowledged this symbolism to be an accurate representation of your life circumstances, the rest of the interpretation is easy to understand.

Your husband lazing in the deckchair suggests that he has had little to do with domestic finances and has left you to shoulder the burden. Furthermore, the fact that he disappears indicates that he resists taking such a responsibility.

It would seem that, in order for you to cope with your son's extra demands, you have tried to increase your income (the hose and buckets). However, the dream also suggests that David's demands are outstripping your earning capacity.

This is clearly reinforced when we consider who was in possession of the water-laden sponge (David is the sponge). This is confirmed because it simply absorbed more resources.

Here, the message is clear: you simply have to put your foot down and be firm with both David and your husband. You must let David know that your finances are not inexhaustible and insist that your husband takes some of the responsibility. Clearly these issues are on the dreamer's mind and she cannot afford to ignore this dream.

Interpretation 99

The fact that you are not married and have no children in real life, yet had a wife waiting in a Rolls Royce which was to take you to your son's wedding, is very positive symbolism. In this instance, a wedding points to a new beginning. The elite car suggests wealth and success connected to this new venture, and the wife represents a mother image: the bearer of your son.

We know that, in real life, you do not have a son, so we must ask what he represents in the dream. And the clue comes in the form of the Easter egg accompanied by the words 'It's for the birth'. If we connect those words with the fact that you do not see your son in the dream, it looks as if he could represent a birth, or hatching. A birth or hatching of what, though?

The answer comes when the professor appears and congratulates you on a bouncing baby boy, then presents you with a scroll. This symbolizes an achievement gained through knowledge, or, more appropriately in this case, the birth of a well-considered idea.

At this point there is a scene-shift effect in which the dream progresses by the law of least effort. It incorporates features – the yellow scroll and the brown Easter egg – into the next scene, where they appear as a yellow suit and a brown carpet. The baptism and the minister's reassuring remarks symbolize a blessing. The party also suggests a happy and successful outcome. Therefore, the message behind your dream is that you will indeed hatch an idea for a new venture that is bound to succeed. However, it seems likely that you might hesitate, as you did in the dream. Nevertheless, you will have the fortitude to go ahead. Good luck!

Interpretation 100

There are many curious phenomena to be encountered during the hours of sleep, and Maureen's description suggests that, during her childhood years, she might have been experiencing the strange REM condition known as false awakenings. False awakenings can come in different varieties, which often confuses dreamers.

Typically, people will be totally convinced that they have awoken in their usual environment and sometimes report seeing visions. The fact that Maureen states that the dream images were superimposed on her surroundings leaves little doubt that these were false awakenings.

In Maureen's questionnaire, she declares that she is proud of her achievements in life and is aware of being psychic, but is still looking for more challenges and fulfilment. If we link this information to Maureen's dream and take into account the fact that, during childhood, they manifested themselves more as visions than dream images, a clear picture emerges. Immediately, we can see that she found herself between the material and the spiritual aspects of her personality.

Next, we can see that, throughout the course of her life, Maureen has resisted following only one path but, on the surface, appears to have maintained an even balance (she stood firm between the two). Initially, then, it is tempting to accept that the dream is telling Maureen that she is leading a well-balanced life.

However, message-bearing dreams rarely recur if there isn't a pertinent reason, so we must look deeper. Maureen asserts that, in the material world, she has achieved much – she has bought a house and is successful in her career – yet still seeks more challenges and fulfilment.

Connect this with her statement that she is psychic and a definite answer is revealed, which is supported by the phenomenon of false awakenings. Indeed, this suggests that Maureen is indeed psychic. However, it would seem that she has paid more attention to material achievements than to spiritual development.

Therefore the message behind the dream is that Maureen should start to work on her spiritual side. She is likely to find the challenge of such a quest far more fulfilling than she realizes.

Interpretation 101

As we approach the new millennium, we receive more and more dreams which contain spiritual elements, and this is a good example. It is also very relevant that Valerie had this dream at a crossroads in her life, when she was considering going back to work, yet was unclear about the nature of employment she should choose.

Spiritual dreams come in various guises, ranging from the obscure (like this one) to the obvious, which can contain angels, religious figures, members of the clergy, etc. In this instance, the setting and Valerie's feelings give the first indication: she felt overwhelmed, it was bright and sunny, there were beautiful flowers, children (innocence) were playing, and everybody was smiling and friendly. However, the most convincing clue arises from her description of the setting: it was like the Garden of Eden.

If we accept that the initial setting symbolizes a spiritual aspect, then the rest of the dream becomes easy to interpret. In contrast, and as if from a vision of the nineteenth century, Valerie noticed a marquee, similar to a hospital tent. These elements suggest a place of healing amid the chaos of life. So, the scene is set – but to what end?

In dream interpretation the use of words is extremely relevant, and the next clue comes in the following phrase, 'Instinctively (meaning that she felt an urge) I walked towards two nurses' (nurses provide another clue).

The next sequence of the dream pulls it all together quite neatly. The nurses inform Valerie that they had been waiting for her (expecting her) to give them a 'hand'. She approached a patient and placed her 'hand' on his head. He then announced that he was cured. This last statement puts the entire dream into context.

It would seem that Valerie's higher self has identified precisely the sort of career she should pursue. It is evident that it encompasses some kind of healing, but not necessarily nursing. Instead, it would seem that it could involve something that incorporates the laying on of hands, such as physiotherapy, aromatherapy, reflexology, chiropody.

The dream also suggests that Valerie could already be aware of her healing abilities. It would seem that she has much to offer that would benefit society. In addition, if she does follow her instincts, she, too, is likely to profit.

Interpretation 102

Amazingly, the unconscious mind is ever vigilant, being on duty 24 hours a day. In fact it never rests nor does it miss a trick. The subconscious has the ability to detect minute changes in the environment around us – changes that the conscious mind would be unlikely to notice.

A good example of this can be found in prodromic dreams (forewarning illness). It is thought that the unconscious mind can detect very small physiological changes, e.g. in the stomach. It then might furnish a dream which, if accurately interpreted, warns of a developing stomach ulcer. Similarly, observation of subtle alterations in our environment can provide dreams that alert us to hitherto unrecognized problems – and this seems to be the case here.

To begin with, Jean finds herself in her living (life) room, which is in darkness. This suggests that there are circumstances in Jean's life about which she is in a state of darkness (an unrecognized problem). This is confirmed by the presence of an unseen third party, who, by placing obstacles in her way, is trying to trip her up.

The next clue comes when we consider Jean's reaction to this: she loses her self-assurance. In other words, we are dealing with an ongoing situation in Jean's life which she hasn't recognized. This same set of circumstances is having the effect of draining her confidence.

Jean made a point of stating that the other person was familiar. This remark suggests that the third party, whom she knows, is responsible for tripping her up or, more appropriately, putting her down, by keeping her in the dark about certain life-circumstances.

If we accept the analysis so far, the message behind the dream becomes chillingly clear: somebody close to Jean is acting with some kind of duplicity towards her and thereby maintaining control over her (by placing obstacles in her path, this individual is keeping her under his or her control).

Nevertheless, the dream suggests that there will be a bright outcome. Jean's ignorance turns to fear (recognizing an unknown threat) and, although she is likely to reach one or two incorrect assumptions (trip up), she will make it to the door (way out of the darkness). When she turns the handle (unlocks the secret), she will be in broad daylight (enlightenment). Good luck, Jean!

Interpretation 103

Dreams sometimes have a beginning, middle, and end and allude to a past, present, and future (element of precognition).

To begin with, Cate finds herself in a village hall packed with people (her community). The fact that she feels frightened suggests a lack of self-confidence and low self-esteem. The presence of the first old schoolfriend indicates that Cate draws a certain amount of comfort from allowing others to make decisions (leading her to a seat). This part of the dream reflects her past and present situation in life.

However, there will come a time when she is likely to leave her community (she left the hall) and take a risk, which, at first, might involve a rough ride (the blizzard conditions). However, she is likely to find the drive to face the challenge, which is symbolized by the mini-car. Indeed, it seems that she is going to feel alone and vulnerable, but, nonetheless, will pursue this path reflected by the country roads, which points to a pleasant change.

Many new ventures in life can appear precarious and uncertain, as symbolized by the road conditions. However, Cate states that the approach of the cliff heralded a feeling that the situation was bigger than her, so she went with it. This indicates that she will be prepared to confront the risk and take the plunge – but into what?

We don't have to look far to find the likely answer. First, the cliff could be symbolizing a male ('Cliff' is a male name). Assuming this to be correct, she next somersaults down the cliff (falls head over heels?). Next the scene changes to sunshine and rolling hills (good omen), and she sees two figures (a couple). They are welcoming and accept her unconditionally. Then we have sweet juice from a pear (or pair).

It would seem, Cate, that, when you reach your 50s, you are going to meet a man. If you accept the risk of a new relationship and take the plunge, you will find your own Garden of Eden, which is likely to bear fruit!

Interpretation 104

Message-bearing dreams all share one thing in common: they awaken dreamers, then force them to give a certain amount of thought to the dream's subject matter.

Sometimes, dreams serve merely to give reassurance, as in this case. In addition, when dreams recur throughout our lives, they are usually plotting some sort of progress, especially when the dream's content changes from time to time. However, in this instance, apart from different designs of aircraft, the dreams are always the same – but why?

To begin with, the dream sets the scene by placing you in an environment in which you grew up. In other words, it establishes a frame of reference. In this particular instance, an aircraft represents a smooth mode of transport that offers the least resistance. Therefore, the planes reflect a means by which you would rather progress through life – encountering fewer obstacles.

In this sense, it would appear that you prefer to take the path of least resistance. Each new plane, therefore, signifies a new challenge or set of circumstances in your life. The fact that they appear to be futuristic reflects your capacity to change, adapt, and accept them.

The fact that most of the dreams occur during daylight means that you are usually aware of these alterations in the environment around you. However, the dreams which reflect dark surroundings suggest that there are times when you are in the dark and not fully conscious of the different circumstances. Nevertheless, it would seem that, on each of these occasions, your subconscious has identified these issues, which enables you to continue adapting and accepting new ideas.

To pull it all together, then, these dreams reflect your gift for being able to go with the flow of things and follow the line of least resistance, because of your ability to change and adapt to new circumstances. If you are able to recall the times when these dreams have recurred, it is likely that they will have coincided with changes in your life situation. These are dreams of reassurance.

Interpretation 105

In this instance, the office block represents a place of business: your present shoe-store. The many flights of stairs symbolize the hard climb (work) necessary to make it a success. Each landing suggests a place where, after another rung of the corporate ladder has been ascended, planning has to be done and decisions taken in order to be able to overcome the next challenge (flight of stairs).

The people who are strewn about the landing signify competitors; by undercutting, etc. they make it more difficult for you to attain your goal. This is confirmed when we consider your remarks concerning obstacles on each of the remaining landings: you had to be careful how you trod or you could go tumbling back down the stairs (fall back to the bottom of the ladder).

Reaching the top of the building reflects your present situation in business: after a considerable struggle, you have flourished. However, you are contemplating opening another shoe-store, and this is symbolized by the adjacent building. The fact that it is neat tells us that any new venture has not yet been cluttered up by obstacles and competition.

It would seem though, that you have two choices on how to proceed, and your dream is cautioning you that there are risks in following the quickest route (jumping the gap or taking a shortcut). Remember your emotional state when you awoke: you were scared to try this option.

The message, then, is that you should retrace the same steps you took to build your first business. No matter how slow and frustrating this approach might be, in the past it proved to be a winning formula. Taking shortcuts in business rarely bodes well for the long term.

Interpretation 106

Some years ago, David Melbourne interpreted a dream for Russell Grant, the famous astrologer, in which he found himself kneeling in front of an archbishop, who was standing beside an altar rail and lit up by some sort of light from behind. It was easily identified as a spiritual dream. Some spiritual dreams aren't as clear-cut and easy to categorize. Nevertheless, on occasion, there are certain criteria which signpost such dreams, and this example contains most of them: an unidentified foreign location, beautiful surroundings, figures in authority, bright light, and extremely loving emotions.

First, the unconscious mind sometimes symbolizes a spiritual realm by likening it to a foreign country that the dreamer is unable to identify. Furthermore, figures of authority sometimes represent higher beings. That they were on 'the other side' of a stream (barrier between the dreamer and that realm) underpins the interpretation so far. Moreover, we have the appearance of the sun (the son).

Next, we notice that, in the first instance, the angel was out of focus and elusive. This reflects things in reality: while we live in the material world, issues of an ethereal nature are often difficult to recognize and acknowledge. However, when things do become clear, there is absolutely no doubt that this is indeed a representation of an angel, and both the halo and smile are good omens.

Now we come to the crux of the dream: the angel pointing to something ahead of you (your future) in the distance (still distant future). In this instance, it seems reasonable to accept that the only way your unconscious mind is able to create a representation of Heaven is to present you with an image of a crystal city or something equally as beautiful. But what is the point of such a dream?

Spiritual dreams often serve the valuable purpose of reassuring dreamers and bolstering their faith, and this seems to be the case here. Apparently, Grant's subconscious wants him to rest assured that his faith is well founded, and that rewards await him at the beginning of a new journey – in the distant future!

Interpretation 107

To begin with, the fact that Rose felt that the penguin was a representation of her daughter cannot be ignored. The subconscious will often leave us with similar lingering feelings upon awakening. In addition, birds do sometimes symbolize females (the term 'bird' is an appropriate colloquialism, especially in the UK).

The fact that the penguin had a threatening beak and used it to bite people, including Rose, provides the first clue as to where the dream is leading. In fact, the pervading theme of this dream is obvious: conflict!

Next, we see that Rose and her husband tried to get away (wanted to escape from certain problems). However, as in this instance, security guards often represent the police force of the mind (self-discipline). The expected arrival of royalty suggests that Rose and her husband were going to have to rise above certain issues to seek a resolution.

The scene then changed, and Rose heard news of a bump involving a car, which she instinctively knew belonged to her daughter (conflict surrounding her daughter). The next segment of the dream then identifies the object of the conflict. There was an older man, whom Rose felt was her daughter's boyfriend, lying (lying = not being honest?) on the floor. Pulling it together then, so far we have Rose, her husband, her daughter, the boyfriend, and conflict.

Bearing this in mind, the rest of the dream is relatively simple to piece together. The unidentified person in the kitchen, with whom the boyfriend was arguing, represents a protective facet of Rose's own personality. The Down's syndrome child represents, unequivocally, innocence and naïveté. Rose also stated that she felt that it was the penguin, which she had earlier sensed was her daughter. Finally, the scene changed again and Rose found herself in her daughter's kitchen among dirty dishes (her daughter had got herself into a mess).

The message, therefore, becomes clear: at the time of the dream, Rose was concerned that her daughter's boyfriend was in some way being duplicitous and perhaps taking her daughter for some sort of ride (he was lying and the centre of an argument, which involved a naïve element – her daughter). Furthermore, the state of the daughter's kitchen symbolized the state of her mind concerning her boyfriend: in a mess! Rose was being warned about him.

Interpretation 108

Dreams often alert us to a past event or place. Sometimes the subconscious has identified circumstances similar to a present-day situation. However, as in this instance, the dream can be trying to identify the root cause of an unrecognized psychosis that has its origins buried in the past.

To begin with, you were pleased with yourself for preparing a meal for friends. This suggests that, at the time of the dream, you wanted to please people, to be liked and accepted. The fact that you went to the great expense of purchasing the delicacies underpins this point and even hints at a certain amount of low self-esteem: you didn't have the confidence to use all your own ingredients.

It is interesting that you describe the creatures as 'beasties', and point out that, in other dreams, the theme has always been the same, including the presence of Nazis. As we know, dreams play on words and bearing this unpleasant subject matter in mind, it seems very likely that the word 'Nazis' translates to 'nasties'.

Viewing this theme and the dream in its entirety, we are able to conclude that, perhaps in childhood situations connected with your peers, your desire to please became an exaggerated need – even unconsciously – to be accepted. In addition, because these dreams persisted into adulthood, it would seem that this need became firmly entrenched in your behaviour, the likely result being lack of confidence and low self-esteem.

The message therefore, is that you should do more to rid yourself of the fear of what others might think about you. This can be achieved by examining this dream (beastie) scientifically (logically), accepting the findings (the interpretation), and then acting accordingly. Good luck!

Appendix

**THE MELBOURNE/HEARNE QUESTIONNAIRE
(SHORT VERSION) FOR DREAM INTERPRETATION**

© Copyright David Melbourne and Dr Keith Hearne 1996

STRICTLY CONFIDENTIAL

Please give as much information as possible, using BLOCK CAPITALS.

A: The Dreamer

NAME: . . . .

ADDRESS: . . . .

. . . .

. . . .

USUAL OCCUPATION: . . . . SEX: M □ F □

. . . .

DATE OF BIRTH: . . . .

TIME & PLACE OF BIRTH*: . . . .

EDUCATION: . . . .

. . . .

. . . .

NATIONALITY: . . . .

MARITAL STATUS: . . . .

NUMBER OF CHILDREN: . . . . RELIGION: . . . .

INTERESTS, HOBBIES: . . . .

. . . .

. . . .

. . . .

WOULD YOU SAY THAT YOU ARE PSYCHIC (i.e. you experience
telepathy, clairvoyance, premonitions, etc.)? □ Yes □ No □ Don't know

GIVE THE *FIRST* NAMES OF PEOPLE SIGNIFICANT TO YOU
(e.g. partner, family, colleagues, friends. These may be represented in
disguised form in the dream): . . . .

. . . .

. . . .

. . . .

* This information is useful for solar/planetary/
lunar influence research into dreams and dreamers.

LIST MATTERS (e.g. relationship problems, career, house, illness, money, decisions to make) THAT ARE PARTICULARLY ON YOUR MIND AT THIS TIME IN ORDER OF CONCERN (most important first). Give a brief summary: . . . .

. . . .

. . . .

. . . .

WAS/IS THERE SOMETHING SPECIAL DUE TO HAPPEN A DAY OR TWO AFTER THE DREAM? □ Yes □ No (If yes, give brief details):

. . . .

. . . .

. . . .

. . . .

B: Dream Report

PROVIDE A *FULL* ACCOUNT OF THE DREAM. Spend some time thinking about your dream and writing the report. Describe *everything* you can remember – even sketch what you saw in some scenes – because sometimes items that seem to be insignificant are in fact very important in the dream analysis. (Use a separate sheet of paper.)

DATE OF DREAM (Night of): . . . .

TIME OF DREAM: . . . .

BED TIME: . . . . .ESTIMATED SLEEP-ONSET TIME: . . . .

(OR OBTAIN A FULL WRITTEN DREAM ACCOUNT, PREFERABLY IMMEDIATELY AFTER THE DREAM)

C: Additional Information

Please provide as much information as possible. This categorized data is useful not only in the interpretation but also for comparison purposes. Various patterns may be noticed between these items in the dreamer over time, or between different people.

DID YOU TAKE ANY MEDICATION BEFORE SLEEP?

□ Yes □ No (If yes, give details): . . . .

. . . .

WERE THE SLEEPING CONDITIONS UNUSUAL (e.g. a different bed)?

□ Yes □ No (If yes, give details): . . . .

. . . .

. . . .

WHAT WERE YOUR THOUGHTS BEFORE SLEEP? . . . .

. . . .

. . . .

IN GENERAL, WERE THESE THOUGHTS:

□ Very pleasant □ Pleasant □ Neutral □ Unpleasant □ Very unpleasant

WOULD YOU DESCRIBE THE DREAM AS A NIGHTMARE?
☐ Yes ☐ No

WERE THE DREAM EVENTS POSSIBLE IN REALITY?
☐ Yes ☐ No

WERE THE EVENTS LAWFUL?
☐ Yes ☐ No

WERE THE EVENTS CUSTOMARY AND NORMAL FOR YOU?
☐ Yes ☐ No

WERE THERE LINKS TO EVENTS THAT HAPPENED IN THE DAY BEFORE?
☐ Yes ☐ No (If yes, give details): . . . .
. . . .
. . . .
. . . .

HAVE YOU HAD THE DREAM BEFORE?
☐ Yes ☐ No

HAVE YOU ANY IDEAS YOURSELF AS TO WHAT THE DREAM MEANS? . . . .
. . . .
. . . .
. . . .
. . . .

ANY OTHER RELEVANT BACKGROUND INFORMATION: . . . .
. . . .
. . . .
. . . .
. . . .

SENSES EXPERIENCED IN DREAM, APART FROM VISUAL:
☐ Hearing ☐ Taste ☐ Smell ☐ Touch ☐ Pain ☐ Sexual

NUMBER OF PERSONS/CREATURES SEEN IN DREAM: . . . .
Briefly describe these persons/creatures (name, sex, age, clothing, behaviour, etc. Continue on separate sheet if necessary): . . . .
. . . .
. . . .
. . . .
. . . .
. . . .
. . . .

SIGNIFICANT THINGS SAID BY DREAM CHARACTERS (indicate who said them): ....

....

....

....

....

EMOTION(S) ON WAKING: ....

....

....

....

PSYCHOLOGICAL STATE ON WAKING:
□ Very unpleasant □ Unpleasant □ Neutral □ Pleasant □ Very pleasant

COLOUR:
□ None □ Some □ Much □ Not noticed

BRIGHTNESS OF DREAM IMAGES:
□ Very bright □ Bright □ In between □ Rather dark □ Very dark

WAS IT A LUCID DREAM (i.e. where you are actually aware that it is a dream while you are still dreaming and can control the events)?
□ Yes □ No □ Not sure

DID THE DREAM OCCUR ON AN ANNIVERSARY OF A SIGNIFICANT EVENT FOR YOU?
□ Yes □ No □ Don't know (If yes, give details): ....

....

....

....

WHICH THINGS STUCK IN YOUR MIND MOST ON WAKING?

....

....

....

....

....

RATE THE STRESS IN YOUR LIFE CURRENTLY:
□ None □ Little □ In between □ Much □ Very much

List of Abbreviations

DPP	dream-producing process
DSPS	delayed sleep-phase syndrome
DTs	delirium tremens
EEG	electroencephalogram
EMG	electromyogram
EOG	electro-oculogram
FAST	false awakening with state-testing
IRA	Irish Republican Army
LSD	lysergic acid diethylamide
MAO	monoamine oxidase
MHQ	Melbourne/Hearne Questionnaire
REM	rapid eye movement
SAD	seasonal affective disorder
TV	television
VIP	very important person
VR	virtual reality
SS	Schutstaffel
SWS	slow-wave sleep

Glossary of Terms

Alpha wave   Brain wave with frequency of 8–13 Hz.

Anima   Female component of the male personality.

Animus   Male component of the female personality.

Archetype   Universal standard or ideal.

Associative imaging   A method of encouraging sleep by reciting associated words, thus distracting the mind from everyday matters and imitating the sort of thinking that occurs during sleep.

Associative pathways   The series of verbal and phonetic (anagrams, puns, homophones), or visual associations by which dreams develop.

Atonia   Lack of muscle tone, or paralysis.

Auto-symbolic phenomenon   The translation of thoughts just before sleep into hypnagogic images.

Beta wave   Brain wave with frequency of 14–30 Hz.

Bruxism   Grinding of the teeth, particularly during sleep.

Centralist   Someone who believes that hypnagogic images are formed in the brain.

Clairvoyance   Seeing at a distance.

Cross-reference flowchart   Scientifically based, analytical approach to deciphering dreams developed by David Melbourne.

Day residue   Events which have occurred during the day that appear in a dream the next night.

Delayed sleep-phase syndrome (DSPS)   Little-known medical condition in which sufferers do not respond normally (i.e. start to feel sleepy) to falling daylight levels.

Delirium tremens (DTs)   Delirious disorder of the brain produced by over-absorption of alcohol.

Delta wave   Brain wave with frequency of 0.5–3 Hz.

Dramatization   Automatic transformation of a waking idea into a dream image.

Dream incubation   The encouragement of dreaming by appropriately mental and physical preparation.

Dysmorphopsia   Distortion of an image.

Ego   Conscious part of the personality representing the self.

Enuresis   Bedwetting.

False awakening   Dreaming of being awake.

Form constants   Universal images which appear in spontaneous hypnagogic imagery and, in wakefulness, as a result of drugs.

Gamma wave   Brain wave with frequency of 30–50 Hz.

Gestalt   Psychology theory which considers the organized whole as being something more than the sum of the parts into which it can be organized.

Hemispheric-alternation sleep   Ability of dolphins and some birds to shut down the left and right hemispheres of the brain alternately.

Homophone   A word that sounds similar to another but has a different meaning.

Hypermnesia   Extreme retentiveness of memory.

Hypnagogic   Occurring during the onset of sleep.

Hypno-oneirography   Tracing of dream images under hypnosis.

Hypnopompic   Occurring after sleep.

Id   Unconscious part of the personality representing the sum total of the primitive instincts.

Initial insomnia   Condition in which the sufferer has difficulty in going to sleep.

K-complex   Sudden negative-to-positive brain waves which occur during SWS in response to a sudden stimulus.

Latent content   The unacceptable, hidden content of dreams.

Light-switch effect   Inability to switch on a light during a dream.

Lucid dreams   In these dreams, the dreamer, although aware that he/she is dreaming, has the same clarity of thought as in wakefulness and, moreover, can manipulate the dream.

Macropsia   Apparent enlargement in size of a perceived image.

Manifest content The symbolic content of dreams, which disguises the latent content.

Micropsia Apparent reduction in size of a perceived image.

Myoclonic jerk A sudden exaggerated movement of the body.

Narcolepsy The condition of immediately entering REM sleep.

Opposites The representation in a dream of the reverse of what it appears to reveal.

Paradoxical sleep Term used to describe REM sleep in animals.

Peripheralist Someone who believes that hypnagogic images are caused by stimulation in the retina.

Phasic REM Stage of REM sleep in which flickering eye movements can be observed beneath the eyelids.

Polygraph Recording machine that traces out amplified signals from electrodes placed on a subject.

Precognition Premonition, or seeing the future.

Prelucid Term used to describe a transitional state in an ordinary dream, when the dreamer is close to deciding whether or not the experience is a dream.

Prodromic Term used to describe a dream which portrays impending illness.

Pseudo-insomnia Overestimated sleeplessness.

Rapid eye-movement (REM) sleep Type of sleep characterized by a fast, mixed-frequency pattern of brain waves. Breathing is rapid and shallow, and flickering eye movements can be detected. Dreams, and sleep paralysis, are linked with REM sleep.

Reticular formation Part of the brain stem believed to stimulate the brain to consciousness.

Scene-shift effect Phenomenon associated with the hypnagogic state, in which one scene effortlessly changes to another, by reusing the pictorial elements.

Seasonal affective disorder (SAD) Depressive condition related to decreasing day length.

Sleep apnea Termination of breathing during sleep, due to blockage of the airways or, more rarely, neurological causes.

Sleep drunkenness Feeling of disorientation and reluctance to wake when roused from stage 4 of SWS.

Sleep-maintenance insomnia In this condition, sufferers fall asleep naturally but wake in the night and find it difficult to go back to sleep.

Sleep terrors Nightmares occurring during SWS. Also known as *pavor nocturnus.*

Slow-wave sleep (SWS) Type of sleep characterized by slow-wave brain activity.

State-dependent Memory effect in which previous dreams can be recalled in subsequent dreams better than in the intervening period of wakefulness.

Superego Unconscious part of the personality which inhibits the ego when it receives unacceptable impulses from the id.

Telepathy Mind-to-mind communication.

Theta wave Brain wave with frequency of 4–7 Hz.

Tonic REM Stage of REM sleep in which the eyes are often quite still.

Trigger effect Waking from an ongoing dream as a result of prompting by the unconscious.

Ultradian Faster than day.

References

Aserinsky, E. & Kleitman, N. (1953) 'Regular periods of eye motility and concomitant phenomena during sleep.' *Science* **118**: 273–4.

Aubrey, J. (1890) *Miscellanies.* Library of Old Authors, Reeves & Turner, London. Originally published in 1696.

Barker, J. C. (1967) 'Premonitions of the Aberfan disaster.' *Journal of the Society for Psychical Research* **44**: 169–81.

Berger, H. (1929) 'Über des Elektenkephalogramm des Menschen.' *Archiv für Psychiatre und Nervenkrankheiten* **87**: 527–70.

Berger, R. J. (1961) 'Tonus of extrinsic laryngeal muscles during sleep and dreaming.' *Science* **134**: 840.

Binz, C.(1878) *Über den Traum.* Bonn. Quoted in Freud (1954).

Burdach, K. F. (1838) *Die Physiologie als Erfahrungswissenschaft.* 2nd edition, vol. 2. Quoted in Freud (1954).

Caton, R. (1875) 'The electric currents of the brain.' *British Medical Journal* **2**: 278.

Cockell, J. (1993) *Yesterday's Children.* Piatkus, London.

Coleridge, S. (1952) Prefatory notes to *Kubla Khan.* In: Ghiselin, B. (ed.) *The Creative Process.* New American Library, New York.

Crick, F. & Mitchison, G. (1986) 'REM sleep and neural nets.' *The Journal of Mind and Behaviour* Spring–Summer.

de Becker, R. (1968) *The Understanding of Dreams, or the Machinations of the Night.* George Allen & Unwin, London.

de Manacéine, M. (1897) *Sleep: Its Physiology, Pathology, Hygiene and Psychology.* Scott, London.

Delage, Y. (1891) 'Essai sur la theorie du rêve.' *Revue industrielle* **2**: 40. Quoted in Freud (1954).

Delage, Y. (1919) *Le rêve.* Les Presses Universitaires de France, Paris.

Delboeuf, I. (1885) *Le sommeil et les rêves.* Paris. Quoted in Freud (1954).

Dement, W. C. (1960) 'The effect of dream deprivation.' *Science* **131**: 1705–07.

Dement, W. C. (1976) *Some Watch While Some Sleep.* San Francisco Book Company, San Francisco.

Dewi-Rees, W. (1971) 'Hallucinations of widowhood.' *British Medical Journal* **4**: 37–41.

Dodds, E. R. (1971) 'Supernormal phenomena in classical antiquity.' *Proceedings of the Society for Psychical Research* **55** (205): 189–237.

Ephron, H. S. & Carrington, P. (1966) 'Rapid eye movement sleep and cortical homeostasis.' *Psychological Review* **73**: 500–26.

Evans, C. & Newman, E. (1964) 'Dreaming: an analogy from computers.' *New Scientist* **24**: 577–9.

Eysenck, H. (1953) *Uses and Abuses of Psychology.* Penguin, Harmondsworth, London.

Faraday, A. (1972) *Dream Power.* Hodder & Stoughton, London.

Faraday, A. (1974) *The Dream Game.* Hodder & Stoughton, London.

Fisher, C. & Dement, W. C. (1963) 'Studies in the psychopathology of sleep and dreams.' *American Journal of Psychiatry* **119** (12): 1160–68.

Fisher, C., Byrne, J., & Edwards, A. (1968) 'NREM and REM nightmares.' *Psychobiology* **5**: 22–222.

Fontana, D. (1993) *The Secret Language of Symbols.* Pavilion Books, London.

Fordham, F. (1953) *An Introduction to Jung's Psychology.* Pelican Books, London.

Foulkes, D. & Vogel, G. (1965) 'Mental activity at sleep onset.' *Journal of Abnormal Psychology* **70**: 231–43.

Fox, O. (1962) *Astral Projection.* University Books Inc., New York.

Freud, S. (1954) *The Interpretation of Dreams.* Translated and edited by Strachey, J. George Allen & Unwin, London. Originally published in 1900.

Garfield, P. (1974) *Creative Dreaming*. Ballantine Books, New York.

Garwell, B. (1996) *Dreams That Come True*. Thorsons, Wellingborough.

Green, C. (1968) *Lucid Dreams*. Institute for Psychophysical Research, Oxford.

Gurney, E., Myers, F. & Podmore, F. (1918) *Phantasms of the Living*. Kegan Paul, Trench, Trubner & Co., London.

Hall, C. (1953) *The Meaning of Dreams*. Harper and Row, New York.

Hartmann, E. (1973) *The Functions of Sleep*. Yale University Press, New Haven & London.

Hearne, K. (1973) *Some Investigations into Hypnotic Dreams Using a New Technique*. BSc project. University of Reading.

Hearne, K. (1975) *Visual Imagery and Evoked Responses*. MSc thesis. Department of Psychology, University of Hull.

Hearne, K. (1978) Lucid Dreams – An Electrophysiological and Psychological Study. PhD thesis, Department of Psychology, University of Liverpool.

Hearne, K. (1981a) 'A light-switch phenomenon in lucid dreams.' *Journal of Mental Imagery* 5 (2): 97–100.

Hearne, K. (1981b) 'Lucid dreams and ESP.' *Journal of the Society for Psychical Research* 51 (787): 7–11.

Hearne, K. (1982) 'Effects of performing certain set tasks in the lucid dream state.' *Perceptual & Motor Skills* 55: 259–62.

Hearne, K. (1984) 'Lucid dreams and psi research.' In: Shapiro, B. & Coly, L. (eds) *Current Trends in Psi Research*. Proceedings of an International Conference held in New Orleans, Louisiana, August 13–14. Parapsychology Foundation, Inc., New York, pp. 192–218.

Hearne, K. (1986) 'An analysis of premonitions deposited over one year, from an apparently gifted subject.' *Journal of the Society for Psychical Research* 53 (804): 376–82.

Hearne, K. (1987) 'A new perspective in dream imagery.' *Journal of Mental Imagery* 11 (2): 75–82.

Hearne, K. (1989) '*Visions of the Future.*' The Aquarian Press, Wellingborough.

Hearne, K. (1990) '*The Dream Machine.*' The Aquarian Press, Wellingborough.

Hearne, K. (1993) 'Hypnosis in the conversion of nightmares to lucid dreams.' *European Journal of Clinical Hypnosis*, 1: 12–17.

Hervey de St-Denys, Marquis d' (1982) *Dreams and How to Guide Them*. Translated by Nicholas Fry. Edited by M. Schatzman. Duckworth, London. Originally published in 1867.

Hildebrandt, F. W. (1875) *Der Traum und seine Verwerthung für's Leben*. Leipzig. Quoted in Freud (1954).

Jasper, H.H. (1958) 'The ten-twenty electrode system of the international federation.' *EEG Journal* 10: 371–75.

Jones, E. (1949) *On the Nightmare*. Hogarth Press, London.

Jouvet, M. (1975) 'The function of dreaming: A neurophysiologist's point of view.' In: Gazzaniga, M. & Blakemore, C. (eds) *Handbook of Psychobiology*. Academic Books, New York.

Jung, C. (1964) *Man and His Symbols*. Aldus Books, London.

Karacan, J., Goodenough, R., & Shapiro, S. (1966) 'Erection cycle during sleep in relation to dream anxiety.' *Archives of General Psychiatry* 15: 183–89.

Kline, P. (1972) *Fact and Fantasy in Freudian Theory*. Methuen, London.

Klüver, H. (1928) *Mescal: The 'Divine' Plant and Its Psychological Effects*. Kegan, Paul, Trench, Trubner, London.

Lienert, G.A. & Othmer, E. (1965) 'Objective correlations of the refreshing effects of sleep.' *Progress in Brain Research* 18: 170–77.

Maury, L. F. A. (1878) *Le sommeil et les rêves*. Paris. Quoted in Freud (1954).

Mavromatis, A. (1987) *Hypnagogia*. Routledge, London. pp.192–3.

McCurdy, H. (1946) 'The history of dream theory.' *Psychological Review* 53: 225–33.

McKellar, P. (1957) *Imagination and Thinking*. Cohen and West, London.

McKenzie, N. (1965) *Dreams and Dreaming*. Aldus Books, London.

Meares, A. (1954) 'Hypnography – a technique in hypnoanalysis.' *Journal of Mental Science* 100: 965–74.

Meddis, R. (1975) 'On the function of sleep.' *Animal Behaviour* 23: 676–91.

Mégroz, R. (1939) *The Dream World*. John Lane. The Bodley Head, London.

Melbourne, D. & Hearne, K. (1997a) *Dream Interpretation – The Secret*. Blandford Press, London.

Melbourne, D. & Hearne, K. (1997b) *The Melbourne/Hearne Questionnaire*

(MHQ). Available from the authors.

Melbourne, D. & Hearne, K. (1998) *The Dream Oracle*. New Holland, London.

Moruzzi, G. & Magoun, H.W. (1949) 'Brain stem reticular formation and activation of the electroencephalogram.' *EEG Journal* 1: 455–73.

Moss, C. (1958) 'Dream symbols as disguises.' *ETC* 14: 267–73.

Oswald, I. (1959) 'Sudden bodily jerks on falling asleep.' *Brain* 82: 92–103.

Pauli, H. (1966) *The Secret of Sarajevo*. Collins, London.

Peek, P. (1991) *African Divinatory Systems – Ways of Knowing*. Indiana University Press.

Perky, C.W. (1910) 'An experimental study of imagination.' *American Journal of Psychology* 21: 422–52.

Popper, K. (1959) *The Logic of Scientific Discovery*. Basic Books, New York.

Price, H. (1949) 'Psychical research and human personality.' *The Hibbert Journal* 47: 105–13.

Radestock, P. (1879) *Schlaf und Traum*. Leipzig. Quoted in Freud (1954).

Rechtschaffen, A. & Kales, A. (1958) *A Manual of Standardised Terminology, Techniques and Scoring System for Sleep Stages of Human Subjects*. Public Health Service, US Government Printing Office, Washington, DC.

Rhine, L.E. (1954) 'Frequencies of types of experiences in spontaneous precognition.' *Journal of Parapsychology* 18: 93–123.

Rhine, L.E. (1955) 'Precognition & intervention.' *Journal of Parapsychology* 19 (1): 1–34.

Robert, W. (1886) *Der Traum als Naturnotwendigkeit erklärt*. Hamburg. Quoted in Freud (1954).

Robinson, C. & Boot, A. (1997) *The Dream Detective*. Warner, London.

Sauneron, S. (1959) *Les songes et leur interprétation dans l'Egypte ancienne*. Paris.

Scherner, A. (1861) *Das Leben des Traumes*. Berlin. Quoted in Freud (1954).

Schleiermacher, F. (1862) *Psychologie*. Berlin. Quoted in Freud (1954).

Segal, S. J., & Nathan, S. (1964) 'The Perky effect: incorporation of an external stimulus into an imagery experience under placebo and control conditions.' *Perceptual & Motor Skills* 18: 385–95.

Silberer, H. (1950) 'Report on a method of eliciting and observing certain symbolic hallucination phenomena.' In: Rappaport, D. (ed.) *The Organisation and Pathology of Thought*. Columbia University Press. Originally published in 1909.

Snyder, F. (1966) 'Towards an evolutionary theory of dreaming.' *American Journal of Psychiatry* 123: 121–36.

Spence, L. (n.d.) *The Magic and Mysteries of Mexico*. Rider & Co.

Spitta, H. (1882) *Die Schlaf- und Traumzustände der menschlichen Seele*. Tübingen. Quoted in Freud (1954).

Strumpell, L. (1877) *Die Natur und Enstehung der Träume*. Leipzig. Quoted in Freud (1954).

Tart, C. (1965) 'Towards the experimental control of dreaming: a review of the literature.' *Psychological Bulletin* LXIV (2).

Time-Life Books, Editors of (1990) *Dreams & Dreaming*. The Time Inc. Book Company, Amsterdam.

Time-Life Books, Editors of (1990) *Psychic Voyages: Mysteries of the Unknown*. The Time Inc. Book Company, Amsterdam.

Ullman, M. (1958) 'Dreams and the therapeutic process.' *Psychiatry* 21: 123–131.

Ullman, M., Krippner, S. & Vaughan, A. (1973) *Dream Telepathy*. MacMillan, New York.

van Eeden, F. (1913) 'A study of dreams.' *Proceedings of the Society for Psychical Research* XXVI (XVII): 431–61.

Weiss, B. (1996) *Only Love is Real*. Piatkus, London.

Index